LLEWELLYN'S
ASTROLOGY DATEBOOK

DAILY
PLANETARY
GUIDE

Printed in the United States of America
Typography property of Llewellyn Worldwide, Ltd.
ISBN: 1-56718-926-1

Cover Art and Design by Tom Grewe
Book Design by Susan Van Sant
Editing and Layout by Cynthia Ahlquist

Special thanks to Leslie Nielsen for astrological proofreading.

Set in Eastern and Pacific Standard Times. (**NOTE:** Although starting and ending dates for **Daylight Savings Time** are marked, all times listed in this datebook are *standard* time.) Ephemeris and aspect data generated by Matrix Software, Big Rapids, MI 49307. Re-use is prohibited.

Published by
LLEWELLYN PUBLICATIONS
P.O. Box 64383
St. Paul, MN 55164-0383, U.S.A.

1996

JANUARY
S	M	T	W	T	F	S
	1	2	3	4	5	6
7	8	9	10	11	12	13
14	15	16	17	18	19	20
21	22	23	24	25	26	27
28	29	30	31			

FEBRUARY
S	M	T	W	T	F	S
				1	2	3
4	5	6	7	8	9	10
11	12	13	14	15	16	17
18	19	20	21	22	23	24
25	26	27	28	29		

MARCH
S	M	T	W	T	F	S
					1	2
3	4	5	6	7	8	9
10	11	12	13	14	15	16
17	18	19	20	21	22	23
24	25	26	27	28	29	30
31						

APRIL
S	M	T	W	T	F	S
	1	2	3	4	5	6
7	8	9	10	11	12	13
14	15	16	17	18	19	20
21	22	23	24	25	26	27
28	29	30				

MAY
S	M	T	W	T	F	S
			1	2	3	4
5	6	7	8	9	10	11
12	13	14	15	16	17	18
19	20	21	22	23	24	25
26	27	28	29	30	31	

JUNE
S	M	T	W	T	F	S
						1
2	3	4	5	6	7	8
9	10	11	12	13	14	15
16	17	18	19	20	21	22
23	24	25	26	27	28	29
30						

JULY
S	M	T	W	T	F	S
	1	2	3	4	5	6
7	8	9	10	11	12	13
14	15	16	17	18	19	20
21	22	23	24	25	26	27
28	29	30	31			

AUGUST
S	M	T	W	T	F	S
				1	2	3
4	5	6	7	8	9	10
11	12	13	14	15	16	17
18	19	20	21	22	23	24
25	26	27	28	29	30	31

SEPTEMBER
S	M	T	W	T	F	S
1	2	3	4	5	6	7
8	9	10	11	12	13	14
15	16	17	18	19	20	21
22	23	24	25	26	27	28
29	30					

OCTOBER
S	M	T	W	T	F	S
		1	2	3	4	5
6	7	8	9	10	11	12
13	14	15	16	17	18	19
20	21	22	23	24	25	26
27	28	29	30	31		

NOVEMBER
S	M	T	W	T	F	S
					1	2
3	4	5	6	7	8	9
10	11	12	13	14	15	16
17	18	19	20	21	22	23
24	25	26	27	28	29	30

DECEMBER
S	M	T	W	T	F	S
1	2	3	4	5	6	7
8	9	10	11	12	13	14
15	16	17	18	19	20	21
22	23	24	25	26	27	28
29	30	31				

1997

JANUARY
S	M	T	W	T	F	S
			1	2	3	4
5	6	7	8	9	10	11
12	13	14	15	16	17	18
19	20	21	22	23	24	25
26	27	28	29	30	31	

FEBRUARY
S	M	T	W	T	F	S
						1
2	3	4	5	6	7	8
9	10	11	12	13	14	15
16	17	18	19	20	21	22
23	24	25	26	27	28	

MARCH
S	M	T	W	T	F	S
						1
2	3	4	5	6	7	8
9	10	11	12	13	14	15
16	17	18	19	20	21	22
23	24	25	26	27	28	29
30	31					

APRIL
S	M	T	W	T	F	S
		1	2	3	4	5
6	7	8	9	10	11	12
13	14	15	16	17	18	19
20	21	22	23	24	25	26
27	28	29	30			

MAY
S	M	T	W	T	F	S
				1	2	3
4	5	6	7	8	9	10
11	12	13	14	15	16	17
18	19	20	21	22	23	24
25	26	27	28	29	30	31

JUNE
S	M	T	W	T	F	S
1	2	3	4	5	6	7
8	9	10	11	12	13	14
15	16	17	18	19	20	21
22	23	24	25	26	27	28
29	30					

JULY
S	M	T	W	T	F	S
		1	2	3	4	5
6	7	8	9	10	11	12
13	14	15	16	17	18	19
20	21	22	23	24	25	26
27	28	29	30	31		

AUGUST
S	M	T	W	T	F	S
					1	2
3	4	5	6	7	8	9
10	11	12	13	14	15	16
17	18	19	20	21	22	23
24	25	26	27	28	29	30
31						

SEPTEMBER
S	M	T	W	T	F	S
	1	2	3	4	5	6
7	8	9	10	11	12	13
14	15	16	17	18	19	20
21	22	23	24	25	26	27
28	29	30				

OCTOBER
S	M	T	W	T	F	S
			1	2	3	4
5	6	7	8	9	10	11
12	13	14	15	16	17	18
19	20	21	22	23	24	25
26	27	28	29	30	31	

NOVEMBER
S	M	T	W	T	F	S
						1
2	3	4	5	6	7	8
9	10	11	12	13	14	15
16	17	18	19	20	21	22
23	24	25	26	27	28	29
30						

DECEMBER
S	M	T	W	T	F	S
	1	2	3	4	5	6
7	8	9	10	11	12	13
14	15	16	17	18	19	20
21	22	23	24	25	26	27
28	29	30	31			

1998

JANUARY
S	M	T	W	T	F	S
				1	2	3
4	5	6	7	8	9	10
11	12	13	14	15	16	17
18	19	20	21	22	23	24
25	26	27	28	29	30	31

FEBRUARY
S	M	T	W	T	F	S
1	2	3	4	5	6	7
8	9	10	11	12	13	14
15	16	17	18	19	20	21
22	23	24	25	26	27	28

MARCH
S	M	T	W	T	F	S
1	2	3	4	5	6	7
8	9	10	11	12	13	14
15	16	17	18	19	20	21
22	23	24	25	26	27	28
29	30	31				

APRIL
S	M	T	W	T	F	S
			1	2	3	4
5	6	7	8	9	10	11
12	13	14	15	16	17	18
19	20	21	22	23	24	25
26	27	28	29	30		

MAY
S	M	T	W	T	F	S
					1	2
3	4	5	6	7	8	9
10	11	12	13	14	15	16
17	18	19	20	21	22	23
24	25	26	27	28	29	30
31						

JUNE
S	M	T	W	T	F	S
	1	2	3	4	5	6
7	8	9	10	11	12	13
14	15	16	17	18	19	20
21	22	23	24	25	26	27
28	29	30				

JULY
S	M	T	W	T	F	S
			1	2	3	4
5	6	7	8	9	10	11
12	13	14	15	16	17	18
19	20	21	22	23	24	25
26	27	28	29	30	31	

AUGUST
S	M	T	W	T	F	S
						1
2	3	4	5	6	7	8
9	10	11	12	13	14	15
16	17	18	19	20	21	22
23	24	25	26	27	28	29
30	31					

SEPTEMBER
S	M	T	W	T	F	S
		1	2	3	4	5
6	7	8	9	10	11	12
13	14	15	16	17	18	19
20	21	22	23	24	25	26
27	28	29	30			

OCTOBER
S	M	T	W	T	F	S
				1	2	3
4	5	6	7	8	9	10
11	12	13	14	15	16	17
18	19	20	21	22	23	24
25	26	27	28	29	30	31

NOVEMBER
S	M	T	W	T	F	S
1	2	3	4	5	6	7
8	9	10	11	12	13	14
15	16	17	18	19	20	21
22	23	24	25	26	27	28
29	30					

DECEMBER
S	M	T	W	T	F	S
		1	2	3	4	5
6	7	8	9	10	11	12
13	14	15	16	17	18	19
20	21	22	23	24	25	26
27	28	29	30	31		

TABLE OF CONTENTS

Introduction to Calendar Astrology

When people hear the word astrology, they usually associate it with the diagnosis of personality traits or predictions of the future. Actually, astrology is much more varied than this. There are many techniques available in astrology that are suited to the many interests that humankind has. In order to use this venerable "science/art" to its maximum, we need to define what it is that we want to know, and which tools we have on hand are suited to the job.

The most common form of astrology is found in the "Sun Sign" columns of newspapers and magazines. These give a very simple and general picture of personality traits and predictions. A much more accurate way to accomplish this task is to set up a horoscope, or birth chart, showing the positions of all the planets and heavenly bodies at the time someone was born. This gives a much deeper and more reliable understanding of a person's character and likely future.

"Calendar astrology" reflects the nature of the calendar itself. Calendars are designed to be read day by day. This is conducive to a certain type of astrological work. Calendar astrology tells us what influences are to be expected in the world at large and in our personal life in a general way in an unfolding pattern. It should be evident that this type of approach cannot give the individualized information that a personal horoscope can. What we see in the calendar are influences that are strongly felt by all individuals, although most of us are unaware of it. However, each person has a personality that is unique and the various astrological configurations will affect each one differently. Since these personality traits are seen in the horoscope, if the reader has a horoscope he or she can more intimately understand the effect of the unfolding astrological configurations upon him/herself. Thus, for maximum results, calendar astrology is best practiced in conjunction with the use of horoscopes. An accurate birth chart can be obtained from **Llewellyn's Personal Services** or any competent astrologer.

Astrological Background

Each day of the year the Sun rises at a different point in the east. If we connect these points into a circular belt around the Earth, we would have the zodiac, or ecliptic. This is the apparent path of the Sun as viewed from our Earth. This imaginary ruler also gives us an accurate and convenient way to measure the planets' positions in the heavens.

This zodiacal ruler is divided into 360 degrees of arc–twelve 30-degree segments that are marked by the astrological signs. There are four major points on the ruler that divide the year into seasons. The zodiacal signs that begin at those four points, or angles, are the Cardinal signs of Aries, Cancer, Libra, and Capricorn.

The Vernal Equinox. The position of the Sun at 0 degrees Aries occurs sometime between March 19th—21st. The date can vary from year to year as our calendar is 365 days per year and the zodiac band is 360 degrees. At the vernal equinox day and night are equal in length. The Sun appears to cross the equator from south to north, when observed from the northern hemisphere.

The Summer Solstice. Throughout the spring, the days lengthen until the longest day of the year, around June 21, when the Sun is at 0 degrees Cancer. The Sun's path reaches its most northern point, the Tropic of Cancer.

The Autumnal Equinox. The Sun crosses the equator going south near September 21, at 0 degrees Libra, and day and night are again equal.

The Winter Solstice. The Sun's path is at its most southern point, the Tropic of Capricorn, around December 21, when the Sun is at 0 degrees Capricorn. This is the shortest day (i.e., least amount of daylight) of the year.

THE ZODIACAL SIGNS

There are twelve signs of the zodiac. Tropical astrology does not deal with the stars or constellations. It is concerned only with the planets, including the Sun and Moon, and their positions in the signs of the zodiac. These signs are divided into different categories to help us better understand their natures.

Elements or Triplicities. Each of the signs is classified as Fire, Earth, Air, or Water. These are the four basic elements. Fire sign personalities are outgoing, energetic, spontaneous, and impulsive. The Fire signs are Aries, Leo, and Sagittarius. Earth sign personalities (Taurus, Virgo, Capricorn) are more stable, conservative, practical, and materialistic. Gemini, Libra, and Aquarius personalities—the Air sign types—are intellectual, sociable, yet detached. Water sign types (Cancer, Scorpio, Pisces) are emotional, receptive, and intuitive.

Qualities or Quadratures. Each sign is also classified as being Cardinal, Fixed, and Mutable. There are four signs in each quadrature, one sign of each element. The Cardinal signs—Aries, Cancer, Libra, and Capricorn—are most powerful signs that occur on the four angles of the chart; their key word: action. Fixed sign types—Taurus, Leo, Scorpio, Aquarius—are persistent, organized, stubborn; their word: strength. Mutable sign types are adaptable, impressionable, tolerant. They are Gemini, Virgo, Sagittarius, and Pisces; their key word: flexibility.

Rulerships. Each planet has one or two signs in which its nature is particularly enhanced. The planets are said to "rule" these signs.

ARIES—March 21–April 19
Element: Fire   **Quality: Cardinal**   **Planet: Mars**

Aries signifies new beginnings, spring, youth, the untried, and is connected with One—The First. This sign is pioneering, exploring, an executive and leader. Aries is self-disciplined, with a dislike of supervision or domination. The Aries mentality is quick, direct, active, and organized. Originality, individuality, and independence are all

Aries qualities. In love you are passionate, impulsive, and idealistic. Your sign is constant and devoted as long as your partner makes you the center of the universe! Negatively, your sign may be stubborn, aggressive, egotistical, tending toward dominating others. Aries acts before thinking, and no Aries ever enjoys being Number Two. Aries never really grows old. Your sense of adventure, curiosity, enthusiasm, and need for variety keep you youthful. You are a social creature, vital, popular, and generally right "up front" where you can be seen and heard.

TAURUS—April 20–May 20

Element: Earth   **Quality: Fixed**   **Planet: Venus**

Taurus is the conservator of the zodiac, maternal/paternal, protective, and nurturing. You are excellent in finishing what other signs begin. There is a natural ability to grow anything as well as a love of land, houses, gardening, and building. Taurus has an ability for turning-practical investments into proven securities, such as government stocks and bonds, banking, and real estate. Your intellect is slow but sure, and while you take your time in making decisions, no one else can make you change your mind. You can be led, but never pushed. Your mentality is thorough and practical. Love and emotional fulfillment are important to all Taureans; marriage, home, family, friends, and pets all come in for the pouring out of your affectionate temperament. You enjoy good food, warm sex, elegant clothes and furnishings. Most Taureans have a flair for the production of beauty combined with utility. Art galleries, museums, beauty parlors, elegant shops, luxury items, expensive equipment are all Taurus-oriented fields. Physically, you can be lazy, indulgent because of your love of good food, wines, and "goodies" in general. Taurus can also be rigid, stubborn, with a dislike of any type of change. Your home base is an emotional necessity, and you take pride in its furnishings being as elegant as you can afford.

GEMINI—May 21–June 20

Element: Air   **Quality: Mutable**   **Planet: Mercury**

As you Geminis are the born communicators of the zodiac, you are fascinated by variety, changes of situations, events, and movement. Travel and the media are your bag! Radio, TV, publishing, lecturing, teaching, writing, and sales are all Gemini-oriented. Quick repartee and a clever tongue are basic Gemini equipment. You are easily bored by routine and detail and have a need for change in all areas of your life. You adore dipping into subjects, picking out points you can adapt, then dropping the remainder of the data. You are a born flirt. You are not a parenting type, but enjoy your offspring, when they begin to talk and think, as companions. Geminis are also likely to change jobs and generally have several employment interests in a lifetime. Geminis make excellent agents, traveling lecturers, writers, and newspeople; deal capably with electronic equipment; and use nimble fingers in creative-artistic products. Many of you are artists, designers, writers and composers, as well as humorists, entertainers, and public relations entrepreneurs. Geminis have a catlike ability to land on their feet in any type of situation, and to learn from it.

CANCER—June 21–July 23
Element: Water   **Quality: Cardinal**   **Planet: Moon**

You Cancer Moon-Children are the nesters of the world, natural parents with a deep love of counseling, feeding, comforting, and protecting. There is also the converse tendency to overdo this quality, and some of you become permissive parents. You have a basic need "to be needed" and give off an aura of sympathy. Intellectually, you tend to fluctuate before making choices. Your mentality is deeply analytical and works well with detail. You need a home base, family, and friends to be happy. Your home is your retreat, your citadel, and safe haven. In love you are devoted, loyal, and empathetic. However, you can also be manipulative, possessive, with an inability to release the past. You may keep your children infantile and your family dependent. Because the Moon is your governing planet, you can be moody, despondent, and depressed, especially during the Moon's full term. Cancers also tend to be overly sensitive and can brood and turn sullen over small, innocent remarks or actions. Because of your native love of earth and growing things, real estate, farms, children, pets, and houses are successful fields for your talents. Cancers are creative. You have a gut-level "knowing" psychic ability which you should trust.

LEO—July 23–August 22
Element: Fire   **Quality: Fixed**   **Planet: Sun**

Leo is the King/Queen syndrome. All Leos enjoy starting at the top! You have the ability to make others enthusiastic, to stimulate people, and are a born actor/actress. Leo governs the entertainment and theatrical fields, and members of this sign adore the limelight. Intellectually, you are direct, forceful, and demanding. Leos are ambitious, making excellent political and military leaders, government executives, teachers, sales people, lawyers, and doctors. As Leo is not only a Fire sign, but a Fixed sign, you can also be stubborn, rigid, and demanding. It will be your way—or else! You love Romance with a capital R. All of the accouterments, such as candlelight, flowers, music, and wine, appeal to your emotional temperament. You are passionate, can be jealous, eager to possess and dominate. As Leo governs the heart, your emotions are quickly moved by those in distress. You will wear yourself out for those you love. Groups associated with benevolent and charitable/loving goals can offer you outlets for your generous nature. As you basically feel the world is your oyster, it may be difficult for you to deal with only one love. Leos adore admiration and need public recognition and constant patting.

VIRGO—August 23–September 22
Element: Earth   Quality: Mutable   Planet: Mercury/Vulcan

Vulcan is the Artisan of the perfect product, and you Virgos have an inward picture of this perfection you find difficult to materialize. This irritant helps explain your constant search for that "perfect" product. Like Diogenes looking for the honest individual, Virgo seeks the perfect person, job, situation, and lifestyle. Virgo has historically been confused with the word Virgin. Actually, Virgo is the Earth Mother.

The male Virgo contains much of the sensitivity and artistic creativity of what the Western World terms "female." The Virgo man has sensitivity, a discretion and sense of discrimination that tones down the arrogance of the macho type. The intellect of your sign is like a strong ray, analyzing, criticizing, researching, and investigating minute details. Companionship on many levels is a Virgo emotional demand, and physical union combines with intellectual communication. You Virgos are slow to make a romantic relationship, but once you do, generally it is enduring and lifelong. Virgos have a natural talent for saving and investing money in practical, proven areas. Virgo types find success in the production of beautiful and usable objects, art galleries, libraries, research and investigative laboratories, and health food outlets. The Virgo philosophy must also appeal to the intellect, to the eye and senses as well, and "make sense."

LIBRA—September 23–October 22

Element: Air　　　**Quality: Cardinal**　　　**Planet: Venus**

Libra has generally been called the "Sign of Balance." Actually, Librans are *seeking* balance. The symbol of the scales depicts your constant weighing of data before reaching conclusions. You Librans also have an emotional desire for relationships, for a love partner who will help make your world for you. Part of the Libra challenge is to learn to be individually and independently oriented. Libra is always "in love with love," putting your pattern on whoever happens to be near! You Librans are not natural physical or emotional parents, and prefer to deal with your children as people and friends. Both female and male members of your sign dislike mess, disorder, noise, and confusion. Intellectually, Libra is connected with beauty, the arts, music, design, law, and counseling. You tend to see yourself in the eyes of others. Librans can be self-indulgent, lazy, jealous, envious, and indecisive. Because you have a need for surface harmony and a pleasant environment, you often bury what you really hate beneath the surface. Being the sign of relationships, Libra needs to extend that duality outward into larger and more varied groups.

SCORPIO—October 23–November 21

Element: Water　　　**Quality: Fixed**　　　**Planet: Pluto**

Scorpio is the All or Nothing vibration. You give it everything you have—or you do not go at all. You Scorpios have a deep need to be devoted to an idea, a philosophy, a belief, or a person. Otherwise, your intense energies deteriorate into excesses in negative fields. Intellectually, your mind is sharp, keen, and razor-edged. Analysis, facts, data, and personal research are all merged before you make a decision or choice. You are also a Fixed sign, giving determination, endurance, as well as stubbornness and rigidity of outlook. You have a deep desire for leadership. It is hard for you to take orders; your natural reaction is to give them! Scorpio governs the sexual organs and the genitals, but this does not especially highlight your love life. You are ardent, swift to fulfill your physical needs, passionate and fiery in romance. You tend to dominate those you love, while you yourself demand freedom and a totally different set of rules.

Scorpios of both sexes may be manipulative, jealous, resentful, and sarcastic when crossed. This sign governs the subconscious mind, dream symbols, what lies beneath the earth and oceans. Scorpio rules the investigative agencies, such as detective organizations. Scorpios are also creative and artistic: painters, dancers, writers, composers, and explorers. Your tenacity and passion for achievement when pointed toward constructive goals bring you recognition.

SAGITTARIUS—November 22–December 21

Element: Fire   Quality: Mutable   Planet: Jupiter

Sagittarius is the traveler of the zodiac. You are the natural student-teacher who remains youthful because of your constantly questioning mind and your active body. You enjoy communicating information that has stimulated you so that teaching, writing, lecturing, publishing, and acting are all natural fields for success. Intellectually, you want direct, clear facts—and you want them now. You have the ability to cut the fat away from data. Exploring, ranging over the world, meeting people with varied backgrounds, and touching all those "wet paint" signs appeals to you. Romantically, you are old-fashioned and sentimental, although your surface personality may appear very modern to others. Sagittarius women demand intellectual freedom and liberty, as well as a very long leash. Given independence, you generally do not stray too far from home. Not given it—you are gone. Sagittarius men take for granted that freedom, and are amazed should disputes arise. The fastest way to end a Sagittarius relationship is to show the leash and rope! They give generously and abundantly, but not when it is demanded. Your sign will be young forever, as long as the exhilaration and stimulation of the unexplored is a potential.

CAPRICORN—December 22–January 19

Element: Earth   Quality: Cardinal   Planet: Saturn

Capricorn is concerned with the past, conserving, and restoring. You have a particular talent for "making do," for refurbishing and recycling. There is a certain Machiavellian aspect of your sign that is clever, persistent, and ambitious. Endurance and patience are also Capricorn traits. Mentally, you have a fine ability for research, investigation, and critical analysis. Like Virgo, you enjoy dissecting formulas, ideas, finances, and any special area that interests you. There is a strange aura of occult ability surrounding your sign, and you often attempt to integrate this inner "knowing" with your outer senses. Capricorn women seek careers and financial independence, and hire others to do the cleaning-up. Male Capricorns are ambitious and persistent. In romance, you are cautious and reserved in expressing emotions. Both male and female Capricorns adore power even in the romantic arena. Capricorns need to have pride in their loved ones, and can be demanding of their energies and affections. Yours is a long-lived sign and you often have several careers. Banking, insurance, health, investigation, medical laboratories, detective agencies, and government investigative organizations appeal to you.

AQUARIUS—January 20–February 18
Element: Air   Quality: Fixed   Planet: Uranus

Aquarius is the madcap of the zodiac, alternating between caring for all humankind, creating innovative yet practical products, and stimulating untried concepts and techniques—and being unreliable, selfish of time, money, and emotion, and irresponsible. Intellectually, you are brilliant, yet stupid when it comes to practical daily affairs. Generally this is due to a lack of interest. Your mind is on something else by the time the problem has been explained. You are the inventor, the explorer, good at beginnings, terrible at finishing. Romantically, you fall into the same pattern. As long as your partner stimulates your intellect, you are the original Funny Valentine. Aquarians are seldom "turned on" by mere physical charms but demand mental fascination. You can be stubborn, rigid, resistant to change or anything new unless it fits into your own inner picture. Reaching out to assist humankind, Aquarians may not see the needs right under their noses in personal family situations. Aquarian men can be sweetly romantic, once their attention is captured. Aquarian women have so many irons in the fire that they too can be emotionally fired up, but with both sexes, don't expect the attention to last long. It is an intellectual sign, not a physical one.

PISCES—February 19–March 20
Element: Water   Quality: Mutable   Planet: Neptune

Pisces is a complex sign. It is a charming sign, nurturing, sympathetic, and fun. Pisceans can also be a pain to others, depending on them to make choices and decisions. Pisces is a strong sign. Intellectually, Pisceans have sufficient patience and detail ability for research, handsome creative products, painting, design, playing an instrument, writing, and acting. Pisces is a natural healer, dealing with emotional problems with great success. In romance, Pisceans are the original hearts and flowers people. Pisces women are old-fashioned and sentimental. Pisces males have a gentle tenderness about love, a sensitivity and warmth which protects and nurtures. Often Pisceans fall in love with someone much older than themselves. They are natural psychics. They have a gut-level intuitive knowing which they should follow. Once they take the reins into their own hands and stop checking in with their loved ones for every decision, their ambitions and goals are easily achieved. They can be passively stubborn, manipulative, secretive, and self-oriented. However, their natural sweetness, desire to give and receive affection, and knack for helping those in distress keep them an important part of our lives.

THE INFLUENCE OF THE MOON

The Moon rules the unconscious, instinctual processes in nature which are devoid of personality. This includes the oceanic tides, plant and animal life, the unconscious in human beings, and the mass mind of the crowd. All are rhythmically attuned to the cycle of the Moon's phases and signs.

Because of this association, the behavior of that which is without personality can be accurately predicted. This is the basic principle upon which

Llewellyn's Moon Sign Book is based. Those who are strongly interested in the subject should turn to this source. However, we include here a short explanation of the crucial points.

Everyone has seen the Moon wax and wane, growing progressively larger and smaller through a period of approximately 29½ days. This circuit from New Moon, when the surface of the Moon is completely dark, to Full Moon, when it is totally lit, and back again, is called the lunation cycle. As the Moon makes one entire trip around the Earth, it reflects the light of the Sun in varying degrees, depending on the angle between the Sun and the Moon as viewed from Earth. During the year, the Moon will make twelve or thirteen such trips, each called a lunation.

This cycle is divided into parts called "phases" or "quarters." There are several methods by which this can be done, and the system used in this calendar will not necessarily correspond to those used in other almanacs and calendars.

The First Quarter begins when the Sun and Moon are in the same place, or conjunct. The Moon is not visible at first, since it rises at the same time as the Sun. But toward the end of this phase, a silver thread can be seen just after sunset as the Moon follows the Sun over the western horizon.

The Second Quarter begins halfway between the New Moon and the Full Moon, when the Sun and Moon are at right angles, or a 90° square, to each other. This half-Moon rises around noon, and sets around midnight, so it can be seen in the western sky during the first half of the night.

The Third Quarter begins with the Full Moon, when the Sun and Moon are opposite one another and the full light of the Sun can shine on the full sphere of the Moon. The round Moon can be seen rising in the east at sunset, and then rising progressively a little later each evening.

The Fourth Quarter begins about halfway between the Full Moon and New Moon, when the Sun and Moon are again at 90°, or square each other. This decreasing Moon rises at midnight and can be seen in the east during the last half of the night, reaching the overhead position just about as the Sun rises.

THE MOON IN THE SIGNS

☽ **MOON IN ARIES** ♈—A time of enthusiasm and beginnings. Tendencies to impulsiveness and snap decisions are accentuated. This is a favorable time for any kind of beginning and for making changes. This is also a good time for work that requires skillful (though not necessarily patient) work with tools, particularly sharp cutting instruments and the like. The first part of the Moon's transit through Aries, when it is closer to Pisces, is a more spiritual time; a sense of rebirth is evident, and the mind is inclined to consider deeper subjects.

Nearing the middle of the transit, the strongest Aries tendencies are felt, which makes this an excellent time to seek inspiration for a direction. Tendencies to bad temper and "selfishness" need to be carefully watched, especially as the Moon approaches Taurus.

☽ **MOON IN TAURUS** ♉—The aggressiveness and verve of Aries "solidifies" into the placid patience of the Bull. People are inclined to be stodgy and cautious. The desire is to protect what one already has, rather than to strike out in search of something new. Because of financial concerns, this is a poor time to seek change. Bankers and others in charge of money are slow to make loans. The first part of the Taurus Moon transit is the most cautious and reserved. The middle area is more placid and calm, a time for rest, or for engaging in those things that require more patience than skill or nimbleness. As the Moon moves toward Gemini, the Taurus solidity gradually gives way to the Gemini quickness and change. Concern is directed more and more toward communication and thought.

☽ **MOON IN GEMINI** ♊—Communication is the key drive of this time, senses of wit and intelligence becoming sharper. Practical concerns tend to be slighted in favor of intellectual pursuits and mental games. People are more changeable than usual. Statements must be taken with a grain of salt. This time is higly favorable for communication, particularly toward the middle of the transit. As the Moon blends into Cancer, more emotiveness becomes apparent in contrast to the highly mental and abstract Gemini mode. Communications tend to be derived more from emotional needs. It is, for example, an excellent time to write letters or to make telephone calls about family matters.

☽ **MOON IN CANCER** ♋—Sensitivity rises sharply in the sign of Cancer, and with it comes a strong drive toward self-indulgence, especially with food and drink. People with natural tendencies toward gullibility must be most prudent during the Moon's transit of Cancer. A sharp tongue should be curbed during the Cancer Moon, when people are more inclined to have their feelings hurt. By the same token, one is to be more watchful of flattery or praise from suspicious sources; the desire to accept it increases with the strong Cancerian need for approval. As the Moon moves toward Leo, Leonine pride blends with Cancerian sensitivity. This can be a time of warmth and friendship, but it is important to be courteous during this phase; a grudge here takes a long time to pass.

☽ **MOON IN LEO** ♌—Pride and circumstance come to the fore now, with matters of display and showmanship getting special priority. The noted Leo generosity becomes evident. Overall vitality increases greatly, with the emphasis on entertainment and romantic pursuits. This is also a good time for dealing with people in positions of power, especially if you appeal to their nobler motives. Conflicts over leadership are more likely to arise in the beginning of this transit, while people in established positions have the edge during the middle of the transit. As the Moon moves toward Virgo, the pride of Leo will blend with the exactness of Virgo, making it a good time for unassuming, yet ultimately ambitious moves toward personal achievement.

☽ **MOON IN VIRGO** ♍—The early phase of Virgo is a good time to relate to matters of the home, as drives for hygiene and upkeep strengthen. An excellent time for dealing with health and dietary concerns. Attention to details is the Virgo forte, so anything that requires painstaking attention is benefited. The Virgo Moon transit is a good time for intellectual matters, though better for those that require exactness rather than innovation. Editing a completed work would be better than attempts at spontaneous creativity. Virgo favors the careful, bargain-hunting shopper.

☽ **MOON IN LIBRA** ♎—With the Moon in Libra, benefits accrue to anything that tends to beautify. Artistic work, especially involving color and color balance, is greatly enhanced. As Libra is also the sign of partnership and union, this transit is an auspicious time for forming partnerships, marriages, and agreements (if the aspects are otherwise favorable). The Moon in Libra accentuates teamwork. Conflicts may be more emotional, and jealousy is possible if relationships aren't stable. An Air sign, Libra favors the eloquent and the charming, though stronger overtones of sarcasm and satire will evolve as the Moon moves toward Scorpio.

☽ **MOON IN SCORPIO** ♏—Your emotional experiences are more likely to be more intense than usual, and you will draw, and be drawn to, unusual people and events. People tend to be suspicious in this phase of the lunar cycle, and are wary and distrustful of anyone seeking information or money from them. As in Cancer, the Moon in Scorpio heightens sensitivity to insult and discourtesy. During this time, people tend to give sharp and accurate criticism. People are most critical during the first and middle parts of the Moon's passage through Scorpio, changing to a lighter, more philosophical mood as the Moon approaches Sagittarius. The last part is the best for dealing with authority.

☽ **MOON IN SAGITTARIUS** ♐—This is the most philosophical of signs, inclining toward higher thinking in all respects. The suspicious reserve of Scorpio gives way to optimism. People who might have displayed suspicions in Scorpio now are honest and direct in their interchanges. People generally tend to bemore humane and more interested in higher thinking (though more intellectual than mystical). A need to get away from routine, and a restlessness occurs. Also, travel is appealing. The Moon in Sagittarius is a good time for sport and adventure, but this sobers quickly as the Moon moves toward Capricorn.

☽ **MOON IN CAPRICORN** ♑—The expansive joviality of Sagittarius withers in the home of Saturn. Pessimism is rampant. Spiritual and intellectual matters are dominated by the concern of Capricorn with the material. This is probably the poorest possible time to seek concession from one in authority or to depart from accepted norms. It is a guardedly acquisitive time. Insensitivity is pervasive, which can frequently lead to malice justified on grounds of necessity (rather than enmity). These trends mellow and are pacified as the Moon approaches Aquarius.

☽ **MOON IN AQUARIUS** ♒—The Moon changes dramatically in Aquarius, as this is the home of Uranus, the revolutionary and electric planet. The flow now is with the innovative, the new, and the different. This transit reinforces the humane and rational in people and favors social concerns. It promotes the gathering of social groups for friendly and convivial interchange. It is also strongly inclined to science and the scientific approach. People tend to react and speak from rational rather than emotional viewpoints.

☽ **MOON IN PISCES** ♓—Things tend to get a bit fuzzy in Pisces. There is a strong undertone of spirituality, though it tends to be expressed in the early and middle part of the transit as a sense of martyrdom. There is difficulty in getting the cold facts of any situation. People are inclined to discuss their troubles and are more easily manipulated. Things are, more than ever, not what they seem and people tend to react with a sense of befuddlement or confusion. They seek the counsel of people they believe to be wiser. It is an excellent time for retreat and contemplation, as this is a natural tendency.

MOON VOID OF COURSE

Just before the Moon enters a new sign it will have one last aspect with one of the planets. Between that last major aspect and the entrance of the Moon into the next sign, it is said to be "void of course." Only the traditional "Ptolemaic" aspects (conjunction, sextile, square, trine, and opposition) are used to calculate the void of course. The asteroids and Chiron do not seem to affect Moon void of course.

The Moon void of course is a peculiar thing. It is hard to understand why it would make any difference whether or not the Moon was finished making major aspects as it approached a new sign. Yet, experience has shown that it does indeed have a significant and reliable effect. It has been found the decisions made while the Moon is void of course never come to fruition in the way intended, and usually not at all. So the astrological rule is to avoid making decisions when the Moon is void of course. Carry on routine activities that have previously been planned.

Many people feel scattered or without direction during the void period. It is a good time for introspection and getting centered and focused.

Often, items purchased during this time are left unused, plagued with mechanical problems, or turn out to be bad investments.

It is nearly impossible in today's world to put off all decisions every time the Moon is void, but try to avoid this period for the most important ones. Or try to make the decision before the Moon is void, and then act on the decision at this time. The world can't stop, but you can do what you can to help things work better for yourself.

PLANETS AND RETROGRADES

THE SUN indicates the psychological bias that will dominate your actions. What you see, and why, is told in the reading for your Sun. The Sun also shows the basic energy patterns of your body and psyche. In many ways, the Sun is the dominant force in your horoscope and your life. Other influences, especially that of the Moon, may modify the Sun's influence, but nothing will cause you to depart very far from the basic solar pattern. Always keep in mind always the basic influence of the Sun and remember all other influences must be interpreted in terms of it, especially insofar as other influences play a visible role in your life. You may think, dream, imagine, hope a thousand things, according to your Moon and your other planets, but the Sun is what you are, and to be your best self in terms of your Sun is to cause your energies to work along the path in which they will have maximum help from planetary vibrations.

THE MOON tells the desire of your life. When you "know what you mean but can't say it," it is your Moon that knows it and your Sun that can't say it. The wordless ecstasy, the mute sorrow, the secret dream, the esoteric picture of yourself that you can't get across to the world, or that the world doesn't comprehend or value—these are the products of the Moon in your horoscope. When you are misunderstood, it is your Moon nature, expressed imperfectly through the Sun sign, that you feel betrayed. Things you know without thought—intuitions, hunches, instincts—are the products of the Moon. Modes of expression that you feel truly reflect your deepest self belong to the Moon: art, letters, creative work of any kind; sometimes love; sometimes business. Whatever you feel is most deeply yourself, whether or not you are able to do anything about it in the outer world, is the product of your Moon and of the sign your Moon occupies at birth.

MERCURY is the sense-impression antenna of your horoscope. Its position by sign indicates your reactions to sights, sounds, odors, tastes, and touch impressions, affording a key to the attitude you have toward the physical world around you. Mercury is the messenger through which your physical body and brain (the Sun) and your inner nature (the Moon) are kept in contact with the outer world, which will appear to you according to the index of Mercury's position by sign in the horoscope. Mercury rules your rational mind.

VENUS is the emotional antenna of your horoscope. Through Venus, impressions come to you from the outer, to which you react emotionally. The position of Venus by sign at the time of your birth gives the key to your attitude toward these emotional experiences. As Mercury is the messenger linking sense impressions (sight, smell, etc.) to the basic nature of your Sun and Moon, so Venus is the messenger linking emotional impressions. If Venus is found in the same sign as the Sun, emotions gain importance in your life, having a direct bearing on your actions. If Venus is in the same sign as the Moon, emotions also gain importance, bearing directly on your inner nature, adding self-confidence, making you sensitive to emotional impressions and frequently indicating you have more love in your heart than you are able to express. If Venus is in the same sign as Mercury, emotional impressions and sense impressions work together; you tend to idealize the world of the senses and sensualize the world of the emotions to interpret emotionally what you see and hear.

MARS is the energy principle in the horoscope. Its position by sign indicates the channels into which energy will most easily be directed. It is the planet through which the activities of the Sun and the desires of the Moon express themselves in action. In the same sign as the Sun, Mars gives abundant energy, sometimes misdirected in temper, temperament, and quarrels. In the same sign as the Moon, it gives a great capacity to make use of the innermost aims, and to make the inner desires articulate and practical. In the same sign as Venus, it quickens emotional reactions and causes you to act on them, makes for ardor and passion in love, and fosters an earthly awareness of emotional realities.

4 JUPITER is the feeler you have out in the world for opportunity. Through it the chances of a lifetime are passed along for consideration according to the basic nature of your Sun and Moon. Jupiter's sign position indicates the places in which you will look for opportunity, the uses to which you wish to put it, and the capacity you have to react and profit by it. Jupiter is ordinarily, and erroneously, called the Planet of Luck. It is "luck" insofar as it is the index of opportunity, but your luck depends less on what comes to you (Jupiter) than on what you do with what comes to you (the total personality). In the same sign as the Sun or Moon, Jupiter gives a direct, and generally effective, response to opportunity and is likely to show forth at its "luckiest." If Jupiter is in the same sign as Mercury, sense impressions are interpreted opportunistically. If Jupiter is in the same sign as Venus, you interpret emotions in such a way as to turn them to your advantage; your feelings work harmoniously with the chances for progress that the world has to offer. If Jupiter is in the same sign as Mars, you follow opportunity with energy, dash, enthusiasm and courage, take long chances, and play your cards wide open.

♄ SATURN indicates the direction that will be taken in life by the self-preservative principle which, in its highest manifestation, ceases to be purely defensive and becomes ambitious and aspirational. Your defense or attack against the world is shown by the sign position of Saturn in the horoscope of birth. If Saturn is in the same sign as the Sun or Moon, defense predominates, and there is danger of introversion. The further Saturn is from the Sun, Moon, and Ascendant, the better for objectivity and extroversion. If Saturn is in the same sign as Mercury, there is a profound and serious reaction to sense impressions; this position generally accompanies a deep and efficient mind. If Saturn is in the same sign as Venus, a defensive attitude toward emotional experience makes for apparent coolness in love and difficulty with the emotions and human relations. If Saturn is in the same sign as Mars, confusion between defensive and aggressive urges can make an indecisive person—or, if the Sun and Moon are strong and the total personality well-developed, a balanced, peaceful, and calm individual of sober judgment and moderate actions may be indicated. If Saturn is in the same sign as Jupiter, the reaction to opportunity is sober and balanced.

♅ URANUS in a general way relates to the neuro-mentality, the creative originality or individuality, and its position by sign in the horoscope tells the direction along which you will seek to express your most characteristic self in creative and original effort. In the same sign as Mercury or the Moon, Uranus suggests acute awareness, a quick reaction to sense impressions and experiences, or a hair-trigger mind. In the same sign as the Sun, it points to great nervous activity, a high-strung nature, an original, creative, or eccentric personality. In the same sign as Mars, Uranus indicates high-speed activity, love of swift motion, and perhaps of danger. In the same sign as Venus, it suggests an unusual reaction to emotional experience, highly idealistic though sensual, original ideas of love and human relations. In the same sign as Saturn, Uranus points to good sense; this can be a practical, creative position, but, more often than not, it sets up a destroying conflict between practicality and originality that can result in a stalemate. In the same sign as Jupiter, Uranus makes opportunity, creates wealth and the means of getting it, and is conducive to the inventive, daring, and executive.

NEPTUNE relates to the deepest wells of the subconscious, inherited mentality and spirituality, indicating what you take deeply for granted in life. Neptune in the same sign as the Sun or Moon indicates that intuitions and hunches—or delusions—dominate; there is a need for rigidly holding to reality. In the same sign as Mercury, sharp sense perceptions, a sensitive mind, perhaps creative, a quivering intensity of reaction to sense experience. In the same sign as Venus, idealistic and romantic (or sentimental) reaction to emotional experience; danger of sensationalism and love of strange pleasures. In the same sign as Mars, energy and intuition that work together to make mastery of life—one of the signs of having angels (or devils) on your side. In the same sign as Jupiter, intuitive response to opportunity generally along practical and money-making lines; one of the signs of security if not indeed of wealth. In the same sign as Saturn, intuitive defense and attack on the world, generally successful unless Saturn is polarized on the negative side; then, danger of delusions and unhappiness.

PLUTO is a planet of extremes—from the lowest criminal and violent level of our society to the heights a person can attain when s/he realizes his/her significance in the collectivity of man. Pluto also rules three important mysteries of life—sex, death, and rebirth—and links them to each other. One level of death symbolized by Pluto is the physical death of an individual, which occurs so that s/he can be reborn into another body to further his/her spiritual development. On another level, an individual can experience a "death" of his/her old self when s/he realizes the deeper significance of life; s/he thus becomes one of the "second born." In a natal horoscope, Pluto signifies our perspective on the world, our conscience and subconscious. Since so many of Pluto's qualities are centered on the deeper mysteries of life, the house position of Pluto, and aspects to it, can show you how to attain a deeper understanding of the importance of the spiritual in your life.

RETROGRADE. When the planets (not including the Sun and Moon) cross the sky, they occasionally appear to move backwards as seen from Earth. Of course, this is only how it looks from our vantage point because of the combined movement of the Earth and planets. The planets never actually go backwards, but the phenomenon still has symbolic significance to the astrologer. When a planet turns backwards it is said to be "retrograde," indicated by the symbol "℞." When it turns forward again it is said to go "direct," indicated by the symbol "D." The point at which the movement changes from one direction to another is called a "station."

When a planet is retrograde, its expression is delayed, or out of kilter with the normal progression of events. Sometimes the functions represented by the planet seem to be obscured or hidden, but more often it is just a matter of delayed timing. Generally, it can be said that whatever is planned during this period will be delayed, but usually it will come to fruition when the retrograde is over. Of course, this applies only to activities ruled by the planet that is retrograde. It is good to be aware that this waiting period does not signal the demise of the projects being undertaken, but only a delay that will straighten out when the planet goes direct.

Activities undertaken when a planet is stationary, about to go direct, are particularly powerful and long-lasting if ruled by that particular planet. Avoid activities when the ruling planet is stationary, going retrograde.

☿ ℞ **MERCURY RETROGRADE.** Although retrogrades of all the planets are of some significance, those involving Mercury and Venus are particularly easy to follow and of personal use, since these are "personal planets."

Mercury rules communications, particularly through informal means—reading and writing, speaking, and short errands. Communication by radio and television comes under the rulership of Uranus, unless it is of a personal nature, so is not considered here. Whenever Mercury goes retrograde, astrologers find that personal communications get fouled up or misunderstood more often. Letters get lost, friends misunderstand each other, more misspellings occur, and so on. So astrologers have developed the rule that when Mercury is retrograde, avoid informal means of communication. Fortunately, the retrograde of Mercury only lasts for short times.

ASTEROIDS AND CHIRON

Shortly after the discovery of the planet Uranus, the first four asteroids were discovered. On New Years Day in 1801, a Sicilian astronomer named Piazzi sighted Ceres between the orbits of Mars and Jupiter. The following year, on March 28, 1802, the asteroid Pallas was sighted; on September 1, 1804, Juno was discovered and on March 29, 1807, Vesta was discovered. While not realized at the time by astrologers, these four asteroids were to play an assisting role to the Moon and Venus in expressing the many-faceted feminine principle. These asteroids, named for four Greek goddesses, came to represent the four aspects of femininity; Ceres—the Mother, Pallas—the Daughter; Juno—the Wife; and Vesta—the Sister. To date, over 2,000 other asteroids have been discovered with ephemerides constantly being developed to assist us in our "Asteroid Watch."

⚳ **CERES** represents what nurtures us and how we go about being nurtured. It represents the principle of unconditional love and acceptance. Ceres is sometimes called the "Great Mother" or "The Great Earth Mother." She gives freely with the principle of sharing and care-giving. When Ceres is in the fire signs (Aries, Leo, or Sagittarius) this nurturing is more inclined to take the form of encouragement and praise. When found in an Earth sign (Taurus, Virgo, or Capricorn) it takes on the form of stabilizing and structuring. When found in an Air sign (Gemini, Libra, or Aquarius) Ceres assists in relating and communicating; and, in a water sign (Cancer, Scorpio, or Pisces) she takes on the role of offering sympathy and understanding. Ceres also represents all that nourishes and, as "Goddess of the Grain," appears prominently in charts of individuals who plant the seeds, tend the land, harvest the crops, are the cooks and bakers, and work as nutritional counselors.

JUNO is the indicator of all one-to-one relationships and our need for compatibility. As Juno represents this need for compatibility, it is our partner or mate, equality, the balance of power, and our individual freedoms. She represents our styles of relating. She gives us a mirror for looking at ourselves to see where we are balanced (or need balance). Juno asks us, "What do I need in an intimate, committed relationship?" In the Fire signs (Aries, Leo, or Sagittarius) shared visions, independence, and passion are important; in Earth signs (Taurus, Virgo, or Capricorn), stability, consistency, and comfort are needed; in Air signs (Gemini, Libra, or Aquarius) there needs to be a verbal exchange; while in water signs (Cancer, Scorpio, or Pisces), emotional rapport, support, and understanding are most important.

PALLAS symbolizes our creative intelligence. She represents our intuition, flashes of genius, keen insights, and our ability to formulate new and original thought. Pallas also represents our abilities to plan strategies that lead us to tangible results. She signifies artistic ability that comes from clear sight and the ability to understand whole patterns. She has the ability to draw the creative artist from within and to give it form. Pallas also governs healing and the holistic approach to healing therapies; such as guided imagery, meditation, visualization, and all mental self-healing techniques. Her primary role in healing is that of balancing the total psyche. Pallas in a Fire sign (Aries, Leo, or Sagittarius) expresses her creative intelligence by becoming inspired and formulating visions; in Earth signs (Taurus, Virgo, or Capricorn) she needs to create new forms and structures; in Air signs (Gemini, Libra, or Aquarius) she develops new ideas and theories; and in water signs (Cancer, Scorpio, or Pisces), her creative intellect tends to be psychic and intuitive.

VESTA seems to symbolize our ability to focus, to dedicate, and aspire to a certain path or goal. She also symbolizes the sacrifices that we make along the way to attain that goal. She represents our ability to work hard and seems to describe where we work for works' sake rather than for any other goal or reward. When Vesta is well aspected in the birth chart, we genuinely like our work. If not, and if there is a strong dislike of our work, we may encounter times of health problems or times where we feel less well. Vesta is how we integrate and focus ourselves. When Vesta is in a Fire sign (Aries, Leo, or Sagittarius) we focus through our inspiration to create; in the Earth signs (Taurus, Virgo, or Capricorn) through developing a physical discipline; in an Air sign (Gemini, Libra, or Aquarius) through learning and sharing ideas; and in a water sign (Cancer, Scorpio, or Pisces) through merging and bonding.

CHIRON (pronounced Ky-ron) was discovered on November 1, 1977 at about 10:00 am (PST). It lies between the orbits of Saturn and Uranus. In the years that have followed its discovery, astrologers and researchers alike have attempted to understand the importance of this "new find." By 1979, some preliminary speculations were in print and have been followed by more detailed work.

Chiron is symbolized by a key, and seems to be a major "key" player in life's lessons. This Chironic key can unlock many doors of our psyche. It can create sonic booms in our lives that require we "do something about it." Chiron shows us the way we can heal ourselves, and with Chiron, we are not without guidance. It is the true holistic healer.

In Greek mythology, Chiron was a teacher who taught not only the arts of war, but also of peace. He taught the necessity of music, art, poetry, astronomy, farming, and healing. He taught students to become whole, learned, and self-sufficient. Chiron is also called "the maverick." Maverick is interpreted to mean "one who acts alone." As Chiron is located in an elliptical orbit (with a 50-year cycle in which to transit the zodiac) between Saturn and Uranus, it appears that one of the lessons Chiron is teaching is how to bring the usefulness of the old structures into the future—the honoring of the old rules but with an update into our contemporary thinking modes. In personal, natal astrology by sign and house position, it indicates our awareness that this is a "turning point" area in our chart. In mundane astrology it is very noticeable in the changing of group consciousness. (Remember Chernobyl and the Challenger disaster—both with significant Chiron activity. We learned a lot, didn't we?)

ASPECTS AND TRANSITS

Aspects are the angles formed between two planets in the sky. Transits are angles formed between a planet as it is now in the sky and the position of a planet sometime in the past, as it is recorded in a horoscope. Thus, a planet can transit its own former position or the former position of another planet.

Aspects indicate current relationships between planets, and transits indicate the influence of present conditions on something established in the past. In defining the meaning of aspects and transits, we can speak of them together because the interpretations are similar.

The major aspects included in *Llewellyn's Daily Planetary Guide* are the conjunction (0 degrees), the semisextile (30 degrees), the semisquare (45 degrees), the sextile (60 degrees), the square (90 degrees), the trine (120 degrees), the sesquiquadrate (135 degrees), the quincunx or inconjunct (150 degrees), and the opposition (180 degrees). In general, those aspects based on a division of the circle by multiples of two are considered the most important, largely because they signify difficulties in relationships and hence are most noticeable. Also of significance is the lesser known quincunx. The conjunction, because it signifies the joining together of two different energies, is also very noticeable. The semi-sextile, the semisquare, the sextile, and the sesquiquadrate have much less influence.

The aspects are roughly divided into two groups, depending on the ease with which humans can deal with the energy involved. The semisquare,

square, quincunx, sesquiquadrate, and opposition are called the difficult or "unfavorable" aspects. The semi-sextile, sextile, and trine are called the "easy" or "favorable" aspects. However, these names have nothing to do with the inherent energy of the aspects themselves, and are just valuations from our perspective.

CONJUNCTION (0°)—When two planets are close to each other (7° for the planets, 12° if the Sun or Moon are involved—these are only rough approximations), the energy of the two planets combine. When the planets are very close together (within half of a degree), they converge to such an extent that the separate energies of each become indistinguishable. The simplicity of this aspect makes it the easiest to understand. However, one should note the differences between the meanings of the planets involved to really appreciate the effect of a conjunction. If the planets are rather opposite in character (like Mars and Venus), if one of them is particularly demanding (like Saturn), or if any of the outer planets (Uranus, Neptune, and Pluto) conjoin the personal, inner planets (Mercury, Venus, and Mars), we will have a combination of energy that will be so out of the ordinary that it will produce distinctive effects, possibly unpleasant ones, although this depends on their reception by humans.

SEMI-SEXTILE (30°)—Two planets semi-sextile to each other will support one another in a very external sense, but will not share any true inner attunement. This aspect should not be considered of great importance.

SEMI-SQUARE (45°)—This aspect denotes a minor irritation. Somewhat like the 90° angle (square) but with less awareness or concern. Many astrologers use this in personal astrology, but it should be noted that it can play a major role in mundane work. (It is a good tool for researchers.)

SEXTILE (60°)—This aspect encourages communication, that is, exchange of understanding, between two planets. However, this interaction is generally not potent enough to contribute significantly to the work of either planet.

SQUARE (90°)—In this aspect the two planets fight against one another, with each trying to get the upper hand, trying to make the other conform to its mode of operation. The fight is continual and can be overcome not by favoring one side or the other—as we so often do—but only by accepting the claims of each and identifying with a higher truth and unity. In this way we accept ourselves (if the aspect is in our natal horoscope) or our challenge from the outside world (if it is a transit) and allow for the true expression of these energies—conflicting, yes, but each valid in its own particular way.

TRINE (120°)—This is the most important of the favorable aspects in that the two planets, rather than merely supporting or communing with each other (semi-sextile and sextile), now share a similarity of purpose. By this we mean they help each other to accomplish their tasks. However, the trine is less often noticed than the square or opposition, probably because people don't count their blessings as often as their curses.

SESQUIQUADRATE (135°)—This aspect is a combination of the square (90°) and the semi-square (45°) and denotes the area of the chart in which there is a conscious need to take action—a strong need to express oneself in activity and to make decisions.

QUINCUNX (150°)—(Also called "inconjunct.") Of all the aspects this is probably the most influential in terms of raising havoc. Its effect is not as noticeable as the other major "unfavorable" aspects, making its effects all the more difficult to deal with.

When a quincunx occurs between two planets, it signifies that there is a slight disharmony between the planets that the conscious mind does not grasp. In fact, the conscious mind assumes that an uplifting integration of the forces of the two planets is not only possible, but just around the corner. This makes the quincunx the aspect of false hopes and aspirations, and expressions that are slightly "off the mark." Often the person experiencing the quincunx feels as if he or she has some problem almost taken care of, and yet the solution continually slips away.

The solution to this problem is harder than it would first appear. It requires not only becoming conscious of the unconscious assumption to correct it; it also requires allowing the planets to manifest in their slightly, although distinctly, disharmonious manner. When this lesson is learned, the quincunxial person will be found to be most fascinating and paradoxical to be around. However, this seldom happens. It appears to be most difficult to become aware of misdirected hopes and aspirations.

OPPOSITION (180°)—While the square produces a quarrel, and the quincunx an unconscious misdirection, the opposition produces a stand-off, a stalemate that is relieved only by compromise. The two planets in opposition each desire to operate in their own fashion and cannot conjoin in expression. The only solution for this is to allow each to have its turn, reassuring the other that its time will soon come, and to once again identify with a higher truth than that found in strife and opposition.

ASPECTS AND TRANSITS TO PLANETS

SUN—When there are transits to the Sun in a birth chart or from the Sun in the sky, the key words are vitality and will. Your Sun sign is how you "impress" others because it's where you feel the most sure of yourself. One of the most important times of the year is when the Sun is traveling through your own Sun sign. This is the beginning of the new year for you. When the transiting Sun is two or four signs from your Sun, you can either rest on your laurels or push for what you want; you are now more likely to make a good impression and a lot of progress. The times when the Sun is three or six signs away from your Sun can indicate either that you are too willful and/or run into people who are boastful and willful, or that you are able to make important decisions and stick to them by putting out extra effort and energy.

You automatically feel a tension when these times come. During easier times, you must consciously "push" yourself because of your tendency to be lazy.

☽ **MOON**—The study of the New Moons, Full Moons, and eclipses helps you know when to begin and end projects. The New Moon means the Sun and Moon are in conjunction (together in the same degree and sign of the zodiac). This is the beginning of a cycle and indicates one project ends so that another can start. The New Moon also indicates the beginning of a new phase of an old project. With the Full Moon, the Sun and Moon are 180° (or six signs) apart. You feel a conscious awareness concerning these same projects. The Full Moon also indicates endings because you get the full view of something and decide to drop it. If these Full Moons are also eclipses, the emphasis is stronger and can last from six months to a year.

☿ **MERCURY**—Transits and aspects always relate to communications, thinking, and learning. If Mercury is involved with other planets in squares or oppositions, there is a tendency toward misunderstanding, confusion, and excessive worry. When Mercury is in an easy aspect, you can communicate more easily so that you will be understood more readily. Mercury aspects also contain a little of the con artist, who promises more than can be delivered. Be cautious when you see these possibilities.

When Mercury goes retrograde (indicated on your calendar by ☿R⟋), it changes the way you and others communicate. You are more likely to communicate about deeper, more subconscious things in your life. You think first, then communicate. It is a time when communications are delayed or not clearly understood. Be cautious during retrograde periods of Mercury about papers you sign because something may be missing. Mercury retrograde can also indicate changes of mind. Beware of making major decisions or purchases during this time. Usually, Mercury retrograde has a stronger effect on Geminis or Virgos because it is their ruling planet.

♀ **VENUS**—Venus, along with Mercury, is never far away from the Sun, just as thinking (Mercury) and your values (Venus) are never far removed from yourself (the Sun). When Venus is emphasized in transits, values, money, and social life are activated. Venus brings with it whatever you value, whether it is money, romance, travel, new clothes, or more freedom. When the aspects to or from Venus are easy, life is smooth and without worry. This is also a time when you see beauty in all things. However, when the aspects are the squares or oppositions, there is more tension involved in spending; your socializing is more forced, you do not feel attractive.

Venus retrograde is a time when you are attracted to bizarre things. It is also a time when money is delayed or your social and romantic life doesn't go as planned.

♂ **MARS**—Initiative, aggression, energy, and sexuality are associated with the planet Mars. If Mars is aspecting a planet in your birth chart, it will energize what that planet means to you. Mars energy is impulsive if you don't structure it. Mars energy is likely to get you into trouble because it makes you act aggressively. You don't want to take "no" for an answer. It does, however, indicate those times when you have extra courage and daring if you need it. When Mars is connected to planets by squares, conjunctions, or oppositions, expect a strong ego thrust coming either from you or to you from others. These are the times to watch your temper. When Mars is aspected by sextiles or trines, you are very confident as you use your initiative to further your goals. People now accept your ego and energy more easily. Mars in your birth chart indicates when you are aggravated and when you aggravate others.

Mars retrograde is an indication of energy impact before it is released. Projects are best planned during these times, and then begun when the planet is direct in motion again.

JUPITER—Jupiter represents opportunities, optimism, and expansion. By transit, you can expect this type of energy from the "Emperor of Planets." With all the aspects of Jupiter, it is wise to be a little conservative to prevent overabundance.

With Jupiter, you expect more than you receive; you are able to exaggerate almost anything under a Jupiter transit. Jupiter works better on the spiritual, mental, and philosophical levels because its orientation is to abstract learning on a higher level. In the material world, it can bring you too much of a good thing—overeating, overconfidence, etc.

Jupiter, on the other hand, brings luck and rewards so that if there are aspects of Jupiter working along with aspects of Saturn, the timer, there are bound to be good results. Saturn and Jupiter work hand in hand to bring you what you have worked and hoped for.

SATURN—The planet of ambition and structure demands discipline and realism, which, with the right attitude (Jupiter), bring rewards. Saturn transits are anything but fun, but they are necessary for achievement in your life. Saturn is the world telling you what you must do, and also what you must give up in order to gain what you really want. Saturn narrows your path during its transits so you aren't distracted by unnecessary things along the way to self-fulfillment.

Saturn affects man-made, consciously-planned activities. It, along with Uranus, is the builder of the zodiac. Every time Saturn aspects another planet, we can expect that the area of life signified by that planet will receive much conscious attention from social institutions and authorities.

URANUS—Uranus is associated with sudden, unpredictable changes. However, seen from a higher viewpoint that encompasses the reality of the spiritual worlds, we can see that what appears to be sudden to us, with our limited physical perception, is actually the logical consequence of actions taken or dictated from a higher realm. It is through Uranus that higher energy can be channeled into the world.

Uranus, when transiting by square or opposition to a planet in your natal chart, forces you through an inner tension to break away from old patterns so that you are more free and detached from things that hold you back. The same freedom of self is likely when the aspect is a sextile or trine, but you may have to work a little harder to free yourself. With the square, opposition, or conjunction, you cannot ignore the call to freedom. Uranus transits also bring unusual people into your life and sometimes take old friends out of your life. When Uranus has moved on, you will have changed; you are more free, and you stay that way.

NEPTUNE—When Neptune transits become prominent, you might not be sure what happened until it's all over. Neptune brings with it a feeling of unreality, fogginess, and idealism. If the aspects of Neptune are the more difficult ones—opposition, square, and conjunction—the results are more hurting, because Neptune is otherworldly, the ideal; humans are not usually ready for universal love or true self-sacrifice. If Neptune transits are used for creativity and spiritual growth, they are handled better and, consequently, they later bring less illusion and disappointment. Always be careful of Neptune transits because they make you want to escape from reality—and you may never want to come back.

PLUTO—The transits of Pluto never happen at a superficial level. Pluto is able to get to the root of the problem, disintegrate it, and leave it. Then you realize the opportunity to build again, but with a better and clearer perspective without all the "garbage." Again, as with Neptune, you are more likely to realize what the transit of Pluto meant after it has been over for a while. Pluto, when it squares, conjuncts, or opposes one of your natal planets, indicates you want to control something or someone in your life. It is really asking you to learn to control yourself. Pluto also influences your obsessions and those things that traditional society does not readily accept. When Pluto transits are in trine or sextile aspects, you more easily gain a new perspective or become involved in something or someone in a deep and intense manner.

Most transits that occur in your birth chart happen at a time in your life when you feel changes are necessary for you to grow in those activated areas. Your attitude toward change is a large factor in whether you find changes easy or difficult. It is always easier to hang on to the past because it is more comfortable and familiar. However, this attitude also keeps you from moving to the next level of your life's cycle. Change is growth, and both are important for self-actualization. Trying to overcome your chart is fighting against your own self-fulfillment. Working with your birth chart helps you feel the most comfortable and the happiest.

ASPECTS AND TRANSITS TO ASTEROIDS AND CHIRON

Though small in size, the asteroids Ceres, Juno, Pallas, and Vesta, as part of the asteroid belt located between Mars and Jupiter, can be our celestial helpmates on our journey to a better understanding of life. They can assist us in grasping the principles of beginning actions and enlarging upon them.While each asteroid is small in comparison to the size of the planets, remember that it can sometimes take only one vote to win an election.

CERES—When Ceres transits one of our natal planets it gives us the opportunity to evaluate and change, if necessary, our attitudes and actions regarding our ability to express love unconditionally. Of course, a clue as to how we might do this is given by the planet being transited. It gives us the opportunity to look at our skills at "givingness," to ourselves and others. The Ceres transit gives us the chance to achieve more balance in our lives and to create and maintain a sound, healthy working relationship with ourselves.

JUNO—While Juno in our birth charts represents our ability to develop one-to-one relationships, by transit it affords us the opportunity to better understand the glitches that have prevented us from developing meaningful relationships. We may have to look at the issues necessary to be centered within ourselves and, thereby, freeing us up to develop truly vital and growing relationships with others. Juno transits shake us loose from our feelings of victimization and give us back our power. The Juno transit gives us the chance to be whole and complete, thereby emanating the gentle, but deep, power of a person who has come to a realization of inner strength developed through sharing with others.

PALLAS—Pallas in our birth charts indicates the area where we can develop a deeper inner knowing and understanding. By transit, Pallas takes just under five years to make its zodiacal journey around our charts. In its journey, it will make contact with the other planets and angles, thereby allowing the energies to be combined and refined, giving us the opportunities to unlock the flow of ideas that may be just below the surface. As Pallas transits our birth charts, we may find that ideas can spring forth at an unbelievable rate. We are seldom still during a transit in which Pallas is one of the key players.

VESTA—Vesta represents pure fire and vital spirit. By transit, it urges us to live out our true desires and motivates us to be our best. As it also represents the hearth (or center), it offers us the opportunity to become focused in our attention and direct our inner fire toward a special cause, project, or ideal. Vesta guides in our spiritual direction. By transit, Vesta brings us to evaluate our "home." That is, the home within ourselves, the home life we experience with our families, or our larger governmental home. Securing and preserving are the major themes during the transit of Vesta.

CHIRON—The transit of Chiron can bring a mentor into our lives. It has a cleansing quality and, much as cleaning out a wound hurts a bit but speeds healing, Chiron transits can hurt while they cleans and heal. When wounds are healed, we find that we have greater freedom to pursue our true creative potential. With the transit of Chiron, the good teacher (mentor) prepares and inspires us. Experience can also be our teacher. Chiron gives us the opportunity to fill out our education—remember Chiron is the believer in "the whole," not "the hole." Chiron shows us that even though we may encounter adversity, we also have the ability to be the healers to others who encounter similar circumstances.

CELESTIAL PHENOMENA FOR 1997

Visibility of the Planets

The planets below are referenced to the constellations, not to the zodiac signs. This information is based on the **astronomical**, not astrological, placement of the planets. Information on Uranus and Neptune assumes use of a telescope. Resource: *Astronomical Phenomena for the Year 1997*, prepared by the U.S. Naval Observatory and the Royal Greenwich Observatory.

MERCURY can be seen low in the east before sunrise, or low in the west after sunset (about the time of the beginning or end of civil twilight). It is visible in the mornings between the following approximate dates: January 8 to March 1, May 4 to June 18, September 8 to October 2, and December 23 to December 31. The planet is brighter at the end of each period (the best conditions in northern latitudes occur during the third week of September, and in southern latitudes from mid-May to the first few days of June). It is visible in the evenings between the following approximate dates: March 21 to April 17, July 3 to August 25, and October 29 to December 11. The planet is brighter at the beginning of each period (the best conditions in northern latitudes occur from the end of March to the beginning of the second week of April, and in southern latitudes from mid-July to mid-August).

VENUS is a brilliant object in the evening sky from the beginning of the year until the end of the third week of February when it becomes too close to the Sun for observation. During the second week of May it reappears in the morning sky where it stays until the end of the year. Venus is in conjunction with Mercury on January 12, with Jupiter on February 6, and with Mars on October 26 and December 22.

MARS can be seen in the morning sky in the constellation of Virgo until a few days after mid-March. It is at opposition on March 17, when it is visible throughout the night. Its eastward elongation gradually decreases, moving into Leo in late March and into Virgo in early June (passing 1°7' N of Spica on August 2). It can be seen in the evening sky only after mid-June, moving into Libra in late August, Scorpius in late September, and Ophiuchus in the second week of October (passing 3°N of Antares on October 11). It then continues into Sagittarius in early November and into Capricornus after mid-December. Mars is in conjunction with Venus on October 26 and December 22.

JUPITER can be seen in the evening sky in Sagittarius the first week of January, after which it is too close to the Sun for observation. It reappears in the morning sky from the beginning of February in Capricornus, in which constellation it remains throughout the year. Its westward elongation gradually increases, and after mid-May it can be seen for more than half the night. It is at opposition on August 9, when it is visible throughout the night. Its eastward elongation then decreases, and after the first week of November until the end of the year it can be seen only in the evening sky.

Jupiter is in conjunction with Venus on February 6 and with Mercury on February 12.

SATURN can be seen in the evening sky in Pisces until mid-March, when it is too close to the Sun for observation. It reappears in the morning sky from mid-April in Cetus. Its westward elongation gradually increases, passing into Pisces again during the second week of April, in which constellation it remains for the rest of the year. It is at opposition on October 10, when it is visible throughout the night. Its eastward elongation then gradually decreases, and for the rest of the year it can be seen for more than half the night.

URANUS is visible as an evening star at the very beginning of the year in Capricornus and remains in this constellation throughout the year. It then is too close to the Sun for observation until mid-February, when it reappears in the morning sky. It is at opposition on July 29, when it can be seen throughout the night, after which its eastward elongation gradually decreases, until from the end of October it can be seen in the evening sky.

NEPTUNE is too close to the Sun for observation until after the first week of February, when it appears in the morning sky in Sagittarius. It passes into Capricornus after the first week of April and into Sagittarius again at the end of May, remaining in this constellation throughout the year. It is at opposition on July 21, when it can be seen throughout the night. Its eastward elongation gradually decreases, and from mid-October until late December it can be seen in the evening sky, after which it again is too close to the Sun for observation.

DO NOT CONFUSE (1) Venus with Mercury around mid-January, at the beginning of the third week in February, and late July to early August; and with Jupiter during the first half of February. On all occasions, Venus is the brighter object. (2) Mars with Venus from mid-October to mid-November and around mid-December when Venus is the brighter object. (3) Jupiter with Mercury around mid-February when Jupiter is the brighter object.

Visibility of Planets in Morning and Evening Twilight

Planet	Morning	Evening
Venus	January 1–February 21	May 12–December 31
Mars	January 1–March 17	March 17–December 31
Jupiter	February 2–August 9	January 1–January 6 August 9–December 31
Saturn	April 18–October 10	January 1–March 13 October 10–December 31

1997 Eclipses

There are four eclipses, two of the Sun and two of the Moon. Times are given in Eastern Standard and, in bold typeface, Pacific Standard. Seconds are expressed as decimal fractions of minutes. The exact time of an eclipse generally differs from the exact time of a New or Full Moon. For solar eclipses, "greatest eclipse" represents the time (converted from Local Mean Time) of the Moon's maximum obscuration of the Sun as viewed from the Earth. For lunar eclipses, "greatest eclipse" represents the time at which the Moon rests at centermost point of its journey through the shadow cast by the Earth passing between it and the Sun. Data reference: Astronomical Phenomena for the Year 1997, prepared jointly by the United States Naval Observatory and the Royal Greenwich Observatory.

MARCH 8
TOTAL ECLIPSE OF THE SUN: 18° ♓ 31'

			Longitude	Latitude
Eclipse begins	6:16.6 PM	**3:16.6 PM**	105°W	19°N
Greatest eclipse	8:53.6 PM	**5:53.6 PM**	154°W	70°N
Eclipse ends	10:30.8 PM	**7:30.8 PM**	146°E	54°N

MARCH 23–24
PARTIAL ECLIPSE OF THE MOON: 3° ♎ 35'

Moon enters penumbra (3/23)	8:40.6 PM	**5:40.6 PM**		
Moon enters umbra	9:57.5 PM	**6:57.5 PM**	43°E	0°S
Middle of eclipse	11:39.4 PM	**8:39.4 PM**		
Moon leaves umbra (3/24 EST; 3/23 PST)	1:21.3 AM	**10:21.3 PM**	93°E	1°S
Moon leaves penumbra (3/24 EST; 3/23 PST)	2:38.1 AM	**11:38.1 PM**		

Visibility: The beginning of the umbral phase is visible in North America except Alaska and northwestern Canada. It is also visible in Central America, South America, Europe, extreme western Asia, Africa except the eastern extremity, Greenland, parts of Antarctica, the eastern South Pacific Ocean, the southeastern North Pacific Ocean, and the Atlantic Ocean; the end is visible in North America except the western Aleutian Islands, Hawaii, the North Island of New Zealand, Central America, South America, most of Greenland, extreme western Europe, the western extremity of Africa, parts of Antarcitica, the eastern half of the Pacific Ocean, the North Atlantic Ocean, and the western South Atlantic Ocean.

SEPTEMBER 1
PARTIAL ECLIPSE OF THE SUN: 9° ♍ 34'

Eclipse begins	4:44.1 PM	**1:44.1 PM**	128°W	25°S
Greatest eclipse	7:03.7 PM	**4:03.7 PM**	114°W	72°S
Eclipse ends	9:23.1 PM	**6:23.1 PM**	138°E	57°S

SEPTEMBER 16
TOTAL ECLIPSE OF THE MOON: 23° ♓ 56'

Moon enters penumbra	11:11.0 AM	**8:11.0 AM**		
Moon enters umbra	12:08.0 PM	**9:08.0 AM**	101°W	3°S
Middle of eclipse	1:46.6 PM	**10:46.6 AM**		
Moon leaves umbra	3:25.2 PM	**12:25.2 PM**	53°W	2°S
Moon leaves penumbra	4:22.2 PM	**1:22.2 PM**		

Visibility: The beginning of the umbral phase is visible in eastern Europe, Asia, the eastern half of Africa, Australia, New Zealand, the western Aleutian Islands, parts of Antarctica, the Indian Ocean, and the western half of the Pacific Ocean; the end is visible in extreme eastern South America, Europe, extreme eastern Greenland, Asia except the extreme east, Africa, Australia except the east coast, parts of Antarctica, the eastern North Atlantic Ocean, most of the South Atlantic Ocean, and the Indian Ocean.

TIME ZONE

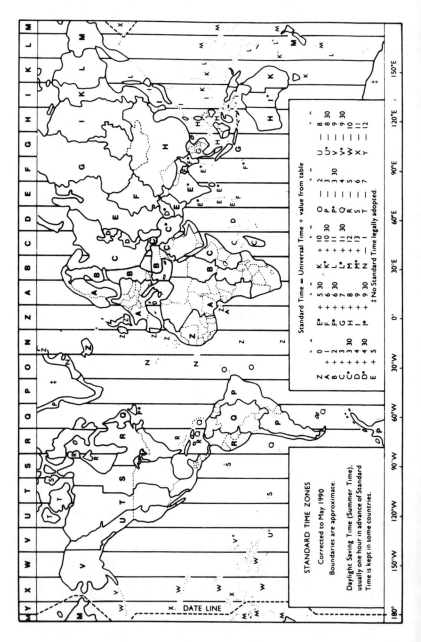

Standard Time = Universal Time + value from table

E*	+ 5 30	K*	+10
F*	+ 6	K*	+10 30
F*	+ 6 30	L*	+11
G	+ 7	L*	+11 30
H	+ 8	M	+12
I	+ 9	M*	+13
I*	+ 9 30		

N	0	O*	− 1
A	+ 1	P	− 2
B	+ 2	P*	− 2 30
C	+ 3	Q	− 3
C*	+ 3 30	R	− 4
D	+ 4	S	− 5
D*	+ 4 30	T	− 6
E	+ 5		

N	0	U	− 7
A	+ 1	U*	− 8 30
B	+ 2	V	− 9
C	+ 3	V*	− 9 30
C*	+ 3 30	W	−10
D	+ 4	X	−11
D*	+ 4 30	Y	−12
E	+ 5		

‡ No Standard Time legally adopted.

STANDARD TIME ZONES

Corrected to May 1990
Boundaries are approximate.

Daylight Saving Time (Summer Time),
usually one hour in advance of Standard
Time is kept in some countries.

DATE LINE

180°   150°W   120°W   90°W   60°W   30°W   0°   30°E   60°E   90°E   120°E   150°E

CONVERSIONS

World Time Zones
Compared to Eastern Standard Time

( ) From Map
(S) Subtract 1 hour
(R) (EST) Used in Datebook
(Q) Add 1 hour
(P) Add 2 hours
(O) Add 3 hours
(N) Add 4 hours
(Z) Add 5 hours
(T) (MST) Subtract 2 hours
(U) (PST) Used in Datebook
    (Subtract 3 hours)
(V) Subtract 4 hours
(W) Subtract 5 hours
(X) Subtract 6 hours

(Y) Subtract 7 hours
(A) Add 6 hours
(B) Add 7 hours
(C) Add 8 hours
(D) Add 9 hours
(E) Add 10 hours
(F) Add 11 hours
(G) Add 12 hours
(H) Add 13 hours
(I) Add 14 hours
(K) Add 15 hours
(L) Add 16 hours
(M) Add 17 hours

Standard Time = Universal Time + Value From Table

	h	m		h	m		h	m
Z	0	00	H	+ 8	00	Q	- 4	00
A	+ 1	00	I	+ 9	00	R	- 5	00
B	+ 2	00	I*	+ 9	30	S	- 6	00
C	+ 3	00	K	+10	00	T	- 7	00
C*	+ 3	30	K*	+10	30	U	- 8	00
D	+ 4	00	L	+11	00	U*	- 8	30
D*	+ 4	30	M	+12	00	V	- 9	00
E	+ 5	00	M*	+13	00	V*	- 9	30
E*	+ 5	30	N	- 1	00	W	- 10	00
F	+ 6	00	O	- 2	00	W*	- 10	30
F*	+ 6	30	P	- 3	00	X	- 11	00
G	+ 7	00	P*	- 3	00	Y	- 12	00

Planetary Stations for 1997

Planet	Begin	EST	PST	End	EST	PST
Mercury	12/23/96	5:40 pm	2:40 pm	01/12/97	3:36 pm	12:36 pm
Mars	02/05/97	7:24 pm	4:24 pm	04/027/97	2:10 pm	11:10 pm
Chiron	02/13/97	9:27 pm	6:27 pm	06/23/97	9:26 am	6:26 am
Pluto	03/08/97	3:36 am	12:36 am	08/13/97	1:34 am (8/12)	10:34 pm
Mercury	04/14/97	6:56 pm	3:56 pm	05/08/97	1:02 pm	10:02 am
Neptune	05/01/97	1:29 pm	10:29 am	10/08/97	6:22 pm	3:22 pm
Uranus	05/12/97	7:16 pm	4:16 pm	10/14/97	3:06 am	12:06 am
Pallas	05/22/97	2:02 pm	11:02 am	09/12/97	7:40 pm	4:40 pm

Planet	Begin	EST	PST	End	EST	PST
Jupiter	06/09/97	6:28 pm	3:28 pm	10/07/97	11:21 pm	8:21 pm
Ceres	07/08/97	1:56 am	10:56 am	10/20/97	1:29 am (10/19)	10:29 pm
Saturn	08/01/97	10:01 am	7:01 am	12/16/97	5:06 am	2:06 am
Mercury	08/17/97	2:43 pm	11:43 am	09/09/97	8:38 pm	5:38 pm
Vesta	08/29/97	5:18 am	2:18 am	12/02/97	1:03 pm	10:03 am
Mercury	12/07/97	11:50 am	8:50 pm	12/27/97	6:36 pm	3:36 pm
Venus	12/26/97	4:17 pm	1:17 pm	02/05/98	4:26 pm	1:26 pm

1997 Graphic Retrograde Ephemeris

(Eastern Standard Time in regular typeface, Pacific Standard Time in **bold typeface**.)

Chart columns: 1996 DEC, 1997 JAN, FEB, MAR, APR, MAY, JUN, JUL, AUG, SEP, OCT, NOV, DEC, 1998 JAN, 1998 FEB

Chart rows (planet symbols): ☿ ♀ ♂ ⚷ ♇ ⚶ ⚵ ♃ ♄ ⚷ ♅ ♆ ♇

32

How to Use Your Daily Planetary Guide

Both Eastern and Pacific times are given in the datebook. The Eastern times are given in the left-hand column in medium typeface. The Pacific times are in the right-hand column in **bold typeface**. Adjustments have not been made for Daylight Savings Time. You need to add one hour to the time given if your locale uses Daylight Savings Time.

The computer program used to compute the ephemeris and the daily data was created by Matrix Software, Big Rapids, Michigan. Re-use is prohibited. It is the same one that is used in *Llewellyn's Astrological Calendar* so that the two are totally compatible. The Calendar is set in Eastern Standard Time.

The void of course Moon is listed to the right of the daily aspect at the exact time that it occurs. It is indicated by "v/c." On days in which it occurs for only one time zone and not the other, it is indicated next to the appropriate column and then repeated on the next day for the other time zone. The ephemeris is shown for midnight, Greenwich Mean Time.

Symbol Key

Planets					
	☉	Sun	⚶	Vesta
	☽	Moon	♃	Jupiter
	☿	Mercury	♄	Saturn
	♀	Venus	⚷	Chiron
	♂	Mars	♅	Uranus
	⚳	Ceres	♆	Neptune
	⚴	Pallas	♇	Pluto
	⚵	Juno		

Signs					
	♈	Aries	♎	Libra
	♉	Taurus	♏	Scorpio
	♊	Gemini	♐	Sagittarius
	♋	Cancer	♑	Capricorn
	♌	Leo	♒	Aquarius
	♍	Virgo	♓	Pisces

Aspects					
	♂	Conjunction	△	Trine
	⋎	Semisextile	⟎	Sesquiquadrate
	∟	Semisquare	⚻	Quincunx
	✶	Sextile	☍	Opposition
	□	Square		

Motion					
	℞	Retrograde	D	Direct

1997 WEEKLY FORECASTS

BY DON LEWIS

January 1–January 5

The year begins with an accent on practical, real-world advancement. Wednesday, the opposition of Moon and Saturn emphasizes material progress and focused effort, while the conjunction of the Sun and Mercury emphasizes mental strength and dissemination of information. Friday, Mars enters Libra for an enthusiastic, assertive energy, and refinements in partnerships. The Moon conjuncts Chiron, promoting insights and healing. On Sunday conjunction of the Moon and Pluto gives desire for, and courage to make, changes.

Personal Notes:

January 6–January 12

Monday Vesta enters Aquarius, giving bright ideas and innovation in vocation. Also Pallas enters Capricorn for creativity in practical matters. Tuesday interaction between the Moon, Venus, Pallas, and Mercury emphasizes originality, cleverness, and problem solving. Wednesday brings the New Moon—focus on what you wish to achieve by the Full Moon. Thursday, conjunctions between the Moon and Ceres, Neptune, Jupiter, Vesta, and Uranus give emotional security and independence, optimism, luck, and the ability to focus on goals. The conjunction of Jupiter and Neptune adds concern for others, but the opposition of Mars and Saturn indicate desired actions held back by circumstances. Venus enters Capricorn, emphasizing pride, ambition, and perseverance. Friday, Venus sextiles Chiron for emotional insights, while Saturday, relations between Venus, Pallas, Mars, and Saturn emphasize creativity and expression, in addition to a rebellious desire for freedom, which may tend to discount emotions. The conjunction of Mercury and Venus on Sunday accents mental harmony and growth in consciousness.

Personal Notes:

1997 Weekly Forecasts

January 13–January 19

On Monday, the Moon conjuncts Saturn and opposes Mars, giving thorough, practical ability with material goals. At mid-week, the Moon conjuncts Juno, strengthening relationships. However, opposition of the Moon and Chiron indicates a need to look at emotions and break through to deeper meanings. Friday, the Sun conjuncts Neptune, giving a highly emotional and sentimental energy—potentially great inspiration and creativity, but a tendency to scatteredness. Saturday, the Moon opposes Pluto, giving action in, or lessons through, relationships or joint ventures. The Sun enters Aquarius on Sunday, and the conjunction of the Sun and Jupiter brings good luck, personal and financial benefit.

Personal Notes:

January 20–January 26

Monday, Mars trines Uranus, giving desire for excitement and exploration, but in the afternoon, opposition of the Moon and Pallas may create a sense of blockage. Tuesday, Jupiter enters Aquarius, giving emphasis on large goals, group projects, and inspiration. Interaction of the Moon, Mercury, and Venus tends toward impulsive action and miscommunication, while the Sun's square of Chiron obscures options. Wednesday, interaction of the Sun and Saturn, and the Moon and Neptune gives practical ambition and attainment of goals, but also unsettled emotions. Thursday is the Full Moon, lending high energy which can be focused to great effect. The opposition of the Moon, Jupiter, and Uranus tends toward over-confidence and must be tempered with judgment. Friday, relations between the Sun, Mars, Uranus, and Pluto give strong will, originality, constructive action, and revitalization of one's role in the world. Friday, Mars sextiles Pluto, giving positive and transformative action.

Personal Notes:

1997 WEEKLY FORECASTS

January 27–February 2

Tuesday, the Moon conjuncts Mars and opposes Saturn for focused, independent action and material advancement. Thursday, the Moon conjuncts Chiron, giving insight into emotions and self, and opportunity for healing. Saturday, Venus conjuncts Neptune, giving a gentle, sensitive energy, and spiritual inspiration and growth. Sunday, the conjunction of the Moon and Pluto and relations between the Sun and the Moon, give emotional harmony, courage, desire, and ability to make positive changes. Sunday, Venus enters Aquarius, which tends to cool emotions but accents ideals and interaction with groups.

Personal Notes:

February 3–February 9

Monday, the Sun conjuncts Venus, giving luck and blessings, unexpected gifts, and good cheer. Tuesday, Venus squares Chiron—working through emotion brings insights. The Moon conjuncts Pallas, accenting self-expression and problem solving. Wednesday, interaction of Uranus and Neptune, Venus and Jupiter, and the Moon and Mercury, accents practical advancement, financial gain, enjoyment of good company, mental clarity and strength, and practical spiritual progress. The Moon conjuncts Neptune, adding imagination and sensitivity. Juno enters Taurus, giving stability in relationships and joy in simple pleasures. On Thursday, conjunctions between the Moon, Venus, Jupiter, and Uranus emphasize pleasure, good luck, and vital, if erratic, energy. Venus sextiles Saturn, strengthening bonds of loyalty, responsibility, and endurance. Friday is the New Moon, so focus your goals for the Full Moon. Venus conjuncts Uranus for restless, easily-bored energy and the possibility of unusual romantic developments. Mercury conjuncts Neptune, lessening ability to focus, but relations between Venus, Mars, and Pluto accent love, money, well-taken actions, and harmony. Saturday, Mercury enters Aquarius, strengthening judgment and communications, especially in groups. Saturn sextiles Ceres, emphasizing a strong, secure emotional base. Sunday, Jupiter sextiles Saturn, giving good sense and practical idealism.

Personal Notes:

1997 WEEKLY FORECASTS

February 10–February 16

Monday, the Moon conjuncts Saturn and opposes Mars, giving ambition, determination, and practical ability. Tuesday afternoon, Mars trines Uranus, enhancing restlessness, desire for adventure, and great vitality. Wednesday, the Moon opposes Chiron, indicating a need to look below surfaces. The conjunction of Mercury and Jupiter gives luck and generosity and eases progress. Relations between Mercury and Mars, Saturn, Pluto, and Uranus accent intelligence and judgment, practical success, strong will, desire for freedom, and an emphasis on new knowledge. Thursday aspects between Jupiter, Mars, and Pluto strengthen self-confidence, optimism, inner-understanding, sincere and helpful actions, and also gain through travel. Friday, Mars sextiles Pluto, accenting mind, understanding, and efficiency, though the opposition of the Moon and Pluto may bring conflict over joint ventures. Saturday Jupiter conjuncts Uranus, accenting judgment, clear intuitions, and creativity. Sunday, Mars opposes Saturn, and responsibilities may postpone desired actions.

Personal Notes:

February 17–February 23

Tuesday, the Sun enters Pisces. The Moon opposes Pallas, and Jupiter squares Juno, accenting emotional restriction, but worldly success. Relationships suffer from lack of time. Wednesday, the trine of Saturn and Pluto gives discipline and practicality, but relations between the Moon, Jupiter, Neptune, and Uranus promote unrealistic expectations and unnecessary risk-taking. Thursday, the Sun trines Chiron, giving insight and breakthroughs in worldly affairs, but the opposition of the Moon and Mercury tends toward erratic impulses and detracts from judgment. Opposition of the Moon and Venus on Friday inhibits emotional security and requires cultivation of love. Saturday is the Full Moon, which brings great energy to focus on our goals. Sunday, the Sun squares Pluto, indicating need for introspection to move beyond false impressions and blocks.

Personal Notes:

1997 WEEKLY FORECASTS

February 24–March 2

Monday, the Moon conjuncts Mars and opposes Saturn, emphasizing independence, ability to focus, and financial or professional advancement. Tuesday, Mercury conjuncts Vesta, giving disciplined mental energy and concentration, especially regarding career goals. Venus enters Pisces on Wednesday, emphasizing gentleness, sensitivity, and romance. The conjunction of the Moon and Chiron indicates insight into self and emotional lessons. Thursday, Mercury enters Pisces, bringing a reactive, sensitive mental energy. Saturday, Saturn sextiles Uranus, and the Moon conjuncts Pluto, highlighting desire for change and advancement, courage, well-executed plans and actions, and great success. Sunday, Mercury conjuncts Venus and squares Pluto, indicating mental harmony, creativity, and growth in consciousness, but also the need to overcome rigidity.

Personal Notes:

March 3–March 9

Monday, Venus squares Pluto, giving a desire for romantic security and revitalization or reform of relationships. Tuesday, the Moon conjuncts Pallas, strengthening creativity, self-expression, and problem solving. Vesta enters Pisces Wednesday, detracting from ability to focus, but accenting compassion and desire to help others, especially in career. Aspects between the Moon, Neptune, and Uranus emphasize imagination but give scattered energy. On Thursday, the Moon conjuncts Jupiter, giving optimism, good luck, and practical gains. Saturday is the New Moon, so focus on those things you wish to accomplish by the Full Moon. Conjunction of the Moon and Venus emphasizes pleasurable pursuits and enjoyment of good company, while the conjunction of the Moon and Mercury makes for mental insights, problem solving, and excellent communications. Mars' entry into Virgo accents skill with details, focus on budget, and cool temperaments. Sunday, the Moon opposes Mars and conjuncts Saturn, emphasizing ambition, perseverance thorough effort, and practical advancement.

Personal Notes:

1997 WEEKLY FORECASTS

March 10–March 16

Monday, Mars trines Neptune, giving practical expression of ideals, advancement of higher goals, and clear perceptions. Tuesday's conjunction of the Sun and Mercury emphasizes mind, teaching, and dissemination of information, but the Moon's opposition to Chiron may give difficulty in integrating new ideas and understanding deeper meanings. Wednesday, the Moon conjuncts Juno, strengthening relationships and partnerships, and giving interpersonal harmony. Friday, the Sun sextiles Pallas, giving creativity, insight, and originality. Oppositions of Mercury and Mars, and of the Moon and Pluto, emphasize ambition and determination, but also over-criticism. Saturday, Mercury enters Aries, giving enthusiasm and impatient desire for progress. Mercury sextiles Neptune, accenting creativity, mysticism, and insights. Sunday, the Sun opposes Mars, giving rashness and need for emotional balance.

Personal Notes:

March 17–March 23

Tuesday, the Moon opposes Neptune, and Mercury trines Pluto, emphasizing unrealistic ideas and expectations, unusual interests, and desire to understand inner workings. Wednesday, aspects between the Moon, Jupiter, and Uranus give self-confidence, strong will, and willingness to take risks. Opposition of Venus and Mars gives strong passions and dislike of restraint. Relations between Mercury and Uranus, and the Sun and Neptune, emphasize creativity, originality, strong communications, and expression of ideals. Thursday, the Sun enters Aries. Mercury conjuncts Saturn, giving ambition, organization, and success, though tending to inhibit emotion. Friday, the Moon opposes Vesta, giving impatience, dislike of discipline, and desire for freedom. Saturday, Venus enters Aries, emphasizing passion and enthusiasm. Interaction between Venus and Neptune, and Mercury and Jupiter, brings harmony, balance, luck, and good judgment, as well as promoting travel and expansion of all sorts. Sunday brings the accentuated energy of the Full Moon, while relations between the Moon, Venus, and Mars give financial and professional advances but inhibit emotional expression.

Personal Notes:

1997 WEEKLY FORECASTS

March 24–March 30

Monday, the Moon opposes Saturn, emphasizing material ambition and ability to focus. Tuesday, the Moon opposes Mercury, giving impulsive action and erratic communications. The Sun trines Pluto, giving luck, advancement, and learning. Wednesday, the Moon conjuncts Chiron, giving insights and breakthroughs. Thursday, Venus trines Pluto, emphasizing emotional balance, kindness, and affection. Friday, the Sun sextiles Uranus, and the Moon conjuncts Pluto, bringing originality, courage, and good planning. Vitality and health are accented. Saturday, Venus sextiles Pluto, promoting romantic and monetary advances and unexpected gains. Sunday, the Sun conjuncts Saturn, giving strength, discipline, and self-restraint. The ability to work hard brings success.

Personal Notes:

March 31–April 6

Monday, Venus conjuncts Saturn, giving concern for others and loyalty, but tending to inhibit emotions. Tuesday, Mercury enters Taurus, giving a very grounded mental energy tending to stubbornness. Development under this transit is slow, but thorough and lasting. Relations between Mercury, Neptune, and Chiron emphasize impracticality, over-emotionalism, and need to break through mental blocks. Wednesday, the Sun conjuncts Venus, giving cheerful, romantic energy and good luck. Relations between the Moon, Jupiter, and Uranus emphasize optimism, independence, personal advancement, and gains. Friday, Chiron enters Scorpio, indicating a period of lessons involving deep emotions, sexual and political passions, and spirituality. Venus sextiles Jupiter, giving optimism, cheerfulness, and monetary advances. Saturday, relations between the Sun and Jupiter, and the Moon and Mars, emphasize ambition, luck, and success. Advances in health issues are accented. Sunday, the Moon conjuncts Saturn for determination, thoroughness, and practicality.

Personal Notes:

1997 WEEKLY FORECASTS

April 7–April 13

Monday brings the New Moon, when we manifest what we wish to achieve by the Full Moon. The Moon conjuncts Venus but opposes Chiron, giving pleasure and enjoyment with others, but inner blockages to work through. Tuesday, the Moon conjuncts Mercury, emphasizing communications and cleverness in problem solving. Wednesday, Mercury squares Uranus, giving independence, inspiration, and trail-blazing new ideas—albeit a need to focus on follow-through. The Moon opposes Pluto Thursday, giving a desire to reform and remake situations, and a tendency toward conflict in partnerships where "space" is needed.

Personal Notes:

April 14–April 20

Monday, the Moon opposes Neptune, giving strong emotions and heightened imagination. Tuesday, opposition of the Moon, Pallas, and Uranus, and aspects between Venus, Chiron, and Neptune, combine to create a sense of emotional blockage—passion overrules good sense or inhibits insight. Wednesday, Venus enters Taurus, giving strong, centered emotions, and accenting home and pleasures. The Moon opposes Jupiter, lending self-confidence and ability to take risks. Friday, the Moon conjuncts Mars while the Sun opposes Chiron, giving independence, strong will, and business and financial advancement, but detracting from inner lessons and insights. Saturday, the Sun enters Taurus. The Sun squares Neptune, and Mercury squares Uranus, giving original ideas and inspirations, development in new and unusual directions, but also a tendency to get carried away. Sunday, the Moon opposes Saturn, accenting ambition and material progress.

Personal Notes:

1997 WEEKLY FORECASTS

April 21–April 27

Monday, the Moon conjuncts Venus, giving inner harmony, creativity, and expansion of consciousness. Tuesday brings the great energy of the Full Moon. The Moon opposes Mercury, then Venus, giving impulsive action but emotional inhibition. Venus squares Uranus, giving potential to upset or revitalize relationships. The conjunction of the Moon and Chiron, however, gives understanding and insight into these emotions and inner healing. Friday, the Moon conjuncts Pluto, giving courage and desire for change and advancement. Conjunction of the Sun and Mercury emphasizes teaching and learning, and mental strength.

Personal Notes:

April 28–May 4

Monday, the Sun squares Uranus, making for impulsive actions and sudden happenings. Tuesday, aspects between the Moon, Neptune, and Uranus heighten imagination and independence, while the trine of Venus and Mars emphasizes harmonious emotions, romance, and pleasure in good company. The Moon conjuncts Jupiter Wednesday, giving good luck and advancement. Venus squares Jupiter Thursday for a restless, expansive energy. Friday, the Moon opposes Mars, accenting ambition and focused action. The Moon opposes Vesta Saturday, emphasizing impatience and desire for freedom from restraint. Sunday, Mercury enters Aries, giving enthusiastic, impulsive energy, and desire for progress. Relations of the Moon and Saturn, Mercury and Neptune, strengthen determination and concentration, but detract from practicality.

Personal Notes:

1997 WEEKLY FORECASTS

May 5–May 11

Monday, the Moon conjuncts Mercury and opposes Chiron, emphasizing mental acuity and problem solving, but obscuring emotional understandings. Tuesday is the New Moon, giving energy to focus our goals toward the Full Moon. Wednesday, the Moon conjuncts Venus and the Sun trines Mars, accenting enjoyment, vitality, and advancement through well-taken action. Opposition of the Moon and Pluto accents desire to reform and increase efficiency, but may bring disagreements in joint projects. Saturday, Venus enters Gemini, emphasizing self-expression and pleasant social exchange. Venus trines Neptune, promoting balance, creativity, and romance. After noon, the Sun squares Jupiter, accenting ambition and self-esteem but stressing the need for good judgment. Sunday, Mercury squares Neptune, emphasizing imagination and sensitivity.

Personal Notes:

May 12–May 18

Monday, Mercury enters Taurus, giving slow but lasting progress, groundedness, and mental stability. Relations between the Moon, Neptune, and Uranus emphasize assertiveness, imagination, and determination. Tuesday, the Moon opposes Jupiter, giving self-confidence and the ability to take risks. Venus opposes Pluto Wednesday, accenting desire for romantic security and the need to reform and revitalize relationships. Friday, the Moon conjuncts Mars, giving independence, and professional and financial advancements. Saturday's trine of Venus and Uranus promotes love, money, and unexpected gains. Pluto trines Vesta, giving rejuvenation or advancement of projects through well-focused effort. Opposition of the Moon and Vesta emphasizes desire for freedom and release from restraint. Sunday's opposition of the Moon and Saturn emphasizes ambition, practicality, and material progress.

Personal Notes:

1997 WEEKLY FORECASTS

May 19–May 25

Monday, the Moon conjuncts Chiron and opposes Mercury, indicating impulsive actions, but also insights into emotions and the subconscious. Tuesday, the Sun enters Gemini. The Sun trines Neptune, emphasizing imagination, creativity, and practical expression of one's ideals. Thursday brings the abundant energy of the Full Moon, and the conjunction of the Moon and Pluto gives desire for change and advancement, and courage to carry this out. Friday, relations between Venus, the Moon, and Saturn give emotional isolation, but emphasize loyalty, ability, and spiritual growth. Saturday, Mercury squares Uranus, accenting independence, mental strength, and trail-blazing new ideas. Sunday, the Sun opposes Pluto, emphasizing material ambitions and advancement, but also the need for inner guidance.

Personal Notes:

May 26–June 1

Monday, relations between the Moon, Neptune, Uranus, and Pallas emphasize independence, self-expression, and assertiveness, in addition to much energy and creativity. Wednesday, relations between Venus, Mars, and Jupiter give strong emotions and the desire for expansion and monetary gain. Thursday, the Sun trines Uranus, accenting vitality, original insights, planning ability, and health issues. Friday, the Moon opposes Mars, emphasizing ambition and assertiveness. The conjunction of the Moon and Saturn Saturday gives determination, thoroughness, and practical advancement.

Personal Notes:

1997 WEEKLY FORECASTS

June 2–June 8

Tuesday, Venus enters Cancer, bringing a gentle, easy-going, sentimental energy. Aspects between Mercury, the Moon, and Jupiter accent mental strength, problem solving, and communication, but also over-confidence and extravagance. Wednesday is the New Moon, when we focus on what we wish to accomplish by the Full Moon. The opposition of the Moon and Pluto emphasizes desire for reform, but may be unsettling for partnerships. Thursday, Mercury trines Mars, giving practical, positive use of action, and mental progress. Friday, the Moon conjuncts Venus, emphasizing pleasure and social interaction. Sunday, Mercury enters Gemini, giving strong, clear mental energy, but also restlessness and over-extension. Mercury trines Neptune, giving creativity and insights, while the sextile of the Sun and Saturn emphasizes goals and ambitions along with ease of advancement. The opposition of the Moon and Neptune heightens emotions and imagination.

Personal Notes:

June 9–June 15

Monday, the Moon opposes Uranus, giving restlessness and desire for freedom. Tuesday, the Moon opposes Jupiter and Pluto, emphasizing assertiveness, risk taking, desire for reform, and advancement. Thursday, the Sun trines Jupiter, giving blessings, harmony, and success. This is especially good for health issues. Friday, the Moon conjuncts Mars, and Mercury trines Uranus, emphasizing originality, inventiveness, and independence. This is good for communications and professional or financial advancement. Sunday, the Moon opposes Saturn and conjuncts Chiron, emphasizing ambition, concentration, material progress, and emotional insights. Understanding and healing the self are accented.

Personal Notes:

1997 WEEKLY FORECASTS

June 16–June 22

Monday, the Sun trines Chiron. New insights bring breakthroughs in lifepath or career, and relationships with others. Tuesday, Mars trines Neptune, accenting practical expressions of ideals and spiritual advancement. Wednesday, Mercury sextiles Saturn, and the Moon conjuncts Pluto, emphasizing discipline, responsibility, positive changes, and successes. This is good for health issues. Thursday, Mars enters Libra, accenting partnerships and enthusiastic progress, but also a need for balance and objectivity. Venus squares Saturn, and the Moon opposes Mercury, giving impulsiveness and emotional inhibition, but the trine of Mercury and Jupiter aids judgment and accents expansion of all sorts. Friday brings the strong energies of the Full Moon. Saturday, the Sun enters Cancer. Sunday, the Moon conjuncts Neptune and opposes Venus while the Sun squares Mars, highlighting strong emotions, imagination, and impulsive desire for gratification.

Personal Notes:

June 23–June 29

Monday, Mercury enters Cancer, giving strong emotions, tenacity, and heightened psychic receptivity. The Moon conjuncts Uranus, accenting great energy, independence, and self-motivation. Tuesday, the Moon conjuncts Jupiter, and Mercury squares Mars, giving optimism, luck, single-minded focus, and success, but also a tendency toward instability and accidents. Wednesday the Sun conjuncts Mercury, emphasizing mental strength, teaching, and disseminating information. Thursday, Mars sextiles Pluto, accenting efficient thought and action, and the ability to see below surfaces and make improvements. Friday, the Moon opposes Mars, and Venus opposes Neptune, accenting ambition, generosity, and optimism, but also the need for practicality. Venus enters Leo Saturday, giving an affectionate, loyal, emotionally self-possessed energy. The Moon conjuncts Saturn and opposes Chiron, emphasizing determination, thoroughness, and responsibility, but inhibiting emotional insight.

Personal Notes:

1997 WEEKLY FORECASTS

June 30–July 6

Tuesday, Venus trines Pluto, accenting harmony, friendship, and unilateral love. The Moon opposes Pluto, giving a desire to reform and revitalize, and bringing possible conflict in joint ventures. Wednesday Mercury squares Saturn, enhancing a need to cultivate patience and the determination to overcome inertia. Friday is the New Moon, the best time to begin projects that we wish to manifest by the Full Moon. Venus sextiles Mars and opposes Uranus, emphasizing harmony, social interaction, romance, and money, but also unexpected challenges and sudden changes. Saturday, Mars trines Uranus, giving desire for excitement, new directions. The conjunction of the Moon and Mercury strengthens the mind, communication, and problem-solving ability. The opposition of the Moon and Neptune accents strong emotion. Sunday, the Moon opposes Uranus, giving self-confidence and desire for freedom. The Moon conjuncts Venus, giving harmony and pleasure in good company.

Personal Notes:

July 7–July 13

Monday, Mercury enters Leo, accenting ambition and confidence, but detracting from ability to focus. Mercury opposes Neptune, and the Moon opposes Jupiter, emphasizing imagination and self-confidence, but also scatteredness, impulsiveness, and risk taking. Wednesday, Mercury trines Pluto, giving a desire to see inner workings and motivations, unusual interests, or circumstances. Friday the Moon conjuncts Mars, Mercury opposes Uranus, and the Sun squares Saturn, emphasizing self-confidence, independence, ambition, and clarity of purpose, but also restlessness and desire for excitement. Financial and professional advancement, and sudden moves and developments, are possible. Saturday, the Moon opposes Saturn, emphasizing ambition, focus, and material advancement. Sunday, the Moon conjuncts Chiron, giving emotional insights, inner learning, and healing.

Personal Notes:

1997 WEEKLY FORECASTS

July 14–July 20

Monday Jupiter sextiles Saturn and Mercury sextiles Mars, emphasizing good judgemnt and practicality, along with the successful achievement of goals. Venus opposes Jupiter, giving confidence but a tendency to overdo. Tuesday, Venus trines Saturn, accenting loyalty and ability. The Moon conjuncts Pluto, accenting courage, risk taking, and desire for change. Friday, the Sun squares Chiron. Ego and worldly concerns tend to obscure insight and inner lessons. Saturday brings the vibrant energy of the Full Moon. Mercury opposes Jupiter and trines Saturn, giving strong opinions and confidence, discipline, material advancement, and success. The Moon conjuncts Neptune, giving strong emotions, imagination, and impulsiveness. Sunday, the Moon conjuncts Uranus, and the Sun opposes Neptune, bringing erratic energy, independence, and strong emotion.

Personal Notes:

July 21–July 27

Monday, the Moon opposes Mercury and Venus, giving impulsiveness and emotional inhibition. The Moon conjuncts Jupiter, bringing good luck and improving judgment. Tuesday, the Sun enters Leo. Venus enters Virgo Wednesday, emphasizing career and skill with details, but inhibiting emotional expression. Friday, the Moon conjuncts Saturn and opposes Mars, accenting ambition, determination, and material advancement. The Sun trines Pluto, giving good luck, positive changes, and learning. Venus squares Pluto, accenting desire for romantic security and progress in relationships. Opposition of the Moon and Chiron tends to inhibit insight and emotional integration of lessons. Saturday, Mercury enters Virgo, emphasizing mental stability, practicality, and clear communications. Mars trines Jupiter, accenting sincere, honest actions and enthusiasm for causes and reform.

Personal Notes:

1997 WEEKLY FORECASTS
July 28–August 3

Monday, the Moon opposes Pluto, giving desire for reform and revitalization, but also bringing conflict in partnerships. Mars opposes Saturn, indicating that desire to take action may be held back by circumstances or necessity. Tuesday, Mercury squares Pluto, and the Sun opposes Uranus, giving strong self will, tenacity, impulsive action, and sudden developments in relationships. Friday, the Moon opposes Neptune, accenting emotions and imagination. Saturday, the Moon opposes Uranus, giving assertiveness, confidence, and strong opinions. Sunday is the New Moon, so focus on the things you wish to accomplish by the Full Moon. The Moon opposes Jupiter, accenting confidence and risk taking.

Personal Notes:

August 4–August 10

Tuesday, the Moon conjuncts Mercury, then Venus, accenting mental strength, cleverness, problem solving, harmony, and social interaction. Friday, the Moon opposes Saturn, emphasizing ambition, ability to focus, and material advancement. Saturday, the Sun opposes Jupiter and the Moon conjuncts Mars, then Chiron, giving independence, great drive for success and recognition, and financial or professional successes; also introspection, learning, and healing. Sunday, Mars conjuncts Chiron and squares Neptune, emphasizing spiritual and emotional insight well expressed through action.

Personal Notes:

1997 WEEKLY FORECASTS
August 11–August 17

Tuesday, the Moon conjuncts Pluto, giving desire for change and the courage to carry it out. The Sun trines Saturn, accenting ambition, practical effort, and attainment of goals. Thursday, Mars enters Scorpio, accenting pride, strong emotions, and the need for security. Friday, Venus trines Neptune, giving balance, creativity, harmony, and romance. Saturday, the Moon conjuncts Neptune, accenting emotions and imagination. Conjunction of the Moon and Uranus gives independence, enthusiasm, and erratic energy. Sunday, Venus enters Libra, giving emotional clarity, balance, and spiritual harmony. The Moon conjuncts Jupiter, accenting good luck, optimism, and advancement.

Personal Notes:

August 18–August 24

The Full Moon on Monday brings great energy. Tuesday, the Moon opposes Mercury, giving restless, impulsive energy. Venus sextiles Pluto, emphasizing friendship, kindness, and unilateral love. Wednesday, the Moon opposes Venus, giving emotional inhibition. Thursday, the Sun sextiles Chiron, giving lessons and insights into one's lifepath and interaction with world. The Moon conjuncts Saturn Thursday, accenting determination, responsibility, and practical advancement. Friday, the Sun enters Virgo, and Venus trines Uranus, accenting love, money, and unexpected gains. The Moon opposes Chiron, then Mars, accenting ambition and difficulty in integrating new ideas and deeper meanings. Saturday, Mars squares Uranus, giving strong emotions, sudden developments, or upheavals. The Moon opposes Pluto Sunday, giving desire to reform and revitalize, but brining possible conflict over how to do this.

Personal Notes:

1997 WEEKLY FORECASTS

August 25–August 31

Monday, the Sun squares Pluto, emphasizing ambition, but also need for introspection. Look beyond surfaces for accurate impressions. Friday, Venus trines Jupiter and sextiles Mars, emphasizing optimism, practical, well-taken action, and monetary gain. Relations between the Moon, Neptune, and Uranus emphasize assertiveness, desire for freedom and strong emotion. Saturday, the Moon opposes Jupiter, giving confidence and risk taking. The Sun conjuncts Mercury Sunday, accenting mental strength, teaching, and dissemination of information.

Personal Notes:

September 1–September 7

Monday is the New Moon, when we focus on what we wish to achieve by the Full Moon. The Moon conjuncts Mercury, strengthening mind, communications, and problem solving. Tuesday, Chiron enters Scorpio, promoting insight and healing in emotions, sexuality, and grand causes. The opposition of Venus and Saturn emphasizes a need to cultivate openness and giving. Friday, the Moon opposes Saturn, accenting ambition, ability to focus, and practical advancement. The conjunction of the Moon and Venus gives pleasure, enjoyment, and social interaction. The opposition of the Moon and Chiron promotes emotional and personal insight and inner healing. Sunday, the Moon conjuncts Mars, giving independence and financial or professional advancement. The square of Mercury and Pluto emphasizes tenacity and perseverance, but suggests a need for flexibility.

Personal Notes:

1997 WEEKLY FORECASTS

September 8–September 14

Monday, the Moon conjuncts Pluto, and the Sun sextiles Mars, giving great vitality, courage, desire for change, and ability to bring change about. Venus squares Neptune Tuesday, accenting generosity and strong emotion, but detracting from judgment. Wednesday, the Sun trines Pallas, giving creative brilliance, insight, and originality. Thursday, Venus enters Scorpio, accenting deep passions, self-assertion, and need for emotional regeneration. Thursday, the Moon conjuncts Pallas, emphasizing great creativity, self-expression, and problem-solving ability. Mercury squares Pluto, giving tenacity and determination, but also a need for flexibility. Friday, the conjunction of the Moon and Neptune emphasizes emotion and imagination, while the conjunction of Venus and Chiron gives insights and revelations in relationships and emotional nature. Saturday, aspects between the Moon, Uranus, and Jupiter give independence, assertiveness, good luck, and gain, though the opposition of Mercury and Ceres tends to bring a feeling of insecurity or isolation.

Personal Notes:

September 15–September 21

Monday, the Moon opposes Mercury, giving restless, impulsive energy. Tuesday brings the high energy of the Full Moon. Venus squares Uranus, giving sudden emotional developments or changes. Thursday, the Moon conjuncts Saturn, then Vesta, giving thoroughness, determination, perseverance, and career or personal advancement. The opposition of the Moon and Chiron, however, detract from emotional insights and integration. Friday, the Sun trines Neptune, giving strong imagination, creativity, and practical expression of idealism in the world. The opposition of the Moon and Venus tends to inhibit emotions. Saturday, the Moon opposes Mars, accenting ambition and worldly advancement. Sunday, the Moon opposes Pluto, giving desire for reform and new directions.

Personal Notes:

1997 WEEKLY FORECASTS

September 22–September 28

The Sun enters Libra Monday. Venus squares Jupiter, bringing restless, expansive energy and tendency to overdo. Wednesday, Mars sextiles Neptune, giving practical expression and advancement of higher ideals. Thursday, the Moon opposes Neptune, then Uranus, emphasizing emotions, imagination, and self-assertion. Friday, the Sun sextiles Pluto, accenting good luck, positive changes, learning, and advancement. The opposition of the Moon and Jupiter enhances confidence, courage, and risk taking. Saturday, the Sun trines Uranus, emphasizing vitality, originality, and good planning. This is excellent for health issues. Venus sextiles Pallas, giving romantic insights, new ideas and approaches. Sunday, Mars enters Sagittarius, giving an impulsive, scattered energy, with an accent on advancement through communications. The Moon opposes Ceres and conjuncts Juno, strengthening relationships, yet giving the need to cultivate love and security.

Personal Notes:

September 29–October 5

Tuesday, Mercury trines Neptune, strengthening creativity, spirituality, visions, and introspection. The Moon conjuncts Mercury, emphasizing mental acuity, new ideas, problem-solving skills, and communications. Wednesday is the New Moon, so focus on the goals you wish to grow by Full Moon. Mercury enters Libra, giving good judgment and desire for perfection, but also vacillation. Thursday, the Moon opposes Saturn, accenting material goals, ambitions, and the ability to focus. Friday, the Moon conjuncts Chiron, giving emotional insights and inner healing. The conjunction of Mars and Pluto gives great strength and fortitude, realism, and the ability to see oneself clearly. Mercury sextiles Pluto, bringing unusual ideas and circumstances, and the ability to see below surfaces. Saturday, Mercury sextiles Mars and trines Uranus, giving inventiveness, originality, practical skill, clear communications, and well-taken action. The Sun trines Jupiter, adding success and blessings, especially good for health issues. Sunday, Mars sextiles Uranus, and the Moon conjuncts Pluto, emphasizing vitality, desire for change, excitement, and challenges. Courage, risk taking, and trail blazing are indicated. Relations between Venus, the Moon, and Neptune add creativity, balance, and harmony. Romance and social interaction are strong.

Personal Notes:

1997 WEEKLY FORECASTS

October 6–October 12

Monday, the Moon conjuncts Mars, giving independence, assertiveness, and financial or professional advancement. Venus enters Sagittarius Wednesday for an affectionate, friendly energy, accenting desire for fun and good times. Mercury trines Jupiter, giving good judgment, optimism, travel, and expansion of all sorts, but the square of Venus and Ceres brings emotional inhibition, romantic insecurity, and uncertainty. Thursday, the Sun opposes Saturn, emphasizing ambition, drive, and clarity of purpose. Conjunction of the Moon and Neptune emphasizes emotions and imagination. Friday, Uranus squares Chiron. Self-will and erratic emotions may obscure insight. The conjunction of the Moon and Uranus gives assertiveness, independence, and much energy. Saturday, the Moon conjuncts Jupiter, giving optimism, good luck, and advancement. Mercury opposes Saturn, bringing mental strength to overcome limitations and obstacles. The conjunction of Venus and Pluto puts great emphasis on love, loyalty, and passion. Sunday, the sextile of Venus and Uranus accents love, money, and unexpected gain.

Personal Notes:

October 13–October 19

Monday, the Sun conjuncts Mercury, emphasizing mental strength, teaching, and dissemination of information. The Sun and Mercury square Pallas; creative energy is scattered and blocked by circumstances. Wednesday is the Full Moon, accenting energy and manifestation. The Moon conjuncts Saturn, giving determination, thoroughness, and practicality. Mars sextiles Jupiter, giving optimism, sincere action, desire for reform, and enthusiasm for causes. The opposition of the Moon and Mercury brings restlessness and impulsive action. Thursday, the Moon opposes Chiron, inhibiting insight and integration. Mercury squares Neptune Friday, giving scattered, unfocused energy. Saturday, the Moon opposes Pluto, giving desire to reform and revitalize. Sunday, Mercury enters Scorpio, accenting mental sharpness, clarity, far-sightedness and deeply-held beliefs. Venus sextiles Jupiter, accenting optimism and monetary advancement. Opposition of the Moon and Mars accents ambitions, but together with opposition of the Moon and Venus tends to inhibit emotion.

Personal Notes:

1997 WEEKLY FORECASTS

October 20–October 26

Monday, the Sun squares Neptune, emphasizing emotion and desires, but detracting from clarity of thought. Tuesday, Mars trines Saturn, accenting ambition, goals, good judgment, and resulting advancement. Wednesday, Mercury squares Uranus, and Venus trines Saturn, emphasizing independence, mental strength, new ideas and directions, practical ability, and personal loyalty. Relations between the Moon, Pallas, and Neptune give a feeling of blockage that must be worked through. Thursday, the Sun enters Scorpio. Mercury conjuncts Chiron, giving mental insights and lessons. The Moon opposes Uranus, then Jupiter, enhancing confidence, assertiveness, and risk taking. Saturday, the Moon opposes Ceres, emphasizing a need for security and a strong emotional base. Sunday, Mars conjuncts Venus, accenting romance, pleasure, good luck, and financial advancement.

Personal Notes:

October 27–November 2

Monday, Mercury squares Jupiter, and the Sun squares Uranus, emphasizing impulsive action, sudden developments, generosity, and desire for freedom from restraint. Wednesday, Ceres enters Pisces, giving sensitivity, concern for others, and spirituality, but also unfocused emotions. The Moon opposes Saturn, accenting ambition, material goals, and practical ability. Thursday, the Sun conjuncts Chiron, giving insights, lessons about lifepath, and direction. The Moon conjuncts Mercury Saturday, accenting mental strength, communications, and problem-solving ability. The Moon conjuncts Pluto Sunday, giving desire for change and revitalization, and the courage to carry it out. This can also indicate strong psychic influences.

Personal Notes:

1997 WEEKLY FORECASTS

November 3–November 9

Monday, the Moon conjuncts Mars, giving independence, assertion, tenacity, and professional advancement. Conjunction of the Moon and Venus Tuesday emphasizes pleasure and social interaction. Wednesday, Venus enters Capricorn, giving passion to worldly ambitions and material goals, but tending to inhibit emotional expression. The Sun squares Jupiter, accenting pride and ambition and the willingness to take risks. Venus sextiles Ceres, giving emotional support and nurturing through relationships. The sextile of Mercury and Neptune emphasizes creativity, spirituality, and inner insights. Thursday, relations between the Moon, Neptune, Uranus, and Pallas accent creativity, originality, independence, and self-expression, in addition to strong emotions and erratic energy. Friday, Mercury enters Sagittarius, giving strong, but unfocused, mental energy and impulsiveness in communications. The Moon conjuncts Jupiter, giving good luck, optimism, and advancement. Saturday, Mars enters Capricorn, emphasizing strength and self-reliance, ambition, and great focus on goals.

Personal Notes:

November 10–November 16

Monday, Mercury conjuncts Pluto, bringing interest in the unusual and obscure, and the desire to see below surfaces and reach deep understandings. Psychic influences are accented. Mercury sextiles Uranus, giving originality, inventiveness, clarity in communications. Tuesday, the Moon conjuncts Saturn, emphasizing thoroughness, determination, and practical ability. The Moon opposes Chiron Thursday, emphasizing a need for integration, inner learning, and resolution. Friday brings the heightened energy of the Full Moon. The sextile of Jupiter and Saturn accents practicality and good sense, success, and achievement of goals. Saturday, Venus sextiles Chiron, giving insights and advancements in relationships. Relations between the Moon, Mercury, and Pluto emphasize desire for reform and revitalization, but also impulsiveness, and miscommunication. Sunday, Neptune conjuncts Pallas giving great, if unfocused, creativity and emotional and spiritual expression.

Personal Notes:

1997 WEEKLY FORECASTS

November 17–November 23

Monday, Mercury trines Saturn and sextiles Jupiter. In addition, the Moon opposes Mars. These aspects emphasize practicality, discipline, good judgment, and ambition; success, travel, and expansion of all sorts are accented. However, opposition of the Moon and Venus tends to inhibit emotions. Wednesday, relations between the Moon, Neptune, and Uranus, and the square of Venus and Saturn, accent emotion and imagination, but also a need for freedom from a feeling of restraint. The sextile of the Sun and Neptune gives strong creativity and practical expression of one's ideals in the world. Thursday, the Moon opposes Jupiter, emphasizing confidence, assertiveness, and risk taking. The Sun enters Sagittarius Friday. The Moon opposes Chiron, emphasizing a need for insight and healing. Mars sextiles Chiron Sunday, giving learning and insight through actions and interactions.

Personal Notes:

November 24–November 30

Tuesday, the Moon opposes Saturn, accenting goals, ambition, and the ability to focus and progress. Mars squares Saturn Thursday, giving a desire for action, which is held back by circumstances or good sense. The Sun conjuncts Pluto, giving great passion, tenacity, and extreme reactions. The sextile of the Sun and Uranus accents creativity, originality, and planning, and is also good for health issues. The conjunction of the Moon and Chiron gives emotional insight, integration, and healing. Saturday is the New Moon, so focus your energy on those things you wish to manifest by the Full Moon. Conjunction of the Moon and Pluto gives desire for change and advancement, and the courage and ability to carry this out; also strong psychic influences. Sunday, Mercury enters Capricorn, giving strong, practical mental energy, determination, and concentration.

Personal Notes:

1997 WEEKLY FORECASTS

December 1–December 7

Monday, the Moon conjuncts Mercury, emphasizing mental strength, cleverness, and problem-solving skills. The conjunction of the Moon and Mars Tuesday accents independence, confidence, financial and professional advancement. Wednesday's conjunction of the Moon and Venus accents pleasure, social interaction. Relations between the Moon and Neptune give strong emotions and imagination. Thursday, the Moon conjuncts Uranus, then Jupiter, giving independence and energy, optimism, good luck, and success. Friday, the Sun trines Saturn, emphasizing ambition, practical effort, progress, and ease of attainment. The Moon conjuncts Ceres Saturday, accenting emotional security, love, and nurturing.

Personal Notes:

December 8–December 14

Monday, the Sun trines Vesta, giving great practical focus and drive, determination, and career advancement. Venus conjuncts Neptune, accenting inspiration, creativity, spirituality, and romance. Relations of the Moon and Saturn highlight material ambitions and progress. The Sun sextiles Jupiter Tuesday, giving harmony, luck, and success; good for health issues. Venus enters Aquarius Thursday, emphasizing involvement with groups or movements, but distracting from individual relationships. On Friday, the opposition of the Moon and Pluto gives desire for change and reform, but may bring disagreements in joint ventures or partnerships. Saturday brings the high energy of the Full Moon. Mercury enters Sagittarius, giving strong but unfocused mental energy and restlessness. Sunday, the Moon opposes Mercury, giving impulsive action and communication.

Personal Notes:

1997 WEEKLY FORECASTS

December 15–December 21

Monday, Venus trines Juno, giving harmony, stability, and pleasure in relationships. Mars conjuncts Neptune, emphasizing strong, clear goals, determination, ability to influence others, advancement, and success. Tuesday, relations between the Moon, Venus, Mars, and Neptune accent strong emotions and imagination, but also assertiveness, ambitions, and goals. The conjunction of the Sun and Mercury emphasizes mental strength, teaching, and dissemination of information. Wednesday, Mars enters Aquarius, giving intellectual expansion, independence, assertiveness, and advancement. The Moon opposes Uranus, giving confidence, tenacity, and desire for freedom from restraints. The conjunction of Uranus and Pallas emphasizes originality and sudden developments in areas of creativity and self-expression. Thursday, the Moon opposes Jupiter, giving confidence, fearlessness, and risk taking. Opposition of the Moon and Ceres Friday brings a need to cultivate emotional security and stabilize one's base. The Sun enters Capricorn Sunday. Mercury sextiles Jupiter, giving optimism and good judgment, and accenting travel and expansion of all sorts.

Personal Notes:

December 22–December 28

Monday, Venus conjuncts Mars, emphasizing passion and pleasure, but also luck and monetary gain and successful dealings with groups or movements. Opposition of the Moon and Saturn emphasizes practicality, goals, and the ability to focus. Tuesday, relations between Vesta, the Moon, and Mercury give great mental focus and dedication, but also emotional desire for freedom from discipline and responsibility. Thursday, the Sun squares Juno, putting an emphasis on worldly goals and personal advancement, but there is also a need to cultivate harmony in relationships. Conjunction of the Moon and Chiron gives introspection and realizations; healing. Mars sextiles Pluto Friday, bringing desire to see below surfaces, make reforms, and enhance efficiency. Conjunction of Mars and Uranus gives courage, persistence, and heightened vitality, while emphasizing the desire to move forward quickly. Saturday, the Moon conjuncts Pluto, emphasizing courage, risk taking, and the ability to make desired changes. The conjunction of the Moon and Mercury gives mental strength, cleverness, problem solving, good ideas, and clarity of communications.

Personal Notes:

1997 WEEKLY FORECASTS

December 29–December 31

Monday is the New Moon. This is the last New Moon of 1997, which will not see fruition until 1998, so focus your goals and desires for the Full Moon with the turn of a new year in mind. Tuesday, the Moon conjuncts Neptune, emphasizing emotions and imagination. Wednesday, relations between the Moon, Venus, Mars, and Uranus give independence, assertiveness, pleasure in relationships and social interaction, and professional advancement. The conjunction of the Moon and Pallas accents great creativity, self-expression, and problem-solving ability.

Personal Notes:

1997
CALENDAR AND ASPECT PAGES

30 MONDAY

3rd ♍

☽	△	☉	2:53	am	
☽	⊡	♃	4:43	am	1:43 am
☽	⊡	⚷	7:56	am	4:56 am
☽	⊡	♆	8:44	am	5:44 am
☽	⊼	⚡	1:45	pm	10:45 am
☽	△	☿	2:31	pm	11:31 am
☽	∟	⚷	3:31	pm	12:31 pm
☽	□	♀	7:49	pm	4:49 pm
☿	□	⚡	8:08	pm	5:08 pm
☽	⊡	♅	9:49	pm	6:49 pm
☽	△	♇	10:25	pm	7:25 pm

31 TUESDAY

3rd ♍

♆	☌	⚷	3:13	am	12:13 am
☽	△	♃	11:42	am	8:42 am
☽	△	♆	3:10	pm	12:10 pm
♀	∟	♅	3:27	pm	12:27 pm
☽	△	⚷	3:41	pm	12:41 pm
☽	□	♀	4:27	pm	1:27 pm
☽	☌	♂	8:03	pm	5:03 pm	☽ v/c
☽	⊻	⚷	9:59	pm	6:59 pm
☽	☍	♄			9:14 pm

☽ enters ♎   9:33 pm   **6:33 pm**

NEW YEAR'S EVE

♑ CAPRICORN ♑

Cardinal • Earth

Rules 10th House

Ruled by Saturn

Rules knees and bones

Keyword: Ambition

Keynote: I USE

1 WEDNESDAY

3rd ♎

☽	☍	♄	12:14	am	
☽	△	♅	4:07	am	1:07 am
☽	⚹	♇	6:20	am	3:20 am
♀	⊻	♇	6:41	am	3:41 am
☿	☌	☉	8:21	pm	5:21 pm
☽	□	☿	8:42	pm	5:42 pm
☽	□	☉	8:46	pm	5:46 pm

4th Quarter   8:46 pm   **5:46 pm**

NEW YEAR'S DAY

2 THURSDAY

4th ♎

☽	☍	♅	3:32 am	**12:32 am**
♇	⊾	♃	5:25 am	**2:25 am**
☽	⊾	♇	11:52 am	**8:52 am**
☽	□	♃	12:03 pm	**9:03 am**
☽	✶	♀	2:18 pm	**11:18 am**
☽	□	♃	11:50 pm	**8:50 pm**
☽	□	♆		**11:11 pm** ☽ v/c

3 FRIDAY

4th ♎

☽	□	♆	2:11 am		☽ v/c
☽	□	♅	5:02 am	**2:02 am**	
☽	✶	♀	5:12 am	**2:12 am**	
☽	⊻	♂	8:10 am	**5:10 am**	
☽	♂	⚷	8:50 am	**5:50 am**	
☽	⊼	♄	10:49 am	**7:49 am**	
☽	□	♅	2:29 pm	**11:29 am**	
☽	⊻	♇	4:27 pm	**1:27 pm**	
☽	⊾	♀	9:46 pm	**6:46 pm**	
☽	✶	☿		**9:26 pm**	
♀	⊻	♅		**9:25 pm**	

♂ enters ♎   3:10 am   **12:10 am**
☽ enters ♏   8:02 am   **5:02 am**

4 SATURDAY

4th ♏

☽	✶	☿	12:26 am	
♀	⊻	♅	12:25 am	
☽	⊾	♀	9:58 am	**6:58 am**
☽	✶	☉	10:35 am	**7:35 am**
☽	⊾	♂	12:36 pm	**9:36 am**
☽	⊼	♅	1:41 pm	**10:41 am**
☽	⊡	♄	2:35 pm	**11:35 am**
♂	⊻	⚷	8:01 pm	**5:01 pm**
☽	✶	♃	9:42 pm	**6:42 pm**
☽	⊾	☿		**10:18 pm**

5 SUNDAY

4th ♏

☽	⊾	☿	1:18 am		
☽	⊻	♀	3:46 am	**12:46 am**	
☽	✶	♃	7:51 am	**4:51 am**	
☽	✶	♆	9:13 am	**6:13 am**	☽ v/c
☽	⊻	♀	1:32 pm	**10:32 am**	
☽	✶	♅	1:51 pm	**10:51 am**	
☽	⊾	☉	3:26 pm	**12:26 pm**	
☽	⊻	⚷	3:30 pm	**12:30 pm**	
☽	✶	♂	3:50 pm	**12:50 pm**	
☽	⊡	♅	5:01 pm	**2:01 pm**	
☽	△	♄	5:15 pm	**2:15 pm**	
☽	✶	♅	8:37 pm	**5:37 pm**	
☽	♂	♇	10:21 pm	**7:21 pm**	
☽	⊾	♃		**9:45 pm**	
☽	⊻	☿		**10:31 pm**	

☽ enters ♐   2:28 pm   **11:28 am**

Eastern Standard Time in medium type
Pacific Standard Time in bold type

6 MONDAY

4th ♐

⚶ enters ♒	6:10 am	**3:10 am**	
⚴ enters ♑	9:04 pm	**6:04 pm**	
☽ ∠ ⚳	12:45 am		
☽ ⚺ ☿	1:31 am		
☽ ∠ ♃	10:10 am	**7:10 am**	
☽ ∠ ♆	11:07 am	**8:07 am**	
☽ ∠ ⚶	4:29 pm	**1:29 pm**	
☽ ∠ ⚷	5:14 pm	**2:14 pm**	
☽ ⚺ ☉	6:59 pm	**3:59 pm**	
☽ △ ⚵	7:16 pm	**4:16 pm**	
☽ ∠ ♅	10:09 pm	**7:09 pm**	
☉ □ ⚵		**9:48 pm**	
☽ ⚺ ⚳		**11:45 pm**	

7 TUESDAY

4th ♐

☽ enters ♑	4:55 pm	**1:55 pm**	
☉ □ ⚵	12:48 am		
☽ ⚺ ⚳	2:45 am		
♀ ⚺ ♃	9:20 am	**6:20 am**	
☽ ⚺ ♃	11:33 am	**8:33 am**	
☽ ☌ ♀	11:43 am	**8:43 am**	☽ v/c
☽ ⚺ ♆	12:08 pm	**9:08 am**	
⚶ □ ⚷	4:11 pm	**1:11 pm**	
♀ ⚺ ♆	4:40 pm	**1:40 pm**	
☽ ☌ ⚴	5:29 pm	**2:29 pm**	
☽ ⚹ ⚷	6:08 pm	**3:08 pm**	
☽ ⚺ ⚶	6:11 pm	**3:11 pm**	
☽ □ ♂	7:13 pm	**4:13 pm**	
☽ □ ♄	7:43 pm	**4:43 pm**	
☽ ⚺ ♅	10:53 pm	**7:53 pm**	
☽ ⚺ ♇		**9:25 pm**	
☽ ☌ ☿		**9:27 pm**	
☿ ⚺ ♇		**10:14 pm**	

8 WEDNESDAY

4th ♑

New Moon	11:26 pm	**8:26 pm**	
☽ ⚺ ♇	12:25 am		
☽ ☌ ☿	12:27 am		
☿ ⚺ ♇	1:14 am		
☽ □ ⚵	9:25 pm	**6:25 pm**	
⚴ ⚹ ⚷	9:46 pm	**6:46 pm**	
☽ ☌ ☉	11:26 pm	**8:26 pm**	
☽ ∠ ♇		**9:32 pm**	

9 THURSDAY

1st ♑

☽ enters ♒	4:59 pm	**1:59 pm**	
♀ enters ♑		**9:32 pm**	
☽ ∠ ♇	12:32 am		
☽ ☌ ⚳	4:37 am	**1:37 am**	
♂ ☍ ♄	5:53 am	**2:53 am**	
♃ ☌ ♆	6:40 am	**3:40 am**	
☿ ⚺ ♅	10:37 am	**7:37 am**	
☽ ☌ ♆	12:29 pm	**9:29 am**	
☽ ☌ ♃	12:33 pm	**9:33 am**	☽ v/c
☽ ⚺ ♀	4:19 pm	**1:19 pm**	
☉ ∠ ♇	4:20 pm	**1:20 pm**	
☽ □ ⚷	6:24 pm	**3:24 pm**	
☽ ⚺ ⚴	6:52 pm	**3:52 pm**	
♄ ⚹ ⚶	7:21 pm	**4:21 pm**	
☽ ⚹ ♄	7:56 pm	**4:56 pm**	
☽ ☌ ⚶	7:57 pm	**4:57 pm**	
☽ △ ♂	8:08 pm	**5:08 pm**	
☽ ⚺ ☿	10:35 pm	**7:35 pm**	
☽ ☌ ♅	11:00 pm	**8:00 pm**	
☽ ⚹ ♇		**9:25 pm**	☽ v/c

10 FRIDAY

1st ≈

☽	⚹	♇	12:25 am			☽ v/c
♂	△	♅	6:26 am	**3:26**	**am**	
☽	∟	♀	6:18 pm	**3:18**	**pm**	
♀	⚹	♂	6:46 pm	**3:46**	**pm**	
☽	∟	♀	7:22 pm	**4:22**	**pm**	
☽	∟	♄	7:52 pm	**4:52**	**pm**	
☽	⊕	♂	8:24 pm	**5:24**	**pm**	
☽	∟	☿	9:54 pm	**6:54**	**pm**	
☽	⚹	⚴	10:24 pm	**7:24**	**pm**	
☽	⚺	☉		**11:35**	**pm**	

♀ enters ♑ 12:32 am

11 SATURDAY

1st ≈

☽	⚺	☉	2:35 am		
☽	⚺	⚵	5:38 am	**2:38**	**am**
☽	⚺	♆	12:23 pm	**9:23**	**am**
♀	♂	♀	12:43 pm	**9:43**	**am**
☽	⚺	♃	1:06 pm	**10:06**	**am**
♀	▢	♄	2:16 pm	**11:16**	**am**
♄	▢	♀	6:14 pm	**3:14**	**pm**
☽	△	♂	6:29 pm	**3:29**	**pm**
☽	⚺	♄	8:03 pm	**5:03**	**pm**
☽	⚹	♀	8:06 pm	**5:06**	**pm**
☽	⚹	♀	8:33 pm	**5:33**	**pm**
☽	⊼	♂	8:54 pm	**5:54**	**pm**
☽	⚺	♅	9:36 pm	**6:36**	**pm**
☽	⚹	☿	9:42 pm	**6:42**	**pm**
☽	⚺	♅	11:09 pm	**8:09**	**pm**
☽	∟	⚴	11:11 pm	**8:11**	**pm**

☿	⚺	♅	9:05 pm
☽	▢	♇	9:31 pm
♀	▢	♂	10:36 pm

☽ enters ♓ 4:51 pm **1:51 pm**

12 SUNDAY

1st ♓

☿	⚺	♅	12:05 am		
☽	▢	♇	12:31 am		
♀	▢	♂	1:36 am		
☽	∟	☉	4:34 am	**1:34**	**am**
☽	∟	⚵	6:32 am	**3:32**	**am**
☿	♂	♀	9:30 am	**6:30**	**am**
☽	∟	♆	12:48 pm	**9:48**	**am**
☽	∟	♃	1:52 pm	**10:52**	**am**
♀	⚺	♅	5:05 pm	**2:05**	**pm**
☽	⊕	♂	7:05 pm	**4:05**	**pm**
☽	∟	♅	11:05 pm	**8:05**	**pm**
☽	∟	♆	11:51 pm	**8:51**	**pm**
☽	⚺	⚴		**9:29**	**pm**

☿ D 3:36 pm **12:36 pm**

JANUARY

S	M	T	W	T	F	S
			1	2	3	4
5	6	7	8	9	10	11
12	13	14	15	16	17	18
19	20	21	22	23	24	25
26	27	28	29	30	31	

13   MONDAY

1st ♓

☽	⊼	♦	12:29 am			
♀	⊼	♅	4:41 am	1:41 am		
☽	✶	☉	7:11 am	4:11 am		
☽	✶	♄	8:02 am	5:02 am		
☽	✶	♆	1:48 pm	10:48 am		
☽	✶	♃	3:15 pm	12:15 pm	☽ v/c	
☽	⊼	♂	8:18 pm	5:18 pm		
♀	⊼	♇	8:24 pm	5:24 pm		
☽	♂	♄	9:58 pm	6:58 pm		
♅	♂	♦	10:57 pm	7:57 pm		
☽	□	♀	11:14 pm	8:14 pm		
☽	☍	♂	11:30 pm	8:30 pm		
☽	□	☿	11:36 pm	8:36 pm		
☽	✶	♅		10:12 pm		
☽	✶	♦		10:16 pm		
☉	♂	♃		11:15 pm		

☽ enters ♈ 6:21 pm **3:21 pm**

☽ △ ♇ 11:31 pm
♇ ⊡ ♦ 11:56 pm

14   TUESDAY

1st ♈

☽	✶	♅	1:12 am		
☽	✶	♦	1:16 am		
☉	♂	♃	2:15 am		
☽	△	♇	2:31 am		
♇	⊡	♦	2:56 am		
☽	□	♀	3:07 am	12:07 am	
♂	□	♀	9:27 pm	6:27 pm	

15   WEDNESDAY

1st ♈

☽	⊡	♇	4:36 am	1:36 am	
☽	♂	♦	5:21 am	2:21 am	
♇	✶	♦	12:52 pm	9:52 am	
☽	□	♄	1:18 pm	10:18 am	
☽	□	☉	3:02 pm	12:02 pm	
☽	□	♆	5:59 pm	2:59 pm	
☽	□	♃	8:19 pm	5:19 pm	☽ v/c
☽	☍	♂		9:57 pm	
☽	⊼	♄		11:47 pm	

2nd Quarter 3:02 pm **12:02 pm**
☽ enters ♉ 10:40 pm **7:40 pm**

16   THURSDAY

2nd ♉

☽	☍	♂	12:57 am		
☽	⊼	♄	2:47 am		
☽	⊼	♂	5:02 am	2:02 am	
☽	△	♀	5:28 am	2:28 am	
☽	△	☿	5:31 am	2:31 am	
☽	□	♅	6:09 am	3:09 am	
☽	⊼	♇	7:26 am	4:26 am	
☽	□	♦	8:09 am	5:09 am	
☽	△	♀	1:28 pm	10:28 am	
☿	⊼	♅		9:59 pm	

17 FRIDAY

2nd ♉

☿	⚺	♅	12:59 am	
☽	⊥	♄	6:19 am	3:19 am
☉	☌	♆	7:34 am	4:34 am
♅	⚺	♀	7:47 am	4:47 am
☽	⊓	♂	8:56 am	5:56 am
☽	⊓	♀	9:47 am	6:47 am
☽	⊓	☿	10:05 am	7:05 am
☽	⚺	⚷	1:30 pm	10:30 am
☽	⊓	♀	8:06 pm	5:06 pm
☽	△	?	9:48 pm	6:48 pm
☽	△	♆		10:09 pm
☽	△	☉		11:37 pm

18 SATURDAY

2nd ♉

☽ enters ♊   5:53 am   **2:53 am**

☽	△	♆	1:09 am		
☽	△	☉	2:37 am		
☽	△	♃	4:27 am	1:27 am	☽ v/c
☿	⚺	♇	6:34 am	3:34 am	
☽	⊼	♂	8:31 am	5:31 am	
☽	✶	♄	10:32 am	7:32 am	
☽	△	♂	1:30 pm	10:30 am	
☽	△	♅	1:59 pm	10:59 am	
☽	⊼	♀	2:50 pm	11:50 am	
☽	☍	♇	3:12 pm	12:12 pm	☽ v/c
☽	⊼	☿	3:39 pm	12:39 pm	
☽	△	⚸	6:14 pm	3:14 pm	
☽	⊥	⚷	6:43 pm	3:43 pm	

19 SUNDAY

2nd ♊

☉ enters ≈   7:42 pm   **4:42 pm**

☽	⊓	?	3:06 am	12:06 am
♇	⚺	♀	3:34 am	12:34 am
☽	⊼	♀	3:36 am	12:36 am
☽	⊓	♆	5:41 am	2:41 am
☉	☌	♃	8:07 am	5:07 am
☽	⊓	♃	9:31 am	6:31 am
☽	⊓	☉	9:37 am	6:37 am
☽	⊓	⚷	1:14 pm	10:14 am
☽	⊓	♅	6:50 pm	3:50 pm
☽	⊓	⚸		9:16 pm
☽	✶	⚷		9:32 pm

SUN ENTERS AQUARIUS

JANUARY

S	M	T	W	T	F	S
			1	2	3	4
5	6	7	8	9	10	11
12	13	14	15	16	17	18
19	20	21	22	23	24	25
26	27	28	29	30	31	

Eastern Standard Time in medium type
Pacific Standard Time in bold type

20 MONDAY

☽	⊡	⚸	12:16 am	
☽	✶	⚷	12:32 am	
☽	⊼	♀	8:59 am	5:59 am
☽	⊼	♆	10:45 am	7:45 am
♂	△	♅	1:54 pm	10:54 am
☽	⊼	♃	3:07 pm	12:07 pm
☽	⊼	☉	5:16 pm	2:16 pm
☽	△	⚷	6:27 pm	3:27 pm
☽	□	♄	8:40 pm	5:40 pm
☽	⊼	♅		9:09 pm
☽	□	♂		9:15 pm
☽	⊼	♇		10:15 pm
☽	☍	♀		11:41 pm

☽ enters ♋   3:29 pm   **12:29 pm**

2nd ♊

MARTIN LUTHER KING, JR. BIRTHDAY

21 TUESDAY

☽	⊼	♅	12:09 am	
☽	□	♂	12:15 am	
☽	⊼	♇	1:15 am	
☽	☍	♀	2:41 am	
☽	☍	☿	5:29 am	2:29 am
☽	⊼	⚸	6:50 am	3:50 am
☉	□	⚷	8:03 am	5:03 am
☽	☍	♀	8:38 pm	5:38 pm

♃ enters ≈   10:12 am   **7:12 am**

2nd ♋

22 WEDNESDAY

☽	⊡	♇	6:56 am	3:56 am	
☉	✶	♄	1:31 pm	10:31 am	
☽	□	✶	1:44 pm	10:44 am	
♆	☌	♀	8:39 pm	5:39 pm	
☽	☍	♆	10:10 pm	7:10 pm	☽ v/c
☽	☍	♀	10:13 pm	7:13 pm	
☿	⊻	⚸	10:39 pm	7:39 pm	

☽ enters ♌

2nd ♋
11:51 pm

23 THURSDAY

☽	☍	♃	3:39 am	12:39 am	
☽	□	⚷	6:06 am	3:06 am	
☽	△	♄	8:34 am	5:34 am	
☽	☍	☉	10:12 am	7:12 am	
☽	☍	♅	12:01 pm	9:01 am	
☽	✶	♂	12:39 pm	9:39 am	
☽	△	♇	12:59 pm	9:59 am	☽ v/c
☽	⊼	♀	4:21 pm	1:21 pm	
☽	☍	⚸	9:18 pm	6:18 pm	
☽	⊼	☿	10:16 pm	7:16 pm	

☽ enters ♌   2:51 am
Full Moon   10:12 am   **7:12 am**

2nd ♌

Eastern Standard Time in medium type
Pacific Standard Time in bold type

24 FRIDAY

3rd ♌

☉	☌	♅	8:53 am	**5:53 am**
☽	⊡	♄	3:01 pm	**12:01 pm**
☽	⊼	♀	3:46 pm	**12:46 pm**
☽	⌊	♂	7:18 pm	**4:18 pm**
☉	△	♂	7:25 pm	**4:25 pm**
☉	✶	♇	7:38 pm	**4:38 pm**
♂	✶	♇	9:19 pm	**6:19 pm**
☽	⊡	♀	11:41 pm	**8:41 pm**

25 SATURDAY

3rd ♌

☽ enters ♍   3:27 pm **12:27 pm**

☽	△	✶	4:30 am	**1:30 am**
☽	⊡	☿	7:32 am	**4:32 am**
☽	⊼	♆	10:53 am	**7:53 am**
☽	⊼	?	12:51 pm	**9:51 am**
☽	⊼	♃	5:30 pm	**2:30 pm**
☽	✶	♅	6:58 pm	**3:58 pm**
☽	⊼	♄	9:42 pm	**6:42 pm**
☽	⊼	♅		10:03 pm
☽	⊡	♀		10:50 pm
☽	☐	♇		10:51 pm
♀	⌊	♇		10:58 pm
☽	⌄	♂		11:06 pm

26 SUNDAY

3rd ♍

☽	⊼	♅	1:03 am	
☽	⊡	♀	1:50 am	
☽	☐	♇	1:51 am	
♀	⌊	♇	1:58 am	
☽	⌄	♂	2:06 am	
☽	⊼	☉	4:38 am	**1:38 am**
☽	△	♀	7:13 am	**4:13 am**
☽	⊡	✶	12:13 pm	**9:13 am**
☽	⊼	♆	12:57 pm	**9:57 am**
☽	△	☿	5:10 pm	**2:10 pm**
☽	⊡	♆	5:30 pm	**2:30 pm**
☽	⊡	?	8:25 pm	**5:25 pm**
☽	⊡	♃		9:38 pm
☽	⌊	♅		10:34 pm

JANUARY

S	M	T	W	T	F	S
			1	2	3	4
5	6	7	8	9	10	11
12	13	14	15	16	17	18
19	20	21	22	23	24	25
26	27	28	29	30	31	

27 MONDAY

3rd ♍

☽	⊡ ♃	12:38 am	
☽	∟ ⚷	1:34 am	
☽	⊡ ♅	7:43 am	4:43 am
☽	△ ♀	11:57 am	8:57 am
☽	⊡ ☉	1:59 am	10:59 am
☽	⊼ ⚸	7:55 pm	4:55 pm
☽	⊡ ♆	8:48 pm	5:48 pm
☽	△ ♆		9:02 pm ☽ v/c

28 TUESDAY

3rd ♍

☽	△ ♆	12:02 am		☽ v/c
☉	⊻ ☿	3:39 am	12:39 am	
☽	△ ♃	3:53 am	12:53 am	
☽	△ ♃	7:38 am	4:38 am	
☽	⊻ ⚷	8:01 am	5:01 am	
☽	⚯ ♄	11:00 am	8:00 am	
☽	△ ♅	2:10 pm	11:10 am	
☽	⚹ ♇	2:46 pm	11:46 am	
☽	♂ ♂	3:28 pm	12:28 pm	
☽	⊡ ♀	9:58 pm	6:58 pm	
☽	△ ☉	11:01 pm	8:01 pm	

☽ enters ♎   4:22 am   **1:22 am**
♃ enters ♒   6:14 pm   **3:14 pm**

29 WEDNESDAY

3rd ♎

☽	△ ⚸	4:19 am	1:19 am
♃	⊡ ⚷	6:49 am	3:49 am
☽	⊡ ☿	12:12 pm	9:12 am
☽	∟ ♇	8:40 pm	5:40 pm

30 THURSDAY

3rd ♎

☽	⊡ ♀	6:49 am	3:49 am	
☽	⚯ ⚸	10:02 am	7:02 am	
☽	⊡ ♆	11:49 am	8:49 am ☽ v/c
☽	⊡ ♃	5:18 pm	2:18 pm	
☽	♂ ⚷	7:27 pm	4:27 pm	
☽	⊡ ♃	8:04 pm	5:04 pm	
☽	⊼ ♄	10:35 pm	7:35 pm	
☽	⊡ ♅		10:27 pm	
☽	⊻ ♇		10:50 pm	
☽	⊻ ♂		11:48 pm	

☽ enters ♏   3:48 pm   **12:48 pm**

31 FRIDAY

3rd ♏
4th Quarter　2:40 pm　**11:40 am**

☽	□	♅	1:27 am	
☽	ⅴ	♇	1:50 am	
☽	ⅴ	♂	2:48 am	
☽	✶	♀	10:26 am	**7:26 am**
☽	□	☉	2:40 pm	**11:40 am**
☽	□	♆	5:03 pm	**2:03 pm**

≈≈≈ **AQUARIUS** ≈≈≈
Fixed • Air
Rules 11th House
Ruled by Uranus
Rules ankles
Keyword: Truth
Keynote: I KNOW

1 SATURDAY

4th ♏
☽ enters ♐　11:51 pm　**8:51 pm**

☽	⊡	♄	3:05 am	**12:05 am**	
☽	✶	☿	4:14 am	**1:14 am**	
☽	∟	♂	7:06 am	**4:06 am**	
♀	□	✶	7:38 am	**4:38 am**	
♀	♂	♆	9:27 am	**6:27 am**	
♆	□	✶	12:42 pm	**9:42 am**	
☽	∟	♀	3:09 pm	**12:09 pm**	
☽	✶	♆	8:18 pm	**5:18 pm**	
☽	⊼	✶	8:34 pm	**5:34 pm**	
☽	✶	♀	9:24 pm	**6:24 pm**	☽ v/c
☿	∟	♇	10:53 pm	**7:53 pm**	
☽	✶	♃		**11:56 pm**	

2 SUNDAY

4th ♐
♀ enters ≈≈　11:27 pm　**8:27 pm**

☽	✶	♃	2:56 am		
☽	ⅴ	♅	3:21 am	**12:21 am**	
☽	✶	♃	4:48 am	**1:48 am**	
☽	△	♄	6:32 am	**3:32 am**	
☽	✶	♅	9:03 am	**6:03 am**	
☽	♂	♇	9:15 am	**6:15 am**	
☽	✶	♂	10:17 am	**7:17 am**	
☽	∟	☿	10:21 am	**7:21 am**	
♃	□	♅	5:37 pm	**2:37 pm**	
☽	ⅴ	♀	6:42 pm	**3:42 pm**	
☽	∟	♆	10:57 pm	**7:57 pm**	
☽	⊡	✶		**9:05 pm**	
☽	✶	☉		**10:22 pm**	☽ v/c　☽ ∟ ♀　11:34 pm
☽	✶	♅		**10:22 pm**	
☉	♂	♆		**10:28 pm**	

GROUND HOG DAY • IMBOLC

3 MONDAY — 4th ♐

Aspect	EST	PST
☽ ⚼ ⚷	12:05 am	
☽ ⚹ ☉	1:22 am	
☽ ⚹ ♆	1:22 am	
☉ ☌ ♆	1:28 am	
☉ ⚻ ♀	2:34 am	
☽ ⚻ ⚷	5:42 am	**2:42 am**
☽ ⚻ ☿	6:02 am	**3:02 am**
☽ ⚻ ♃	7:30 am	**4:30 am**
☽ ⚻ ♅	11:15 am	**8:15 am**
☽ ⚺ ☿	3:05 pm	**12:05 pm**
☽ ⚺ ♆		**9:35 pm**
☽ △ ⚷		**11:30 pm**

☽ v/c

4 TUESDAY — 4th ♐

Aspect	EST	PST
☽ ⚺ ♆	12:35 am	
☽ △ ⚷	2:30 am	
☽ ⚻ ♅	3:48 am	**12:48 am**
☽ ⚻ ☉	4:47 am	**1:47 am**
☽ ⚺ ♀	6:26 am	**3:26 am**
☽ ⚹ ⚷	7:04 am	**4:04 am**
☽ ⚺ ☿	8:03 am	**5:03 am**
☽ ⚺ ♃	9:11 am	**6:11 am**
☽ □ ♄	10:17 am	**7:17 am**
☽ ⚺ ♅	12:29 pm	**9:29 am**
☽ ⚺ ♇	12:32 pm	**9:32 am**
☽ □ ♂	1:32 pm	**10:32 am**
♀ □ ⚷	1:50 pm	**10:50 am**
☽ ☌ ♀	10:35 pm	**7:35 pm**

☽ enters ♑ — 3:44 am / **12:44 am**

5 WEDNESDAY — 4th ♑

Aspect	EST	PST
☽ ⚺ ♆	5:18 am	**2:18 am**
♅ ⚹ ♇	5:46 am	**2:46 am**
☽ ⚺ ☉	7:10 am	**4:10 am**
♀ ☌ ☿	9:04 am	**6:04 am**
☽ ⚻ ♇	12:56 pm	**9:56 am**
♀ ☌ ♃	8:48 pm	**5:48 pm**
☽ ☌ ☿	9:17 pm	**6:17 pm**
☽ ☌ ♆		**10:29 pm**

☽ v/c

♂ ℞ — 7:24 pm / **4:24 pm**
⚶ enters ♉ — 3:23 pm / **12:23 pm**

6 THURSDAY — 4th ♑

Aspect	EST	PST
☽ ☌ ♆	1:29 am	
☽ □ ⚷	4:47 am	**1:47 am**
♀ ⚹ ♄	6:34 am	**3:34 am**
☽ □ ⚶	7:34 am	**4:34 am**
☽ ☌ ☿	9:45 am	**6:45 am**
☽ ☌ ♃	10:17 am	**7:17 am**
☽ ⚹ ♄	10:55 am	**7:55 am**
☽ ☌ ♀	11:16 am	**8:16 am**
☽ ⚹ ♇	12:48 pm	**9:48 am**
☽ ☌ ♅	12:53 pm	**9:53 am**
☽ △ ♂	1:43 pm	**10:43 am**
☽ ⚺ ♀	11:37 pm	**8:37 pm**

☽ v/c

☽ enters ≈ — 4:21 am / **1:21 am**

7 FRIDAY

4th ≈

♀	✶	♇	6:06 am	**3:06 am**		
☽	♂	♆	6:35 am	**3:35 am**		
♀	♂	♅	7:44 am	**4:44 am**		
☽	♂	☉	10:06 am	**7:06 am**	☽ v/c	
☽	∟	♄	10:40 am	**7:40 am**		
☽	⊞	♂	1:16 pm	**10:16 am**		
♀	△	♂	4:33 pm	**1:33 pm**		
☉	∟	♄	7:22 pm	**4:22 pm**		
☿	♂	♆	7:31 pm	**4:31 pm**		
☽	∟	♀	11:46 pm	**8:46 pm**		
☽	⊻	♆		**9:49 pm**		
☽	⊻	☿		**10:21 pm**		

New Moon   10:06 am   **7:06 am**

8 SATURDAY

1st ≈

☽	⊻	♆	12:49 am		
☽	⊻	☿	1:21 am		
☽	✶	♃	5:33 am	**2:33 am**	
☽	△	♅	6:48 am	**3:48 am**	
☽	⊻	♀	10:11 am	**7:11 am**	
☽	⊻	♃	10:12 am	**7:12 am**	
☽	⊻	♄	10:25 am	**7:25 am**	
♃	♂	♀	11:40 am	**8:40 am**	
☽	☐	♇	12:02 pm	**9:02 am**	
☽	⊻	♅	12:15 pm	**9:15 am**	
☽	⊼	♂	12:50 pm	**9:50 am**	
☽	⊻	♀	2:42 pm	**11:42 am**	
♄	✶	♃	9:54 pm	**6:54 pm**	
☽	✶	☿		**9:04 pm**	
☽	∟	♆		**9:36 pm**	

☽ enters ♓   3:34 am   **12:34 am**
☿ enters ≈   **9:53 pm**

9 SUNDAY

1st ♓

☽	✶	♀	12:04 am		
☽	∟	♆	12:36 am		
☽	∟	☿	3:34 am	**12:34 am**	
☽	∟	♃	6:09 am	**3:09 am**	
☽	⊞	♃	6:37 am	**3:37 am**	
☽	⊻	♆	7:38 am	**4:38 am**	
☉	⊞	♂	8:24 am	**5:24 am**	
☽	∟	♃	10:25 am	**7:25 am**	
♃	✶	♄	10:36 am	**7:36 am**	
☽	∟	♃	10:40 am	**7:40 am**	
☽	∟	♅	12:13 pm	**9:13 am**	
☽	⊻	☉	12:59 pm	**9:59 am**	
☽	∟	♀	4:49 pm	**1:49 pm**	
✶	♂	♃	8:36 pm	**5:36 pm**	
☽	✶	♆		**9:46 pm**	☽ v/c

☿ enters ≈   12:53 am

FEBRUARY

S	M	T	W	T	F	S
						1
2	3	4	5	6	7	8
9	10	11	12	13	14	15
16	17	18	19	20	21	22
23	24	25	26	27	28	

Eastern Standard Time in medium type
Pacific Standard Time in bold type

10 MONDAY

1st ♓

☽	✶	♆	12:46	am		☽ v/c
☽	✶	☿	6:24	am	3:24	am
☽	⊼	♅	6:53	am	3:53	am
☽	⊻	♃	7:14	am	4:14	am
☽	∟	♆	8:48	am	5:48	am
☽	♂	♄	10:57	am	7:57	am
☽	✶	♃	11:10	am	8:10	am
☿	□	♅	11:16	am	8:16	am
☽	✶	♇	11:42	am	8:42	am
☽	△	♇	12:21	pm	9:21	am
☽	✶	♅	12:43	pm	9:43	am
☽	♂	♂	12:58	pm	9:58	am
☽	∟	☉	3:13	pm	12:13	pm
☿	□	♃	6:39	pm	3:39	pm
☽	✶	♀	7:39	pm	4:39	pm
☽	□	♀			11:12	pm

☽ enters ♈   3:30 am   **12:30 am**

11 TUESDAY

1st ♈

☽	□	♀	2:12	am		
☽	✶	♃	10:43	am	7:43	am
♇	✶	♃	1:07	pm	10:07	am
☽	⊞	♇	1:29	pm	10:29	am
☽	✶	☉	6:22	pm	3:22	pm
♂	△	♅	7:08	pm	4:08	pm

12 WEDNESDAY

1st ♈

☽	□	♆	3:11	am	12:11	am	☽ v/c
♂	△	♃	4:08	am	1:08	am
☿	✶	♄	6:33	am	3:33	am
♅	♂	♃	7:48	am	4:48	am
☽	♂	♃	9:35	am	6:35	am
☽	♂	♃	11:51	am	8:51	am
☿	♂	♃	1:22	pm	10:22	am
☽	⊻	♄	2:17	pm	11:17	am
☽	□	♃	2:59	pm	11:59	am
☽	□	☿	3:10	pm	12:10	pm
☽	⊼	♇	3:27	pm	12:27	pm
☽	⊼	♂	3:47	pm	12:47	pm
☽	□	♅	3:59	pm	12:59	pm
☽	□	♃	4:12	pm	1:12	pm
☿	✶	♇	5:47	pm	2:47	pm
☿	△	♂	8:29	pm	5:29	pm

☽ enters ♉   5:57 am   **2:57 am**

☿   ♂   ♅   10:56 pm   **7:56 pm**

LINCOLN'S BIRTHDAY • ASH WEDNESDAY

13 THURSDAY

1st ♉

☿	♂	♃	3:29	am	12:29	am
☽	□	♀	4:29	am	1:29	am
☽	△	♀	7:40	am	4:40	am
♄	∟	♃	12:56	pm	9:56	am
☽	∟	♄	5:19	pm	2:19	pm
☽	□	♃	5:27	pm	2:27	pm
☽	⊞	♂	6:27	pm	3:27	pm
♃	✶	♇	7:42	pm	4:42	pm
♂	△	♃			9:08	pm

♃ ℞   9:27 pm   **6:27 pm**

14 FRIDAY

♂ △ ♃	12:08 am		
☽ □ ☉	3:58 am	12:58 am	
♂ ✶ ♇	8:06 am	5:06 am	
☽ △ ♆	9:05 am	6:05 am	☽ v/c
☽ ⊼ ♀	11:52 am	8:52 am	
♂ ⊼ ♅	2:53 pm	11:53 am	
☽ ⊼ ⚷	3:47 pm	12:47 pm	
☽ ⌄ ⚷	8:27 pm	5:27 pm	
☽ ✶ ♄	9:16 pm	6:16 pm	
☽ ☍ ♂	9:59 pm	6:59 pm	
☽ ☍ ♇	10:07 pm	7:07 pm	
☽ △ ♃	10:34 pm	7:34 pm	
☽ △ ♅	10:53 pm	7:53 pm	
☽ △ ♏		9:35 pm	

1st ♉

2nd Quarter   3:58 am   **12:58 am**
☽ enters Ⅱ   11:54 am   **8:54 am**

VALENTINE'S DAY

15 SATURDAY

☽ △ ♏	12:35 am		
♀ ⌄ ♀	3:08 am	12:08 am	
☽ △ ☿	5:08 am	2:08 am	
☽ ⊼ ♆	1:22 pm	10:22 am	
☽ ⊼ ♀	4:59 pm	1:59 pm	
☽ △ ♀	6:05 pm	3:05 pm	
☽ ⊼ ⚷	8:11 pm	5:11 pm	
♃ ♂ ♅	9:23 pm	6:23 pm	
♄ ⌄ ♆	10:31 pm	7:31 pm	
☽ ∟ ♆		11:11 pm	

2nd Ⅱ

16 SUNDAY

☽ ∟ ♆	2:11 am		
☽ ⊼ ♅	3:36 am	12:36 am	
☽ ⊼ ♃	3:41 am	12:41 am	
♂ ⊼ ♆	3:42 am	12:42 am	
☽ △ ⚷	4:09 am	1:09 am	
☽ ⊼ ♏	6:09 am	3:09 am	
♂ ☍ ♄	12:14 pm	9:14 am	
☽ ⊼ ☿	2:00 pm	11:00 am	
♇ ⊼ ♆	3:22 pm	12:22 pm	
☽ △ ☉	5:56 pm	2:56 pm	☽ v/c
☽ ⊼ ♆	6:25 pm	3:25 pm	
☉ ⌄ ♆	11:54 pm	8:54 pm	
☽ △ ⚷		10:18 pm	
☽ ⊼ ♀		11:28 pm	

2nd Ⅱ

☽ enters ♋   9:13 pm   **6:13 pm**

FEBRUARY

S	M	T	W	T	F	S
						1
2	3	4	5	6	7	8
9	10	11	12	13	14	15
16	17	18	19	20	21	22
23	24	25	26	27	28	

17 MONDAY

2nd ♋

☽	△	♀	1:18	am	
☽	⊼	♀	2:28	am	
☽	□	♂	7:11	am	4:11 am
☽	□	♄	7:35	am	4:35 am
☽	⊼	♇	8:01	am	5:01 am
☽	✶	♆	8:43	am	5:43 am
☽	⊼	♅	9:01	am	6:01 am
☽	⊼	♃	9:32	am	6:32 am
☽	⊼	⚷	10:44	am	7:44 am
☽	⊼	?	12:27	pm	9:27 am
♅	□	♆	4:34	pm	1:34 pm
☽	⊼	☿	11:53	pm	8:53 pm
☽	⊼	☉			11:12 pm

18 TUESDAY

2nd ♋

☉ enters ♓   9:51 am   **6:51 am**

☽	⊼	☉	2:12	am	
☽	☍	♀	5:29	am	2:29 am
☽	⊼	♀	11:38	am	8:38 am
☽	⊼	♇	1:50	pm	10:50 am
☽	⊼	⚷	5:54	pm	2:54 pm
♃	□	♆	6:22	pm	3:22 pm
♀	⊼	♂	7:52	pm	4:52 pm

SUN ENTERS PISCES

19 WEDNESDAY

2nd ♋

☽ enters ♌   8:53 am   **5:53 am**

☽	☍	♆	6:10	am	3:10 am	☽ v/c
♀	∟	♄	8:40	am	5:40 am	
☽	⊼	☉	11:01	am	8:01 am	
♄	△	♇	11:44	am	8:44 am	
☽	□	♀	1:02	pm	10:02 am	
☽	✶	♂	6:19	pm	3:19 pm	
☽	△	♇	8:01	pm	5:01 pm	
☽	△	♄	8:05	pm	5:05 pm	
☽	☍	♅	9:17	pm	6:17 pm	
☽	☍	♃	10:41	pm	7:41 pm	
☽	□	♆	11:25	pm	8:25 pm	
☽	☍	?			11:31 pm	

20 THURSDAY

2nd ♌

☽	☍	?	2:31	am	
☿	⊻	♀	4:42	am	1:42 am
☉	△	♀	10:37	am	7:37 am
☉	∟	♀	12:55	pm	9:55 am
☽	⊼	♀	7:45	pm	4:45 pm
☽	☍	☿	9:36	pm	6:36 pm
☽	∟	♂			9:12 pm
☽	⊼	♄			11:45 pm

21 FRIDAY

☽	∟	♂	12:12 am	
☽	⊡	♄	2:45 am	
☽	☍	♀	7:17 am	**4:17 am** ☽ v/c
☽	☍	♆	9:14 am	**6:14 am**
☿	⊡	♂	2:43 pm	**11:43 am**
☽	⊼	♆	7:04 pm	**4:04 pm**
☽	⚹	⚷		**10:45 pm**

2nd ♌

☽ enters ♍   9:38 pm   **6:38 pm**

22 SATURDAY

☽	⚹	⚷	1:45 am	
☽	⊡	♀	3:08 am	**12:08 am**
☽	☍	☉	5:27 am	**2:27 am**
☽	⊻	♂	6:09 am	**3:09 am**
☽	□	♇	8:54 am	**5:54 am**
☽	⊼	♄	9:30 am	**6:30 am**
☽	⊼	♅	10:24 am	**7:24 am**
☉	⊼	♂	12:21 pm	**9:21 am**
☽	⊼	♃	12:43 pm	**9:43 am**
♀	♂	♆	12:59 pm	**9:59 am**
☿	∟	♄	1:14 pm	**10:14 am**
☽	△	⚹	3:03 pm	**12:03 pm**
☽	⊼	♀	5:25 pm	**2:25 pm**
☽	⊡	♆		**10:36 pm**

2nd ♍

Full Moon   5:27 am   **2:27 am**

23 SUNDAY

☽	⊡	♆	1:36 am	
☽	∟	⚷	8:08 am	**5:08 am**
☽	△	♀	10:28 am	**7:28 am**
☽	⊡	♅	4:56 pm	**1:56 pm**
☽	⊡	♃	7:41 pm	**4:41 pm**
☽	⊼	☿	8:17 pm	**5:17 pm**
☉	□	♇	10:17 pm	**7:17 pm**
☽	⊡	⚹	10:50 pm	**7:50 pm**
☽	⊼	♆		**9:47 pm**
☽	⊡	♀		**9:48 pm**

3rd ♍

FEBRUARY

S	M	T	W	T	F	S
						1
2	3	4	5	6	7	8
9	10	11	12	13	14	15
16	17	18	19	20	21	22
23	24	25	26	27	28	

24   MONDAY

3rd ♍

☽ ⊼ ♆	12:47 am		
☽ ⊓ ♄	12:48 am		
☽ ⊼ ♀	3:17 am	12:17 am	
☽ △ ♆	7:59 am	4:59 am	☽ v/c
☉ ⊼ ♄	10:41 am	7:41 am	
☽ ⊻ ♂	2:22 pm	11:22 am	
☽ ☌ ♂	5:40 pm	2:40 pm	
☉ ⊻ ♅	6:35 pm	3:35 pm	
☽ ⚹ ♇	9:33 pm	6:33 pm	
☽ ☍ ♄	10:42 pm	7:42 pm	
☽ △ ♅	11:16 pm	8:16 pm	
☽ ⊼ ☉	11:40 pm	8:40 pm	
☽ △ ♃		11:25 pm	

☽ enters ♎   10:23 am   **7:23 am**

25   TUESDAY

3rd ♎

☽ △ ♃	2:25 am		
☽ ⊼ ♆	6:21 am	3:21 am	
☽ ⊓ ☿	7:21 am	4:21 am	
☽ △ ♄	7:54 am	4:54 am	
☽ ⊓ ♆	8:14 am	5:14 am	
☽ ⊓ ♀	12:51 pm	9:51 am	
☿ ☌ ♆	3:58 pm	12:58 pm	
☽ ☐ ♀		9:25 pm	
♀ ⊻ ♆		10:16 pm	

26   WEDNESDAY

3rd ♎

☽ ☐ ♀	12:25 am		
♀ ⊻ ♆	1:16 am		
☽ ∟ ♇	3:26 am	12:26 am	
☽ ⊓ ☉	8:11 am	5:11 am	
☽ △ ♆	3:13 pm	12:13 pm	
☉ ⊻ ♃	4:53 pm	1:53 pm	
☽ △ ☿	5:52 pm	2:52 pm	
☽ ☐ ♆	7:47 pm	4:47 pm	
☽ △ ♀	9:49 pm	6:49 pm	☽ v/c
☽ ☌ ♂		10:41 pm	

☽ enters ♏   9:56 pm   **6:56 pm**
♀ enters ♓   11:01 pm   **8:01 pm**

27   THURSDAY

3rd ♏

☽ ☌ ♂	1:41 am		
☽ ⊻ ♂	3:48 am	12:48 am	
☿ ⊻ ♆	7:46 am	4:46 am	
☽ ⊻ ♇	8:47 am	5:47 am	
☽ ⊼ ♄	10:24 am	7:24 am	
☽ ☐ ♅	10:39 am	7:39 am	
☽ ☐ ♃	2:30 pm	11:30 am	
☽ △ ☉	3:59 pm	12:59 pm	
☽ ☍ ♆	7:49 pm	4:49 pm	
☽ ☐ ♀	8:34 pm	5:34 pm	

☿ enters ♓   10:54 pm   **7:54 pm**

28 FRIDAY

3rd ♏

☽	∟	♂	7:58 am	**4:58 am**	
♀	△	♅	11:15 am	**8:15 am**	
☽	✶	♀	12:08 pm	**9:08 am**	
☽	⊡	♄	3:17 pm	**12:17 pm**	
♀	⊼	♂	11:06 pm	**8:06 pm**	
☿	△	♅		**9:37 pm**	
☽	□	♆		**11:59 pm**	

♓ PISCES ♓
Mutable • Water
Rules 12th House
Ruled by Neptune
Rules feet
Keyword: Unity
Keynote: I BELIEVE

1 SATURDAY

3rd ♏

☽ enters ♐   7:01 am   **4:01 am**

☿	△	♅	12:37 am			
☽	□	♆	2:59 am			
☽	✶	♆	5:06 am	**2:06 am**	☽ v/c	
☿	⊼	♂	7:48 am	**4:48 am**		
♄	✶	♅	8:24 am	**5:24 am**		
☽	⊻	♅	10:26 am	**7:26 am**		
☽	✶	♂	11:21 am	**8:21 am**		
☽	□	☿	11:59 am	**8:59 am**		
☽	□	♀	12:57 pm	**9:57 am**		
☽	∟	♀	4:44 pm	**1:44 pm**		
☽	♂	♇	5:17 pm	**2:17 pm**		
☽	✶	♅	7:15 pm	**4:15 pm**		
☽	△	♄	7:18 pm	**4:18 pm**		
☽	✶	♃	11:36 pm	**8:36 pm**		

2 SUNDAY

3rd ♐

4th Quarter   4:38 am   **1:38 am**

☽	□	☉	4:38 am	**1:38 am**	☽ v/c	
☽	⊼	✶	5:58 am	**2:58 am**		
☽	✶	♃	5:59 am	**2:59 am**		
?	□	✶	7:29 am	**4:29 am**		
☽	∟	♆	8:30 am	**5:30 am**		
☿	♂	♀	9:32 am	**6:32 am**		
☽	∟	♅	1:32 pm	**10:32 am**		
♇	∟	♀	2:21 pm	**11:21 am**		
☽	⊻	♀	8:22 pm	**5:22 pm**		
☽	∟	♅	10:13 pm	**7:13 pm**		
☽	∟	♃		**11:45 pm**		
☿	□	♇		**11:59 pm**		

3 MONDAY

4th ♐

☽ enters ♑ 12:39 pm **9:39 am**

☽ ∠ ♃	2:45	am		
☿ □ ♇	2:59	am		
☿ ∠ ⚴	5:50	am	**2:50**	**am**
♂ ⚺ ⚷	6:49	am	**3:49**	**am**
☉ ⚺ ⚳	8:47	am	**5:47**	**am**
☽ ∠ ⚳	9:15	am	**6:15**	**am**
☽ ⚼ ⚵	9:33	am	**6:33**	**am**
♀ □ ♇	10:31	am	**7:31**	**am**
☽ ✶ ⚶	10:55	am	**7:55**	**am**
☽ ⚺ ♆	10:59	am	**7:59**	**am**
♆ ⚺ ⚶	12:33	pm	**9:33**	**am**
☽ □ ♂	3:34	pm	**12:34**	**pm**
☽ ✶ ⚷	3:44	pm	**12:44**	**pm**
☉ ✶ ⚵	5:15	pm	**2:15**	**pm**
♀ ∠ ⚴	5:45	pm	**2:45**	**pm**
☿ ⚺ ♅	6:39	pm	**3:39**	**pm**
☿ ⚺ ♄	8:59	pm	**5:59**	**pm**
☽ ⚺ ♇	10:16	pm	**7:16**	**pm**
☽ ✶ ♀	11:24	pm	**8:24**	**pm**
☽ ⚺ ♅			**9:17**	**pm**
☽ □ ♄			**9:35**	**pm**
☽ ✶ ☿			**10:05**	**pm**

4 TUESDAY

4th ♑

☽ ⚺ ♅	12:17	am		
☽ □ ♄	12:35	am		
☽ ✶ ☿	1:05	am		
☽ ⚺ ♃	4:58	am	**1:58**	**am**
☉ ∠ ♆	9:33	am	**6:33**	**am**
♀ ⚺ ♅	9:38	am	**6:38**	**am**
☽ ⚺ ⚳	11:33	am	**8:33**	**am**
☽ △ ⚵	12:09	pm	**9:09**	**am**
☽ ✶ ☉	12:48	pm	**9:48**	**am**
☽ ∠ ⚶	1:25	pm	**10:25**	**am**
♀ ⚺ ♄	2:02	pm	**11:02**	**am**
☽ ∠ ♇	11:29	pm	**8:29**	**pm**
☽ ☌ ⚴			**9:48**	**pm**
☽ ∠ ♀			**11:57**	**pm**

5 WEDNESDAY

4th ♑

⚶ enters ♓ 10:32 am **7:32 am**
☽ enters ♒ 2:55 pm **11:55 am**

☽ ☌ ⚴	12:48	am			
☽ ∠ ♀	2:57	am			
☽ ∠ ☿	5:48	am	**2:48**	**am**	
☿ ⚺ ♃	10:47	am	**7:47**	**am**	
☽ ☌ ♆	1:26	pm	**10:26**	**am**	☽ v/c
☽ ⚺ ⚶	3:04	pm	**12:04**	**pm**	
☽ ∠ ☉	3:25	pm	**12:25**	**pm**	
☽ △ ♂	4:35	pm	**1:35**	**pm**	
☽ □ ⚷	5:43	pm	**2:43**	**pm**	
☽ ✶ ♇			**9:00**	**pm**	
☽ ☌ ♅			**11:04**	**pm**	
☽ ✶ ♄			**11:36**	**pm**	

6 THURSDAY

4th ♒

☽ ✶ ♇	12:00	am			
☽ ☌ ♅	2:04	am			
☽ ✶ ♄	2:36	am			
☽ ⚺ ♀	5:38	am	**2:38**	**am**	
☽ ☌ ♃	7:05	am	**4:05**	**am**	☽ v/c
☽ ⚺ ☿	9:36	am	**6:36**	**am**	
☽ ☌ ⚳	1:53	pm	**10:53**	**am**	
☽ □ ⚵	3:01	pm	**12:01**	**pm**	
☽ ⚼ ♂	4:12	pm	**1:12**	**pm**	
☽ ⚺ ☉	5:20	pm	**2:20**	**pm**	
♂ ⚻ ⚶	5:56	pm	**2:56**	**pm**	
☉ ⚼ ⚷			**9:03**	**pm**	
♀ ⚺ ♃			**11:15**	**pm**	
☽ ⚺ ⚴			**11:23**	**pm**	
☽ ∠ ♄			**11:48**	**pm**	

7 FRIDAY

4th ≈

		EST		PST	
☉	⊡	⚷	12:03 am		
♀	⊻	♃	2:15 am		
☽	⊻	♀	2:23 am		
☽	∟	♄	2:48 am		
♂	⊡	♅	11:38 am	**8:38 am**	
☽	⊻	Ψ	1:37 pm	**10:37 am**	
☽	⊼	♂	3:30 pm	**12:30 pm**	
☽	☌	⚸	4:45 pm	**1:45 pm**	
☽	△	⚷	5:33 pm	**2:33 pm**	
☿	∟	Ψ	7:03 pm	**4:03 pm**	
☽	□	♇	11:49 pm	**8:49 pm**	
☽	⊻	♅		**10:59 pm**	
☽	∟	♀		**11:39 pm**	
☽	⊻	♄		**11:45 pm**	

☽ enters ♓   2:57 pm   **11:57 am**

8 SATURDAY

4th ♓

			EST	PST	
☽	⊻	♅	1:59 am		
☽	∟	♀	2:39 am		
☽	⊻	♄	2:45 am		
☿	⊻	♃	3:26 am	**12:26 am**	
☽	⊻	♃	7:26 am	**4:26 am**	
☽	☌	♀	9:36 am	**6:36 am**	
☽	∟	Ψ	1:23 pm	**10:23 am**	
☽	⊻	♃	2:40 pm	**11:40 am**	
⚸	△	⚷	3:04 pm	**12:04 pm**	
♂	⊡	♃	3:12 pm	**12:12 pm**	
☽	☌	☿	3:57 pm	**12:57 pm**	
☽	⚹	♅	4:21 pm	**1:21 pm**	
☽	⊡	⚷	5:13 pm	**2:13 pm**	
☽	☌	☉	8:15 pm	**5:15 pm**	
☿	⚹	♅	8:17 pm	**5:17 pm**	
☽	∟	♅		**10:50 pm**	

☿ ⊡ ⚷   **10:57 pm**
☽ ⚹ ♀   **11:56 pm**

♇ R   3:36 am   **12:36 am**
♂ enters ♏   2:49 pm   **11:49 am**
New Moon   8:15 pm   **5:15 pm**

TOTAL ECLIPSE OF THE SUN 18° ♓ 31'

9 SUNDAY

1st ♓

			EST	PST	
☽	∟	♅	1:50 am		
☿	⊡	⚷	1:57 am		
☽	⚹	♀	2:56 am		
☽	∟	♃	7:34 am	**4:34 am**	
☽	⚹	Ψ	1:17 pm	**10:17 am**	
☽	☍	♂	1:59 pm	**10:59 am**	☽ v/c
☽	∟	♃	3:08 pm	**12:08 pm**	
☽	⊼	⚷	5:03 pm	**2:03 pm**	
☽	∟	♅	5:08 pm	**2:08 pm**	
☽	⊻	⚸	6:01 pm	**3:01 pm**	
☽	△	♇	11:33 pm	**8:33 pm**	
☽	⚹	♅		**10:55 pm**	
☽	☌	♄		**11:55 pm**	

☽ enters ♈   2:33 pm   **11:33 am**

MARCH

S	M	T	W	T	F	S
						1
2	3	4	5	6	7	8
9	10	11	12	13	14	15
16	17	18	19	20	21	22
23	24	25	26	27	28	29
30	31					

Eastern Standard Time in medium type
Pacific Standard Time in bold type

1997　　　　　　　　　　　　　　MARCH　　　　　　　　　　　　　　1997

10　MONDAY
1st ♈

☽	⚹	♅	1:55 am	
☽	♂	♄	2:55 am	
☽	⚹	♃	8:01 am	5:01 am
♀	∟	♆	8:30 am	5:30 am
☽	⊻	♀	1:59 pm	10:59 am
☽	⚹	♇	4:01 pm	1:01 pm
♂	△	♆	4:59 pm	1:59 pm
☽	⊻	⚸	6:21 pm	3:21 pm
☽	∟	⚷	7:12 pm	4:12 pm
☽	⊻	☿	11:20 pm	8:20 pm
☽	⊡	♇	11:59 pm	8:59 pm
☽	⊻	☉		9:06 pm

11　TUESDAY
1st ♈
☽ enters ♉　3:38 pm　**12:38 pm**

☽	⊻	☉	12:06 am	
☽	□	♀	4:34 am	1:34 am
☿	♂	☉	10:34 am	7:34 am
☽	⊼	♂	1:48 pm	10:48 am
☽	□	♆	2:23 pm	11:23 am	☽ v/c
☽	∟	♀	5:11 pm	2:11 pm
☽	☍	⚷	6:06 pm	3:06 pm
☽	⚹	⚷	9:05 pm	6:05 pm
♀	⊻	♃	10:53 pm	7:53 pm
☿	∟	♅	11:36 pm	8:36 pm
☽	⊼	♇		10:06 pm

12　WEDNESDAY
1st ♉

☽	⊼	♇	1:06 am	
☽	∟	☉	3:08 am	12:08 am
♀	⊡	⚷	3:15 am	12:15 am
☽	□	♅	3:46 am	12:46 am
☽	∟	☿	4:25 am	1:25 am
☽	⊻	♄	5:06 am	2:06 am
☽	□	♃	10:49 am	7:49 am
☉	∟	♅	12:29 pm	9:29 am
☽	⊡	♂	2:41 pm	11:41 am
☽	□	♃	7:57 pm	4:57 pm
☿	⚹	♀	8:56 pm	5:56 pm
☽	⚹	♀	9:26 pm	6:26 pm
☽	♂	⚷	11:09 pm	8:09 pm

13　THURSDAY
1st ♉
☽ enters ♊　7:49 pm　**4:49 pm**

☽	⚹	☉	7:14 am	4:14 am
☽	∟	♄	7:27 am	4:27 am
☽	△	♀	9:10 am	6:10 am
☽	⚹	☿	10:55 am	7:55 am
☽	△	♂	4:24 pm	1:24 pm
☽	△	♆	6:35 pm	3:35 pm	☽ v/c
☽	⊼	⚷	10:16 pm	7:16 pm

14 FRIDAY

1st ♊

		EST		PST	
☽	□	⚵	3:43 am	12:43	am
♀	⚹	⚶	5:46 am	2:46	am
☽	☍	♇	5:58 am	2:58	am
☿	⊥	♃	6:39 am	3:39	am
☽	△	♅	9:02 am	6:02	am
☽	⚹	♄	10:47 am	7:47	am
☽	⊡	♀	12:58 pm	9:58	am
☽	△	♃	5:17 pm	2:17	pm
☿	☍	♂	7:06 pm	4:06	pm
☉	⚹	♀	8:03 pm	5:03	pm
☽	⊡	♆	10:07 pm	7:07	pm
☽	⊡	⚵		10:47	pm

15 SATURDAY

1st ♊

2nd Quarter   7:06 pm   **4:06 pm**
☿ enters ♈   11:13 pm   **8:13 pm**

			EST		PST	
☽	⊡	⚵	1:47 am			
☽	△	⚶	3:50 am	12:50	am	
☽	⊻	⚵	8:08 am	5:08	am	
☽	□	♀	9:44 am	6:44	am	
☽	⊡	♅	1:08 pm	10:08	am	
☿	⚹	♆	3:30 pm	12:30	pm	
☽	⊼	♀	5:48 pm	2:48	pm	
☽	□	☉	7:06 pm	4:06	pm	
☽	⊡	♃	10:03 pm	7:03	pm	
☽	□	♂	10:31 pm	7:31	pm	☽ v/c
☽	⊼	♆		11:38	pm	

16 SUNDAY

2nd ♊

☽ enters ♋   3:51 am   **12:51 am**

			EST		PST	
☽	⊼	♆	2:38 am			
☽	□	☿	4:44 am	1:44	am	
☽	△	⚵	6:14 am	3:14	am	
♂	⊡	♃	8:23 am	5:23	am	
☽	⊡	⚶	9:20 am	6:20	am	
☿	⊼	⚵	1:58 pm	10:58	am	
☽	⊥	⚶	2:14 pm	11:14	am	
♇	□	⚵	2:35 pm	11:35	am	
☽	△	⚵	2:40 pm	11:40	am	
☽	⊼	♇	2:40 pm	11:40	am	
☽	⊼	♅	6:10 pm	3:10	pm	
☽	□	♄	8:24 pm	5:24	pm	
♀	⊥	♅	9:27 pm	6:27	pm	
☉	☍	♂		11:55	pm	

MARCH

S	M	T	W	T	F	S
						1
2	3	4	5	6	7	8
9	10	11	12	13	14	15
16	17	18	19	20	21	22
23	24	25	26	27	28	29
30	31					

17 MONDAY

2nd ♋

☉	☍	♂	2:55 am	
☽	⊼	♃	3:42 am	12:42 am
☿	∟	♄	2:48 pm	11:48 am
☽	⊼	♄	3:43 pm	12:43 pm
☉	∟	♃	4:42 pm	1:42 pm
☽	⊡	♇	8:15 pm	5:15 pm
☽	✳	♥	9:14 pm	6:14 pm
☽	⊡	♆	9:32 pm	6:32 pm
☽	△	♀		11:54 pm

ST. PATRICK'S DAY

18 TUESDAY

2nd ♋

☽ enters ♌   3:08 pm   **12:08 pm**

☽	△	♀	2:54 am		
☽	☍	♀	6:08 am	3:08 am	
☽	✳	♂	7:42 am	4:42 am	
☽	△	☉	11:20 am	8:20 am	
☽	☍	♆	1:59 pm	10:59 am	☽ v/c
☽	☐	♅	5:22 pm	2:22 pm	
☿	△	♇	6:17 pm	3:17 pm	
☽	△	♇		11:22 pm	

19 WEDNESDAY

2nd ♌

☽	△	♇	2:22 am		
☽	△	☿	4:01 am	1:01 am	
☽	⊼	♆	5:00 am	2:00 am	
☽	☍	♅	6:14 am	3:14 am	
☽	△	♄	8:58 am	5:58 am	
♂	△	♀	10:26 am	7:26 am	
☿	∟	♥	10:38 am	7:38 am	
☿	⊻	♆	11:32 am	8:32 am	
☽	⊡	♀	12:41 pm	9:41 am	
☽	∟	♂	1:00 pm	10:00 am	
♀	☍	♂	3:08 pm	12:08 pm	
☽	☍	♃	4:54 pm	1:54 pm	☽ v/c
☿	✳	♅	5:30 pm	2:30 pm	
♀	✳	♀	6:30 pm	3:30 pm	
☉	✳	♆	7:51 pm	4:51 pm	
☽	⊡	☉	8:26 pm	5:26 pm	

20 THURSDAY

2nd ♌

☉ enters ♈   8:55 am   **5:55 am**

☽	☍	♄	6:06 am	3:06 am
☿	♂	♄	11:15 am	8:15 am
☽	☐	♥	12:48 pm	9:48 am
♅	⊻	♆	1:14 pm	10:14 am
☽	⊡	♄	3:46 pm	12:46 pm
☽	⊡	☿	4:37 pm	1:37 pm
☽	⊻	♂	6:31 pm	3:31 pm
☽	⊼	♀	8:24 pm	5:24 pm
☽	⊼	♀	10:45 pm	7:45 pm
☽	⊼	♆		11:57 pm

SPRING EQUINOX • SUN ENTERS ARIES

Eastern Standard Time in medium type
Pacific Standard Time in bold type

21 FRIDAY

2nd ♌

☽	⊼	♆	2:57 am	
☽	⊼	☉	5:44 am	**2:44 am**
☽	⚹	♀	5:56 am	**2:56 am**
☉	⊼	♀	7:57 am	**4:57 am**
♀	⎵	♃	11:30 am	**8:30 am**
☽	□	♇	3:16 pm	**12:16 pm**
☽	⊼	♅	7:23 pm	**4:23 pm**
☽	☍	♆	8:35 pm	**5:35 pm**
☽	⊼	♄	10:34 pm	**7:34 pm**

☽ enters ♍   3:59 am   **12:59 am**

22 SATURDAY

2nd ♍

☽	⊡	♀	3:37 am	**12:37 am**
☽	⊼	☿	5:10 am	**2:10 am**
☽	⊼	♃	6:51 am	**3:51 am**
☽	⊡	♆	9:26 am	**6:26 am**
☽	⎵	♀	12:12 pm	**9:12 am**
♀	⚹	♆	3:12 pm	**12:12 pm**
☿	⚹	♃	4:23 pm	**1:23 pm**
☽	⊼	♀	8:50 pm	**5:50 pm**
☽	⊡	♅		**10:48 pm**

♀ enters ♈   **9:26 pm**

PURIM BEGINS

23 SUNDAY

2nd ♍

☽	⊡	♅	1:48 am	
☽	△	⚹	4:33 am	**1:33 am**
☽	♂	♂	5:21 am	**2:21 am**
☽	△	♀	10:36 am	**7:36 am**
☽	⊡	♃	1:34 pm	**10:34 am**
♂	△	⚹	8:59 am	**11:59 am**
☽	△	♆	3:40 pm	**12:40 pm**	☽ v/c
♀	⊼	♀	4:03 pm	**1:03 pm**
☽	⊻	♀	6:12 pm	**3:12 pm**
☽	☍	♀	6:27 pm	**3:27 pm**
♄	⎵	⚹	9:50 pm	**6:50 pm**
☽	☍	☉	11:45 pm	**8:45 pm**

♀ enters ♈   12:26 am
☽ enters ♎   4:35 pm   **1:35 pm**
Full Moon   11:45 pm   **8:45 pm**

PARTIAL ECLIPSE OF THE MOON 3° ♎ 35'

PURIM ENDS • PALM SUNDAY

MARCH

S	M	T	W	T	F	S
						1
2	3	4	5	6	7	8
9	10	11	12	13	14	15
16	17	18	19	20	21	22
23	24	25	26	27	28	29
30	31					

Eastern Standard Time in medium type
Pacific Standard Time in bold type

24 MONDAY
3rd ♎

☽	⚹	♇	3:37	am	**12:37**	**am**
☽	⊓	♄	3:48	am	**12:48**	**am**
☽	△	♅	7:54	am	**4:54**	**am**
☽	⊼	♆	11:25	am	**8:25**	**am**
☽	☍	♄	11:26	am	**8:26**	**am**
☽	⊓	⚹	11:57	am	**8:57**	**am**
♄	⊻	♆	11:58	am	**8:58**	**am**
☽	△	♃	7:52	pm	**4:52**	**pm**

25 TUESDAY
3rd ♎

♂	△	⚹	2:38	am			
☽	☍	☿	4:28	am	**1:28**	**am**	
☽	∟	♇	9:14	am	**6:14**	**am**	
☽	△	♃	10:19	am	**7:19**	**am**	
☽	⊻	♂	3:02	pm	**12:02**	**pm**	
☽	⊓	♆	6:09	pm	**3:09**	**pm**	
☽	⊼	⚹	6:50	pm	**3:50**	**pm**	
☉	△	♇	10:23	pm	**7:23**	**pm**	
☽	□	♀	11:15	pm	**8:15**	**pm**	
☽	□	♆			**11:55**	**pm**	☽ v/c

26 WEDNESDAY
3rd ♎

☽ enters ♏   3:43 am **12:43 am**

☽	□	♆	2:55	am			☽ v/c
☽	♂	☿	4:57	am	**1:57**	**am**	
☿	⊓	♇	12:03	pm	**9:03**	**am**	
☽	⊼	♀	12:05	pm	**9:05**	**am**	
☽	⊻	♇	2:20	pm	**11:20**	**am**	
☽	⊼	☉	3:43	pm	**12:43**	**pm**	
☽	□	♅	6:41	pm	**3:41**	**pm**	
☽	∟	♂	7:13	pm	**4:13**	**pm**	
☽	⊼	♄	10:31	pm	**7:31**	**pm**	
☽	△	♆			**9:17**	**pm**	
☉	∟	♃			**10:54**	**pm**	

27 THURSDAY
3rd ♏

☽	△	♆	12:17	am		
☉	∟	♃	1:54	am		
☿	⚹	♃	3:42	am	**12:42**	**am**
☽	□	♃	6:57	am	**3:57**	**am**
♀	△	♇	10:35	am	**7:35**	**am**
♂	⊓	♅	11:51	am	**8:51**	**am**
☿	⊼	♂	5:51	pm	**2:51**	**pm**
☽	⊓	♀	7:47	pm	**4:47**	**pm**
☽	□	♃	9:35	pm	**6:35**	**pm**
☽	⊓	☉	10:40	pm	**7:40**	**pm**
☽	⚹	♂	10:54	pm	**7:54**	**pm**
☽	⊼	☿	11:52	pm	**8:52**	**pm**

28 FRIDAY

☽	⊼	♄	3:12 am	**12:12 am**	
☉	✶	♅	6:30 am	**3:30 am**	
☽	⚹	♅	6:45 am	**3:45 am**	
☽	✶	♀	9:37 am	**6:37 am**	
☽	✶	♆	11:59 am	**8:59 am**	☽ v/c
☽	⊻	☿	1:35 pm	**10:35 am**	
♀	∟	♃	8:48 pm	**5:48 pm**	
♂	⊼	♃	10:07 pm	**7:07 pm**	
☽	♂	♇	10:49 pm	**7:49 pm**	
☽	△	♀		**11:40 pm**	

3rd ♏

☽ enters ♐   12:40 pm   **9:40 am**

GOOD FRIDAY

29 SATURDAY

☽	△	♀	2:40 am		
☽	✶	♅	3:11 am	**12:11 am**	
☽	△	☉	4:49 am	**1:49 am**	
☽	△	♄	7:14 am	**4:14 am**	
☽	⊼	☿	7:48 am	**4:48 am**	
♀	✶	♅	8:17 am	**5:17 am**	
☽	□	♆	10:32 am	**7:32 am**	
☽	∟	♀	1:48 pm	**10:48 am**	
☽	✶	♃	3:33 pm	**12:33 pm**	
☽	∟	♆	3:36 pm	**12:36 pm**	
☽	∟	☿	4:58 pm	**1:58 pm**	

3rd ♐

30 SUNDAY

☽	□	♂	4:35 am	**1:35 am**	
☽	✶	♃	6:12 am	**3:12 am**	
☽	∟	♅	6:28 am	**3:28 am**	
☽	△	☿	2:32 pm	**11:32 am**	☽ v/c
☿	∟	♆	3:12 pm	**12:12 pm**	
☽	⊼	♆	3:51 pm	**12:51 pm**	
☽	⊻	♀	5:17 pm	**2:17 pm**	
☉	♂	♄	5:19 pm	**2:19 pm**	
☽	⊻	♆	6:33 pm	**3:33 pm**	
☽	∟	♃	6:49 pm	**3:49 pm**	
☽	✶	☿	7:43 pm	**4:43 pm**	

3rd ♐

☽ enters ♑   7:07 pm   **4:07 pm**

EASTER SUNDAY

MARCH

S	M	T	W	T	F	S
						1
2	3	4	5	6	7	8
9	10	11	12	13	14	15
16	17	18	19	20	21	22
23	24	25	26	27	28	29
30	31					

Eastern Standard Time in medium type
Pacific Standard Time in bold type

31 MONDAY

3rd ♏
4th Quarter   2:39 pm   **11:39 am**

☽	⊻	♇	4:45 am	**1:45**	**am**
♀	♂	♄	7:48 am	**4:48**	**am**
☿	⊻	♅	8:19 am	**5:19**	**am**
☽	⊻	♅	9:05 am	**6:05**	**am**
☽	∟	⚷	9:27 am	**6:27**	**am**
☽	□	♄	1:18 pm	**10:18**	**am**
☽	□	♀	1:48 pm	**10:48**	**am**
☽	□	☉	2:39 pm	**11:39**	**am**
☽	✷	⚵	5:54 pm	**2:54**	**pm**
☽	⊡	⚷	7:16 pm	**4:16**	**pm**
☿	□	♀	8:05 pm	**5:05**	**pm**
☽	⊻	♃	9:25 pm	**6:25**	**pm**

♈ **ARIES** ♈
Cardinal • Fire
Rules 1st House
Ruled by Mars
Rules head
Keyword: Action
Keynote: I AM

1 TUESDAY

4th ♏
☿ enters ♉   8:44 am   **5:44 am**
☽ enters ≈   10:59 pm   **7:59 pm**

☿	□	♆	3:39 am	**12:39**	**am**
☽	∟	♇	6:44 am	**3:44**	**am**
☽	△	♂	7:56 am	**4:56**	**am**
☽	⊻	⚷	11:59 am	**8:59**	**am**
☿	♂	⚵	12:28 pm	**9:28**	**am**
☽	∟	⚵	8:30 pm	**5:30**	**pm**
☽	△	♅	9:59 pm	**6:59**	**pm**
☽	♂	♀	10:11 pm	**7:11**	**pm**
☽	♂	♆	10:31 pm	**7:31**	**pm**	☽ v/c
☽	□	⚵	11:18 pm	**8:18**	**pm**
☽	□	☿		**9:31**	**pm**

APRIL FOOL'S DAY

2 WEDNESDAY

4th ≈
⚵ enters ♊   11:15 pm   **8:15 pm**

☽	□	☿	12:31 am		
♀	△	♅	6:38 am	**3:38**	**am**
☽	✷	♇	8:07 am	**5:07**	**am**
♀	♂	☉	8:45 am	**5:45**	**am**
☽	⊡	♂	8:46 am	**5:46**	**am**
♆	△	♅	11:23 am	**8:23**	**am**
☽	♂	♅	12:26 pm	**9:26**	**am**
☽	✷	♄	4:48 pm	**1:48**	**pm**
♆	♂	♀	5:45 pm	**2:45**	**pm**
☽	✷	☉	9:23 pm	**6:23**	**pm**
☽	✷	♀	9:37 pm	**6:37**	**pm**
☽	⊻	⚵	10:30 pm	**7:30**	**pm**
☽	♂	♃		**9:45**	**pm**	☽ v/c

3 THURSDAY

4th ♒

⚴ enters ♒	8:26 pm	**5:26 pm**	
☽ enters ♓		**9:43 pm**	

☽ ☌ ♃	12:45 am		☽ v/c
⚵ ⚻ ⚷	3:29 am	**12:29 am**	
☽ ⚻ ♂	9:09 am	**6:09 am**	
♀ ⚺ ⚶	1:44 pm	**10:44 am**	
☽ ☌ ⚳	3:18 pm	**12:18 pm**	
☽ ∠ ♄	5:46 pm	**2:46 pm**	
☽ ∠ ☉	11:50 pm	**8:50 pm**	
⚴ □ ⚷		**9:02 pm**	
☽ ⚺ ♆		**9:18 pm**	
☽ ∠ ♀		**9:35 pm**	
☽ △ ⚷		**9:46 pm**	
☽ ⚺ ⚴		**9:47 pm**	
☽ □ ⚵		**10:43 pm**	

4 FRIDAY

4th ♓

☽ enters ♓	12:43 am	
⚷ enters ♏	11:59 am	**8:59 am**

⚴ □ ⚷	12:02 am	
☽ ⚺ ♆	12:18 am	
☽ ∠ ♀	12:35 am	
☽ △ ⚷	12:46 am	
☽ ⚺ ⚴	12:47 am	
☽ □ ⚵	1:43 am	
☉ ⚺ ⚶	4:24 am	**1:24 am**
☽ ⚹ ☿	6:43 am	**3:43 am**
☽ □ ♇	9:30 am	**6:30 am**
♆ ∠ ⚶	9:34 am	**6:34 am**
☽ ⚺ ♅	1:51 pm	**10:51 am**
♀ ⚹ ♃	3:29 pm	**12:29 pm**
☽ ⚺ ♄	6:24 pm	**3:24 pm**
⚶ ⚼ ⚷	8:38 pm	**5:38 pm**
♀ ∠ ⚵		**9:21 pm**
☽ ∠ ♆		**9:41 pm**
☽ ⚼ ⚷		**10:00 pm**
☽ ☌ ⚶		**10:11 pm**
☽ ∠ ⚴		**10:33 pm**
☽ ⚺ ☉		**10:56 pm**
☽ ⚺ ♃		**11:19 pm**

5 SATURDAY

4th ♓

☽ enters ♈		**10:20 pm**

♀ ∠ ⚵	12:21 am		
☽ ∠ ♆	12:41 am		
☽ ⚼ ⚷	1:00 am		
☽ ☌ ⚶	1:11 am		
☽ ∠ ⚴	1:33 am		
☽ ⚺ ☉	1:56 am		
☽ ⚺ ♃	2:19 am		
☽ ⚺ ♀	3:10 am	**12:10 am**	
☉ ⚹ ♃	8:40 am	**5:40 am**	
☽ ∠ ☿	8:56 am	**5:56 am**	
☽ ☍ ♂	9:01 am	**6:01 am**	
☿ ⚼ ♂	9:57 am	**6:57 am**	
☽ ∠ ♅	2:10 pm	**11:10 am**	
☽ ⚺ ⚳	5:09 pm	**2:09 pm**	
☿ ⚻ ♇	9:32 pm	**6:32 pm**	
⚴ ∠ ⚶	11:31 pm	**8:31 pm**	
☽ ⚹ ♆		**9:58 pm**	☽ v/c
☽ ⚻ ⚷		**10:08 pm**	
☽ ⚹ ⚴		**11:12 pm**	
☽ ∠ ♃		**11:51 pm**	

6 SUNDAY

4th ♈

☽ enters ♈	1:20 am	

☽ ⚹ ♆	12:58 am		☽ v/c
☽ ⚻ ⚷	1:08 am		
☽ ⚹ ⚴	2:12 am		
☽ ∠ ♃	2:51 am		
☽ ⚹ ⚵	4:14 am	**1:14 am**	
☽ △ ♇	10:01 am	**7:01 am**	
☽ ⚺ ☿	10:52 am	**7:52 am**	
☽ ⚹ ♅	2:30 pm	**11:30 am**	
☉ ∠ ⚵	2:42 pm	**11:42 am**	
☽ ∠ ⚳	6:01 pm	**3:01 pm**	
☽ ☌ ♄	7:23 pm	**4:23 pm**	

DAYLIGHT SAVINGS BEGINS

(Aspect times ***not*** adjusted for Daylight Savings)

7 MONDAY
4th ♈

☽	⊼	♆	3:25 am	**12:25 am**	
☽	⚹	♃	3:30 am	**12:30 am**	
☽	⊏	♅	5:35 am	**2:35 am**	
☽	☌	☉	6:02 am	**3:02 am**	
♆	□	⚷	6:48 am	**3:48 am**	
♃	⊼	♆	6:57 am	**3:57 am**	
☽	☌	♀	8:16 am	**5:16 am**	
☽	⊼	♂	8:50 am	**5:50 am**	
☽	⊡	♇	10:26 am	**7:26 am**	
♀	⊼	♂	1:45 pm	**10:45 am**	
☽	⚹	♃	7:08 pm	**4:08 pm**	
☽	☍	⚷		**10:54 pm**	
☽	□	♆		**11:01 pm**	☽ v/c

New Moon   6:02 am   **3:02 am**
☽ enters ♉   **11:21 pm**

8 TUESDAY
1st ♉

☽	☍	⚷	1:54 am		
☽	□	♆	2:01 am		☽ v/c
☽	□	♀	4:02 am	**1:02 am**	
☽	⊏	♆	4:57 am	**1:57 am**	
☽	⊼	♅	7:19 am	**4:19 am**	
☽	⊡	♂	9:12 am	**6:12 am**	
♀	⊡	♇	9:28 am	**6:28 am**	
☽	⊼	♇	11:14 am	**8:14 am**	
☽	☌	☿	3:02 pm	**12:02 pm**	
☉	⊼	♂	3:41 pm	**12:41 pm**	
☽	□	♅	4:01 pm	**1:01 pm**	
☽	⊼	♄	9:26 pm	**6:26 pm**	

☽ enters ♉   2:21 am

9 WEDNESDAY
1st ♉

☽	□	♃	6:02 am	**3:02 am**
☽	⚹	♆	7:06 am	**4:06 am**
☽	△	♂	10:08 am	**7:08 am**
☽	⊼	☉	11:53 am	**8:53 am**
☿	□	♅	2:47 pm	**11:47 am**
☽	⊼	♀	3:20 pm	**12:20 pm**
☉	⊡	♇	10:32 pm	**7:32 pm**
☽	□	♃	11:05 pm	**8:05 pm**
☽	⊏	♄	11:24 pm	**8:24 pm**

10 THURSDAY
1st ♉

☽	⊼	⚷	4:43 am	**1:43 am**	
☽	△	♆	5:10 am	**2:10 am**	☽ v/c
☽	△	♀	8:06 am	**5:06 am**	
☽	☌	♅	12:57 pm	**9:57 am**	
☽	☍	♇	2:50 pm	**11:50 am**	
☽	⊏	☉	4:08 pm	**1:08 pm**	
☽	△	♅	8:05 pm	**5:05 pm**	
♄	⊏	♃	8:06 pm	**5:06 pm**	
☽	⊏	♀	8:19 pm	**5:19 pm**	
☽	⊼	☿	9:09 pm	**6:09 pm**	
☽	⚹	♄		**11:14 pm**	

☽ enters ♊   5:28 am   **2:28 am**

11 FRIDAY

1st ♊

☽	✶	♄	2:14 am		
☽	⊡	♅	7:20 am	4:20	am
☽	⊡	♆	7:59 am	4:59	am
☽	⊡	♀	11:28 am	8:28	am
☽	△	♃	11:35 am	8:35	am
☽	□	⚷	2:04 pm	11:04	am
☽	□	♂	2:27 pm	11:27	am
♂	☍	⚷	9:33 pm	6:33	pm
☽	✶	☉	9:33 pm	6:33	pm
☽	⊡	♅	11:29 pm	8:29	pm
☽	∟	☿		10:18	pm
☽	✶	♀		11:34	pm	☽ v/c

12 SATURDAY

1st ♊

☽ enters ♋   12:03 pm   **9:03 am**

☽	∟	☿	1:18 am		
☽	✶	♀	2:34 am			☽ v/c
☽	△	♃	6:37 am	3:37	am
♇	☍	⚹	8:33 am	5:33	am
☽	△	♅	10:55 am	7:55	am
☽	⊼	♆	11:47 am	8:47	am
☽	⊼	♀	3:50 pm	12:50	pm
☽	⊡	♃	3:50 pm	12:50	pm
☽	⊼	♇	10:01 pm	7:01	pm
☽	⊻	⚹	10:40 pm	7:40	pm

13 SUNDAY

1st ♋

☽	⊼	♅	3:51 am	12:51	am
☽	✶	☿	6:12 am	3:12	am
☽	□	♄	10:54 am	7:54	am
☽	⊡	♃	11:56 am	8:56	am
☽	⊼	♃	9:04 pm	6:04	pm
☽	✶	♂	10:31 pm	7:31	pm
☽	△	⚷		10:16	pm

APRIL

S	M	T	W	T	F	S
		1	2	3	4	5
6	7	8	9	10	11	12
13	14	15	16	17	18	19
20	21	22	23	24	25	26
27	28	29	30			

Eastern Standard Time in medium type
Pacific Standard Time in bold type

14 MONDAY

			EST	PST
☽	△	⚷	1:16 am	
☽	⊡	♇	3:02 am	12:02 am
☽	⅃	♃	5:09 am	2:09 am
♀	⚹	?	9:56 am	6:56 am
☽	□	☉	11:59 am	8:59 am
☽	⊼	♀	6:11 pm	3:11 pm
☽	□	♀	6:53 pm	3:53 pm
☽	□	⚷	8:48 pm	5:48 pm
☽	☍	♆	10:07 pm	7:07 pm ☽ v/c

1st ♋

	EST	PST
2nd Quarter	11:59 am	**8:59 am**
☿ ℞	6:56 pm	**3:56 pm**
☽ enters ♌	10:22 pm	**7:22 pm**

15 TUESDAY

2nd ♌

			EST	PST
☽	☍	♀	3:23 am	12:23 am
☽	⅃	♂	3:49 am	12:49 am
☽	⊡	⚷	8:15 am	5:15 am
☽	△	♇	8:48 am	5:48 am
♀	☍	⚷	12:27 pm	9:27 am
☽	⚹	♃	12:29 pm	9:29 am
☽	☍	♅	3:08 pm	12:08 pm
☽	□	☿	5:39 pm	2:39 pm
♂	⊡	♀	6:14 pm	3:14 pm
☽	△	♄	11:01 pm	8:01 pm
♀	□	♆		11:35 pm

16 WEDNESDAY

2nd ♌

			EST	PST
♀	□	♆	2:35 am	
♂	⊼	♃	6:13 am	3:13 am
☽	⚺	♂	9:41 am	6:41 am
☽	☍	♃	9:46 am	6:46 am
☽	⊼	⚷	3:48 pm	12:48 pm

	EST	PST
♀ enters ♉	4:42 am	**1:42 am**

17 THURSDAY

2nd ♌

			EST	PST
☽	⊡	♄	5:47 am	2:47 am
☽	△	☉	5:52 am	2:52 am ☽ v/c
☽	☍	?	8:25 am	5:25 am
☽	⚹	⚷	9:01 am	6:01 am
☽	⊼	♆	10:48 am	7:48 am
☽	△	♀	2:33 pm	11:33 am
☽	⊼	♀	5:08 pm	2:08 pm
☽	□	♇	9:30 pm	6:30 pm
♅	△	⚷	10:38 pm	7:38 pm
♀	⊡	♂		10:38 pm
?	△	⚷		11:33 pm

	EST	PST
☽ enters ♍	11:00 am	**8:00 am**

18 FRIDAY

2nd ♍

♀	⊼	♂	1:38	am		
?	△	⚷	2:33	am		
☽	⊼	♅	4:07	am	1:07	am
☽	□	⚷	4:23	am	1:23	am
☽	△	☿	5:27	am	2:27	am
☽	⊼	♄	12:34	pm	9:34	am
☽	⊡	☉	3:04	pm	12:04	pm
☽	∟	⚷	3:16	pm	12:16	pm
☽	⊡	♆	5:17	pm	2:17	pm
☉	☍	⚷	5:19	pm	2:19	pm
☿	⊻	♅	6:39	pm	3:39	pm
♀	□	♀	7:04	pm	4:04	pm
☽	♂	♂	9:56	pm	6:56	pm
☽	⊼	♃	11:26	pm	8:26	pm
☽	⊡	♀			9:02	pm

☽ ⊡ ♀   9:31 pm
☉ ⚹ ?   10:57 pm

19 SATURDAY

2nd ♍

☉ enters ♉   8:03 pm   **5:03 pm**
☽ enters ♎   11:37 pm   **8:37 pm**

☽	⊡	♀	12:02	am		
☽	⊡	♀	12:31	am		
☉	⚹	♃	1:57	am		
☽	☍	♇	7:09	am	4:09	am
☽	⊡	♅	10:29	am	7:29	am
☽	⊡	☿	10:50	am	7:50	am
☉	□	♆	6:02	pm	3:02	pm
☿	□	♅	7:49	pm	4:49	pm
☽	⊻	⚷	9:16	pm	6:16	pm
☽	⊼	?	10:41	pm	7:41	pm
☽	△	♆	11:27	pm	8:27	pm	☽ v/c
☽	⊼	☉	11:56	pm	8:56	pm

SUN ENTERS TAURUS

20 SUNDAY

2nd ♎

☽	⊡	♃	5:52	am	2:52	am
☽	△	♀	6:33	am	3:33	am
♀	⊼	♇	7:56	am	4:56	am
☽	⚹	♇	9:47	am	6:47	am
☽	⊼	♀	9:59	am	6:59	am
☽	⊼	☿	3:37	pm	12:37	pm
☽	△	♅	4:26	pm	1:26	pm
☽	△	⚷	7:31	pm	4:31	pm
☽	☍	♄			10:09	pm

APRIL

S	M	T	W	T	F	S
		1	2	3	4	5
6	7	8	9	10	11	12
13	14	15	16	17	18	19
20	21	22	23	24	25	26
27	28	29	30			

21 MONDAY

2nd ♎

☽	♂	♄	1:09 am	
☽	⊡	♆	5:07 am	**2:07 am**
♆	⊼	♆	5:36 am	**2:36 am**
☿	∟	♇	7:18 am	**4:18 am**
☽	⊻	♂	9:09 am	**6:09 am**
☽	△	♃	11:45 am	**8:45 am**
☽	∟	♇	3:12 pm	**12:12 pm**
☉	⊡	♂	7:57 pm	**4:57 pm**
☽	⊼	♇	8:48 pm	**5:48 pm**
☿	♂	♀		**10:55 pm**
☽	⊡	♇		**11:10 pm**

♃ enters ♓   11:18 am   **8:18 am**

PASSOVER BEGINS

22 TUESDAY

2nd ♎

Full Moon   3:34 pm   **12:34 pm**
☽ enters ♏   10:20 am   **7:20 am**

☿	♂	♀	1:55 am		
☽	⊡	♇	2:10 am		
☽	♂	♇	7:42 am	**4:42 am**	
☽	⊡	♆	10:12 am	**7:12 am**	☽ v/c
☽	△	♃	10:54 am	**7:54 am**	
☽	∟	♂	1:57 pm	**10:57 am**	
☽	♂	☉	3:34 pm	**12:34 pm**	
☽	⊡	♀	5:47 pm	**2:47 pm**	
☽	⊻	♇	7:59 pm	**4:59 pm**	
☽	♂	☿	11:10 pm	**8:10 pm**	
♅	∟	♇		**9:47 pm**	
♀	⊡	♅		**10:56 pm**	
☽	⊡	♅		**11:31 pm**	
♀	∟	♇		**11:34 pm**	
☽	♂	♀		**11:35 pm**	
☽	⊡	♇		**11:35 pm**	

23 WEDNESDAY

3rd ♏

♅	∟	♇	12:47 am	
♀	⊡	♅	1:56 am	
☽	⊡	♅	2:31 am	
♀	∟	♇	2:34 am	
☽	♂	♀	2:35 am	
☽	⊡	♇	2:35 am	
☽	⊼	♇	8:05 am	**5:05 am**
☽	⊼	♄	11:20 am	**8:20 am**
☽	⁎	♂	6:10 pm	**3:10 pm**
☽	⊡	♃	9:32 pm	**6:32 pm**
☉	⊡	♀		**10:35 pm**

24 THURSDAY

3rd ♏

☽ enters ♐   6:33 pm   **3:33 pm**

☉	⊡	♀	1:35 am		
☽	△	♇	7:40 am	**4:40 am**	
☽	⊡	♄	3:28 pm	**12:28 pm**	
☽	⊻	♇	3:42 pm	**12:42 pm**	
☽	⁎	♆	6:26 pm	**3:26 pm**	☽ v/c
☽	⊡	♃	8:25 pm	**5:25 pm**	
☉	⊼	♇	11:26 pm	**8:26 pm**	
☽	⁎	♀		**11:23 pm**	

25 FRIDAY
3rd ♐

☽ ✶ ♀	2:23 am		
☽ ♂ ♇	3:42 am	12:42 am	
☽ ⊼ ☉	4:03 am	1:03 am	
☽ ⊼ ☿	4:13 am	1:13 am	
☿ ♂ ☉	5:32 am	2:32 am	
☽ ✶ ♅	10:08 am	7:08 am	
☿ ⊼ ♇	2:50 pm	11:50 am	
☽ ⊼ ♀	3:50 pm	12:50 pm	
☽ ☍ ⚶	5:51 pm	2:51 pm	
☽ ∟ ⚷	6:51 pm	3:51 pm	
☽ △ ♄	7:02 pm	4:02 pm	
☽ ∟ ♆	9:42 pm	6:42 pm	
☽ □ ♂		9:56 pm	

26 SATURDAY
3rd ♐
9:33 pm

☽ enters ♑

☽ □ ♂	12:56 am		
☽ ✶ ♃	4:52 am	1:52 am	☽ v/c
☽ ∟ ♀	5:48 am	2:48 am	
☽ ⬚ ☿	5:59 am	2:59 am	
☿ □ ♀	9:02 am	6:02 am	
☽ ⬚ ☉	9:14 am	6:14 am	
☽ ∟ ♅	1:07 pm	10:07 am	
✶ ⬚ ⚶	2:47 pm	11:47 am	
☽ □ ⚵	3:59 pm	12:59 pm	
☽ ⬚ ♀	9:23 pm	6:23 pm	
☽ ✶ ⚶	9:30 pm	6:30 pm	
☽ ⊻ ♆		9:28 pm	

27 SUNDAY
3rd ♑

☽ enters ♑   12:33 am
♂ D   2:10 pm   **11:10 am**

☽ ⊻ ♆	12:28 am		
☽ ✶ ♃	3:33 am	12:33 am	
♄ ✶ ⚶	4:59 am	1:59 am	
♀ ⊻ ♄	5:38 am	2:38 am	
♀ ⊻ ⚶	6:04 am	3:04 am	
☽ △ ☿	7:22 am	4:22 am	
☽ ∟ ♃	7:45 am	4:45 am	
☽ ⊻ ♀	8:43 am	5:43 am	
☽ ⊻ ♇	9:18 am	6:18 am	
☽ △ ☉	1:50 pm	10:50 am	
☽ ⊻ ♅	3:39 pm	12:39 pm	
☽ □ ♄		9:40 pm	
☽ ⊼ ⚶		10:20 pm	
☽ △ ♀		11:22 pm	

APRIL

S	M	T	W	T	F	S
		1	2	3	4	5
6	7	8	9	10	11	12
13	14	15	16	17	18	19
20	21	22	23	24	25	26
27	28	29	30			

28 MONDAY

3rd ♑

☽	□	♄	12:40 am		
☽	⊼	♅	1:20 am		
☽	△	♀	2:22 am		
☽	△	♂	5:55 am	2:55 am	
☽	∟	?	6:24 am	3:24 am	
☽	⊻	♃	10:13 am	7:13 am	
☽	∟	♇	11:27 am	8:27 am	
☉	□	♅	3:44 pm	12:44 pm	
☽	✶	♆	10:17 pm	7:17 pm	
☽	□	⚷		10:36 pm	

29 TUESDAY

3rd ♑

4th Quarter   9:37 pm   **6:37 pm**
☽ enters ♒   4:51 am   **1:51 am**

☽	□	⚷	1:36 am		
☽	⊡	♅	4:25 am	1:25 am	
☽	♂	♆	4:46 am	1:46 am	☽ v/c
☽	⊡	♂	7:52 am	4:52 am	
♇	✶	♀	8:42 am	5:42 am	
☽	⊻	?	8:52 am	5:52 am	
☽	□	☿	9:11 am	6:11 am	
☽	✶	♇	1:15 pm	10:15 am	
☽	♂	♀	1:19 pm	10:19 am	
♆	⊡	♅	1:19 pm	10:19 am	
☿	✶	?	2:04 pm	11:04 am	
♀	△	♂	6:32 pm	3:32 pm	
☽	♂	♅	7:35 pm	4:35 pm	
☽	□	☉	9:37 pm	6:37 pm	
☽	∟	♆		9:51 pm	

PASSOVER ENDS

30 WEDNESDAY

4th ♒

☽	∟	♆	12:51 am		
☽	✶	♄	4:45 am	1:45 am	
☽	△	♅	7:07 am	4:07 am	
☽	⊼	♂	9:31 am	6:31 am	
☽	□	♀	10:55 am	7:55 am	
☽	♂	♃	2:05 pm	11:05 am	☽ v/c
☿	⊡	♂	3:30 pm	12:30 pm	

♀ **TAURUS** ♀

Fixed • Earth
Rules 2nd House
Ruled By Venus
Rules the throat
Keyword: Stability
Keynote: I HAVE

1997　　　　　　　　　　**MAY**　　　　　　　　　1997

1 THURSDAY

☽	⊻	♆	3:06 am	12:06 am
☽	△	♀	4:24 am	1:24 am
☽	∟	♄	6:21 am	3:21 am
☽	⊻	♆	7:46 am	4:46 am
☽	✳	☿	10:10 am	7:10 am
☽	♂	♀	12:49 pm	9:49 am
☽	□	♇	3:59 pm	12:59 pm
☽	⊻	♀	4:35 pm	1:35 pm
♀	∟	✳	6:36 pm	3:36 pm
☽	⊻	♅	10:19 pm	7:19 pm
♀	□	♃		11:43 pm

4th ≈≈

☽ enters ♓ 7:50 am **4:50 am**
♆ ℞ 1:29 pm **10:29 pm**

BELTANE

2 FRIDAY

4th ♓

♀	□	♃	2:43 am	
☽	✳	☉	3:57 am	12:57 am
☽	⊡	♀	5:26 am	2:26 am
☽	⊻	♄	7:42 am	4:42 am
☽	∟	♆	8:55 am	5:55 am
☽	∟	☿	10:29 am	7:29 am
☽	□	✳	11:40 am	8:40 am
☽	♂	♂	12:08 pm	9:08 am
♆	⊼	♀	2:48 pm	11:48 am
☽	⊻	♃	4:52 pm	1:52 pm
☽	∟	♀	5:53 pm	2:53 pm
☽	✳	♀	6:04 pm	3:04 pm
☽	∟	♅	11:23 pm	8:23 pm
♂	□	✳		9:57 pm

3 SATURDAY

4th ♓

☽ enters ♈ 9:59 am **6:59 am**

♂	□	✳	12:57 am	
☽	⊼	♀	6:20 am	3:20 am
☽	∟	☉	6:47 am	3:47 am
☽	♂	♆	6:54 am	3:54 am
☉	∟	♆	9:54 am	6:54 am
☽	✳	♆	9:55 am	6:55 am	☽ v/c
☽	⊻	☿	10:46 am	7:46 am
☽	⊻	♀	3:54 pm	12:54 pm
☽	△	♇	5:59 pm	2:59 pm
☽	∟	♃	6:02 pm	3:02 pm
☽	✳	♀	7:04 pm	4:04 pm
☽	∟	♀	9:23 pm	6:23 pm
☽	✳	♅		9:22 pm

4 SUNDAY

4th ♈

☿ enters ♈ 8:48 pm **5:48 pm**

☽	✳	♅	12:22 am	
☽	⊻	☉	9:34 am	6:34 am
☽	♂	♄	10:06 am	7:06 am
☽	⊼	♂	2:22 pm	11:22 am
☽	✳	✳	3:41 pm	12:41 pm
☽	∟	♀	5:24 pm	2:24 pm
☉	⊻	♄	6:20 pm	3:20 pm
☽	⊡	♇	6:56 pm	3:56 pm
☽	✳	♃	7:14 pm	4:14 pm
☿	□	♆		9:42 pm
☽	⊻	♀		9:45 pm

5 MONDAY

☿	□	♆	12:42 am		
☽	⊼	♀	12:45 am		
☽	☍	⚷	8:08 am	5:08 am	
☽	⊼	⚸	10:34 am	7:34 am	
☽	☌	☿	11:48 am	8:48 am	
☽	□	♆	11:59 am	8:59 am	☽ v/c
☽	⊡	♂	3:39 pm	12:39 pm	
☽	∟	♃	5:52 pm	2:52 pm	
☽	✳	♄	7:03 pm	4:03 pm	
☽	⊼	♇	8:04 pm	5:04 pm	
☽	□	♀	9:39 pm	6:39 pm	
☽	□	♅		11:41 pm	

4th ♈

☽ enters ♉   12:04 pm   **9:04 am**

6 TUESDAY

☽	□	♅	2:41 am		
☽	∟	⚸	12:46 pm	9:46 am	
☽	⊼	♄	12:59 pm	9:59 am	
☿	⊼	⚸	2:32 pm	11:32 am	
☽	☌	☉	3:47 pm	12:47 pm	
☽	△	♂	5:18 pm	2:18 pm	
☽	⊼	♃	8:25 pm	5:25 pm	
☽	□	♃	10:20 pm	7:20 pm	

4th ♉

New Moon   3:47 pm   **12:47 pm**

7 WEDNESDAY

♆	✳	⚸	8:26 am	5:26 am	
☽	☌	♀	8:35 am	5:35 am	
☽	⊼	⚷	10:59 am	7:59 am	
☽	⊼	☿	2:29 pm	11:29 am	
☽	∟	♄	3:04 pm	12:04 pm	
☽	△	♆	3:15 pm	12:15 pm	☽ v/c
☽	✳	⚸	3:29 pm	12:29 pm	
☉	△	♂	4:30 pm	1:30 pm	
♇	□	♃	8:39 pm	5:39 pm	
☽	☍	♇	11:34 pm	8:34 pm	
☽	□	♃	11:38 pm	8:38 pm	
☽	△	♀		10:40 pm	

1st ♉

⚸ enters ♈   11:12 am   **8:12 am**
☽ enters ♊   3:21 pm   **12:21 pm**

8 THURSDAY

☽	△	♀	1:40 am		
☽	△	♅	6:35 am	3:35 am	
♀	⊼	⚷	10:20 am	7:20 am	
☽	⊡	⚷	1:16 pm	10:16 am	
☽	∟	☿	4:56 pm	1:56 pm	
☽	⊡	♆	5:46 pm	2:46 pm	
☽	✳	♄	5:49 pm	2:49 pm	
☽	□	♂	10:22 pm	7:22 pm	
☽	⊼	☉		9:25 pm	

1st ♊

☿ D   1:02 pm   **10:02 am**

9 FRIDAY

1st ♊

☽	⊻	☉	12:25 am	
☽	☌	⚸	3:32 am	**12:32 am**
☽	△	♃	3:36 am	**12:36 am**
☽	⌷	♀	4:40 am	**1:40 am**
♃	△	⚸	5:18 am	**2:18 am**
☽	⌷	♅	9:34 am	**6:34 am**
☽	△	♅	4:19 pm	**1:19 pm**
☽	⊻	♀	7:38 pm	**4:38 pm**
☽	✶	☿	8:22 pm	**5:22 pm** ☽ v/c
☽	⊼	♆	9:06 pm	**6:06 pm**
☽	□	♇	11:15 pm	**8:15 pm**

☽ enters ♋   9:13 pm   **6:13 pm**

10 SATURDAY

1st ♋

☿	⊻	♀	4:06 am	**1:06 am**
☽	⊼	♇	5:50 am	**2:50 am**
☽	∟	☉	6:13 am	**3:13 am**
☽	△	♃	7:09 am	**4:09 am**
☽	⌷	♃	7:27 am	**4:27 am**
☽	⊼	♀	8:32 am	**5:32 am**
♀	⌷	⚸	10:23 am	**7:23 am**
♀	△	♆	11:07 am	**8:07 am**
☽	⊼	♅	1:25 pm	**10:25 am**
♀	∟	♄	3:50 pm	**12:50 pm**
☉	□	♃		**9:16 pm**
☽	□	♄		**10:52 pm**
☽	∟	♀		**11:52 pm**

♀ enters ♊   12:20 pm   **9:20 am**

11 SUNDAY

1st ♋

☉	□	♃	12:16 am	
☽	□	♄	1:52 am	
☽	∟	♀	2:52 am	
☽	✶	♂	6:54 am	**3:54 am**
☽	⌷	♇	10:17 am	**7:17 am**
☽	⊼	♃	12:13 pm	**9:13 pm**
☽	⌷	♃	12:19 pm	**9:19 am**
☽	✶	☉	1:08 pm	**10:08 am**
☽	⊻	⚸	2:24 pm	**11:24 am**
☿	□	♆	11:16 pm	**8:16 pm**
☽	□	♇		**10:03 pm**

MOTHER'S DAY

MAY

S	M	T	W	T	F	S
				1	2	3
4	5	6	7	8	9	10
11	12	13	14	15	16	17
18	19	20	21	22	23	24
25	26	27	28	29	30	31

12 MONDAY

1st ♋

☽	□	♆	1:03	am		
♀	✶	⚷	4:32	am	1:32	am
☽	☍	♆	6:25	am	3:25	am	☽ v/c
☽	□	☿	6:35	am	3:35	am
☽	△	⚷	10:50	am	7:50	am
☽	✶	♀	11:18	am	8:18	am
☽	⊥	♂	12:34	pm	9:34	am
☽	△	♇	3:35	pm	12:35	pm
☽	⊼	♄	6:21	pm	3:21	pm
☽	☍	♀	6:53	pm	3:53	pm
☽	⊥	✶	9:19	pm	6:19	pm
☽	☍	♅	11:44	pm	8:44	pm
☉	⊻	✶			11:02	pm

☿ enters ♉	5:25 am	**2:25 am**
☽ enters ♌	6:33 am	**3:33 am**
♅ ℞	7:16 pm	**4:16 pm**

13 TUESDAY

1st ♌

☉	⊻	✶	2:02	am		
☽	△	♄	1:24	pm	10:24	am
☽	⊡	⚷	5:54	pm	2:54	pm
☽	⊻	♂	6:59	pm	3:59	pm
☽	☍	♃			9:08	pm

14 WEDNESDAY

1st ♌

☽	☍	♃	12:08	am		
♀	⊻	♀	3:22	am	12:22	am
♀	☍	♇	4:45	am	1:45	am
☽	✶	✶	4:56	am	1:56	am
☽	□	☉	5:56	am	2:56	am	☽ v/c
☽	✶	⚷	12:43	pm	9:43	am
☽	⊼	♆	6:34	pm	3:34	pm
☽	⊡	♄	8:02	pm	5:02	pm
☽	△	☿	8:46	pm	5:46	pm
☽	⊼	⚷			10:26	pm
♅	⊡	✶			10:29	pm

| 2nd Quarter | 5:56 am | **2:56 am** |
| ☽ enters ♍ | 6:44 pm | **3:44 pm** |

15 THURSDAY

2nd ♍

☽	⊼	⚷	1:26	am		
♅	⊡	✶	1:29	am		
☽	□	♇	3:53	am	12:53	am
☽	□	♀	6:38	am	3:38	am
☽	⊼	♀	7:41	am	4:41	am
☽	☍	♃	8:10	am	5:10	am
☽	⊼	♅	12:22	pm	9:22	am
♀	△	♀	5:02	pm	2:02	pm
☽	⊥	⚷	7:02	pm	4:02	pm
♀	□	♃			9:35	pm
☽	⊡	♆			10:01	pm
☽	⊼	♄			11:46	pm

16 FRIDAY

2nd ♍

♀	□	♃	12:35	am		
☽	⊡	♆	1:01	am		
☽	⊼	♄	2:46	am		
☽	⊡	☿	4:38	am	1:38	am
☽	♂	♂	8:50	am	5:50	am
☽	⊼	♃	1:24	pm	10:24	am
☽	⊡	♀	2:13	pm	11:13	am
☽	⊡	♅	6:44	pm	3:44	pm
☽	□	⚹	8:47	pm	5:47	pm
☽	△	☉			9:08	pm
☽	⊻	⚷			10:12	pm

17 SATURDAY

2nd ♍

☽ enters ♎   7:28 am   **4:28 am**

☽	△	☉	12:08	am			
☽	⊻	⚷	1:12	am			
☽	△	♆	7:15	am	4:15	am	☽ v/c
☽	⊼	☿	12:27	pm	9:27	am	
☉	⊼	⚷	12:42	pm	9:42	am	
♀	△	♅	1:31	pm	10:31	am	
☽	☍	⚳	4:16	pm	1:16	pm	
☽	⚹	♇	4:19	pm	1:19	pm	
♇	△	⚳	5:45	pm	2:45	pm	
☽	⊡	♃	7:39	pm	4:39	pm	
☽	△	♀	8:21	pm	5:21	pm	
☽	⊼	♃	9:52	pm	6:52	pm	
☽	△	♅			9:43	pm	
☽	△	♀			10:58	pm	

18 SUNDAY

2nd ♎

☽	△	♅	12:43	am		
☽	△	♀	1:58	am		
☽	⊡	☉	8:34	am	5:34	am
☽	☍	♄	3:13	pm	12:13	pm
☽	⊻	♂	9:37	pm	6:37	pm
☽	∟	♇	9:47	pm	6:47	pm
☽	△	♃			10:16	pm

	MAY					
S	M	T	W	T	F	S
				1	2	3
4	5	6	7	8	9	10
11	12	13	14	15	16	17
18	19	20	21	22	23	24
25	26	27	28	29	30	31

Eastern Standard Time in medium type
Pacific Standard Time in bold type

19 MONDAY

2nd ♎

☽ enters ♏   6:12 pm   **3:12 pm**

Aspect	EST	PST	
☽ △ ♃	1:16 am		
☽ ⚻ ♇	3:50 am	**12:50 am**	
☽ ⚻ ♀	10:28 am	**7:28 am**	
☽ △ ♅	10:47 am	**7:47 am**	
☽ ☌ ⚷	11:57 am	**8:57 am**	
☽ ⚻ ☉	4:07 pm	**1:07 pm**	
☽ □ ♆	5:57 pm	**2:57 pm**	☽ v/c
♀ ⚻ ⚷	9:55 pm		
☿ ⚻ ♇	10:59 pm		
☽ ⚺ ♇	11:30 pm		
☽ ☍ ☿	11:32 pm		
☽ ⚼ ♂	11:57 pm		

20 TUESDAY

2nd ♏

☉ enters ♊   7:18 pm   **4:18 pm**

Aspect	EST	PST
♀ ⚻ ⚷	12:55 am	
☿ ⚻ ♇	1:59 am	
☽ ⚺ ♇	2:30 am	
☽ ☍ ☿	2:32 am	
☽ ⚼ ♂	2:57 am	
☽ ⚻ ♆	4:34 am	**1:34 am**
☽ □ ♀	6:34 am	**3:34 am**
☽ △ ♃	8:58 am	**5:58 am**
☽ □ ♅	10:34 am	**7:34 am**
☽ △ ⚷	10:37 am	**7:37 am**
☿ ⚻ ♂	11:15 am	**8:15 am**
☉ △ ♆	3:52 pm	**12:52 pm**
☽ ⚻ ♅	4:30 pm	**1:30 pm**
☽ ⚻ ♀	5:54 pm	**2:54 pm**
☽ ⚻ ♄	9:47 pm	

SUN ENTERS GEMINI

21 WEDNESDAY

2nd ♏

☽ enters ♐   **10:51 pm**

Aspect	EST	PST	
☽ ⚻ ♄	12:47 am		
☽ ✶ ♂	7:27 am	**4:27 am**	
☽ ⚻ ♅	9:25 am	**6:25 am**	
☽ □ ♃	10:07 am	**7:07 am**	
☽ ⚺ ⚷	7:42 am	**4:42 am**	
☽ ⚻ ♅	9:18 pm	**6:18 pm**	
☽ ✶ ♆	10:35 pm		☽ v/c

22 THURSDAY

2nd ♐

Full Moon   4:14 am   **1:14 am**
☽ enters ♐   1:51 am
♀ R℞   2:02 pm   **11:02 am**

Aspect	EST	PST	
☽ ✶ ♆	1:35 am		☽ v/c
☽ ☍ ☉	4:14 am	**1:14 am**	
☽ ⚻ ♄	4:22 am	**1:22 am**	
☉ ⚼ ♄	6:27 am	**3:27 am**	
☿ ⚺ ♅	9:10 am	**6:10 am**	
☽ ☌ ♇	9:36 am	**6:36 am**	
♃ ⚼ ♅	10:43 am	**7:43 am**	
☿ □ ♀	1:14 pm	**10:14 am**	
☽ △ ⚷	1:26 pm	**10:26 am**	
☽ ✶ ♀	1:36 pm	**10:36 am**	
☽ ⚻ ☿	1:37 pm	**10:37 am**	
♀ ⚻ ♆	2:20 pm	**11:20 am**	
☽ □ ♃	4:46 pm	**1:46 pm**	
☽ ✶ ♅	5:20 pm	**2:20 pm**	
♀ ✶ ⚷	6:24 pm	**3:24 pm**	
☽ ⚼ ⚷	10:30 pm	**7:30 pm**	

Eastern Standard Time in medium type
Pacific Standard Time in bold type

23 FRIDAY

3rd ♐

☽	⊾	♆	4:20 am	**1:20 am**		
☽	☍	♀	5:44 am	**2:44 am**		
☽	△	♄	7:17 am	**4:17 am**		
☽	□	♂	2:16 pm	**11:16 am**		
☽	✶	♃	3:59 pm	**12:59 pm**	☽ v/c	
☽	⊾	♀	4:06 pm	**1:06 pm**		
☽	⊡	☿	6:11 pm	**3:11 pm**		
☽	⊾	♅	7:45 pm	**4:45 pm**		
♀	✶	♄		**9:23 pm**		
☽	✶	⚷		**9:45 pm**		
♅	⊼	♆		**10:57 pm**		

24 SATURDAY

3rd ♐
☽ enters ♑   6:51 am   **3:51 am**

♀	✶	♄	12:23 am		
☽	✶	⚷	12:45 am		
♅	⊼	♆	1:57 am		
☽	☍	✶	4:43 am	**1:43 am**	
☽	⊻	♆	6:33 am	**3:33 am**	
☽	⊼	☉	1:05 pm	**10:05 am**	
☽	⊻	♇	2:12 pm	**11:12 am**	
☿	□	♅	2:59 pm	**11:59 am**	
☽	⊻	♀	6:08 pm	**3:08 pm**	
☽	⊾	♃	6:09 pm	**3:09 pm**	
☿	✶	♆	6:25 pm	**3:25 pm**	
☽	□	♆	7:37 pm	**4:37 pm**	
☽	⊻	♅	9:44 pm	**6:44 pm**	
☽	✶	♆	10:04 pm	**7:04 pm**	
☽	△	☿	10:18 pm	**7:18 pm**	

25 SUNDAY

3rd ♑

☉	☍	♇	4:57 am	**1:57 am**	
☽	□	♄	11:40 am	**8:40 am**	
☽	⊼	♀	2:47 pm	**11:47 am**	
☽	⊾	♇	3:56 pm	**12:56 pm**	
☽	⊡	☉	4:46 pm	**1:46 pm**	
☽	△	♂	7:09 pm	**4:09 pm**	
☽	⊻	♃	7:59 pm	**4:59 pm**	
☽	⊾	♆		**9:10 pm**	
♆	⊼	✶		**10:07 pm**	

MAY

S	M	T	W	T	F	S
				1	2	3
4	5	6	7	8	9	10
11	12	13	14	15	16	17
18	19	20	21	22	23	24
25	26	27	28	29	30	31

26 MONDAY

3rd ♑

☽ ∟ ♃	12:10 am			
♇ ⊼ ✶	1:07 am			
☽ □ ♅	4:10 am	**1:10 am**		
☽ ♂ ♆	9:59 am	**6:59 am**	☽ v/c	
☽ ⊼ ✶	10:22 am	**7:22 am**		
☽ ✶ ♇	5:28 pm	**2:28 pm**		
☽ ⊡ ♀	6:48 pm	**3:48 pm**		
☽ △ ☉	8:12 pm	**5:12 pm**		
☽ ⊡ ♂	9:14 pm	**6:14 pm**		
☽ ♂ ♀	9:22 pm	**6:22 pm**		
☽ ✶ ♆		**9:26 pm**		
☽ ♂ ♅		**9:57 pm**		
☽ ⊻ ♃		**11:05 pm**		
♂ ⊡ ♀		**11:33 pm**		

☿ enters ♋	9:40 am	**6:40 am**
☽ enters ♒	10:20 am	**7:20 am**

MEMORIAL DAY, OBSERVED

27 TUESDAY

3rd ♒

☽ ✶ ♆	12:26 am			
☽ ♂ ♅	12:57 am			
☽ ⊻ ♃	2:05 am			
♂ ⊡ ♀	2:33 am			
☽ □ ☿	6:00 am	**3:00 am**		
☉ △ ♀	12:45 pm	**9:45 am**		
☽ ⊡ ✶	12:54 pm	**9:54 am**		
☽ ✶ ♄	3:07 pm	**12:07 pm**		
♅ ✶ ♆	6:14 pm	**3:14 pm**		
♂ ⊼ ♃	6:17 pm	**3:17 pm**		
☽ △ ♀	10:42 pm	**7:42 pm**		
☽ ♂ ♃	11:10 pm	**8:10 pm**	☽ v/c	
☽ ⊼ ♂	11:16 pm	**8:16 pm**		
♀ ⊡ ♀	11:37 pm	**8:37 pm**		
☽ ∟ ♆		**11:39 pm**		

28 WEDNESDAY

3rd ♒

☽ ∟ ♆	2:39 am	
♀ △ ♃	4:19 am	**1:19 am**
☽ △ ♅	6:59 am	**3:59 am**
♀ □ ♂	7:10 am	**4:10 am**
☽ ⊻ ♆	12:54 pm	**9:54 am**
☽ △ ✶	3:24 pm	**12:24 pm**
☽ ∟ ♄	4:45 pm	**1:45 pm**
☽ □ ♇	8:19 pm	**5:19 pm**
☽ ⊻ ♀		**9:10 pm**
☽ □ ☉		**11:51 pm**

4th Quarter	**11:51 pm**	
☽ enters ♓	1:18 pm	**10:18 am**

29 THURSDAY

4th ♓

☽ ⊻ ♀	12:10 am	
☽ □ ☉	2:51 am	
☽ ⊻ ♅	3:51 am	**12:51 am**
☽ ⊻ ♆	4:52 am	**1:52 am**
☽ ♂ ♃	5:45 am	**2:45 am**
☽ ⊡ ♂	8:23 am	**5:23 am**
☽ ✶ ☿	1:51 pm	**10:51 am**
☽ ∟ ♆	2:21 pm	**11:21 am**
♀ ⊡ ♅	5:03 pm	**2:03 pm**
☉ △ ♅	5:16 pm	**2:16 pm**
☽ ⊻ ♄	6:24 pm	**3:24 pm**
☽ ∟ ♀		**10:35 pm**
☽ ⊻ ♃		**11:16 pm**

4th Quarter	2:51 am

30 FRIDAY

4th ♓

☽	∟	♀	1:35 am	
☽	⊻	♃	2:16 am	
☽	☍	♂	3:22 am	12:22 am
☽	∟	♅	5:19 am	2:19 am
☽	□	♀	6:30 am	3:30 am
☽	⊼	☿	9:48 am	6:48 am
☽	✳	♆	3:51 pm	12:51 pm	☽ v/c
☽	∟	☿	6:01 pm	3:01 pm
☽	□	♆	8:30 pm	5:30 pm
☽	△	♇	11:14 pm	8:14 pm

☽ enters ♈   4:18 pm   **1:18 pm**

31 SATURDAY

4th ♈

☽	✳	♀	3:03 am	12:03 am
☽	∟	♃	3:53 am	12:53 am
☉	✳	♆	4:11 am	1:11 am
☽	✳	♅	6:51 am	3:51 am
☉	□	♆	7:34 am	4:34 am
☽	♂	♆	9:26 am	6:26 am
☽	⊻	♆	9:32 am	6:32 am
☽	✳	☉	9:39 am	6:39 am
♆	⊻	♆	4:41 pm	1:41 pm
☿	⊻	♄	4:47 pm	1:47 pm
♀	△	☿	7:30 pm	4:30 pm
☽	♂	♄	9:54 pm	6:54 pm
☽	⊻	☿	10:26 pm	7:26 pm
☽	⊼	♇		9:50 pm

♊ GEMINI ♊

Mutable • Air

Rules 3rd House

Ruled by Mercury

Rules shoulders, arms

Keyword: Diversity

Keynote: I THINK

1 SUNDAY

4th ♈

☽	⊼	♇	12:50 am	
☽	✳	♃	5:36 am	2:36 am
☽	⊼	♂	7:48 am	4:48 am
☉	⊼	♀	9:10 am	6:10 am
☿	∟	♆	10:09 am	7:09 am
☽	∟	♆	11:35 am	8:35 am
☽	☍	♀	12:57 pm	9:57 am
☽	∟	☉	1:14 pm	10:14 am
☽	✳	♀	2:41 pm	11:41 am
☽	□	♆	7:09 pm	4:09 pm	☽ v/c
☽	✳	♆		11:02 pm
☽	⊼	♇		11:34 pm

☽ enters ♉   7:39 pm   **4:39 pm**

2 MONDAY

4th ♉

☽	✶	♅	2:02 am	
☽	⊼	♇	2:34 am	
☽	□	♀	6:18 am	3:18 am
☽	⊡	♂	10:18 am	7:18 am
☽	□	♅	10:21 am	7:21 am
♂	⊡	♅	11:45 am	8:45 am
☽	✶	♃	1:49 pm	10:49 am
☽	⊻	♆	2:31 pm	11:31 am
♇	⊼	♅	2:55 pm	11:55 am
☽	⊻	☉	5:04 pm	2:04 pm
☽	∟	♀	7:07 pm	4:07 pm
☽	⊻	♄		11:02 pm

3 TUESDAY

4th ♉

♀ enters ♋   11:18 pm   **8:18 pm**
☽ enters ♊   11:55 pm   **8:55 pm**

☽	⊻	♄	2:02 am	
☽	∟	✶	5:10 am	2:10 am
☽	☌	☿	8:23 am	5:23 am
☽	□	♃	9:37 am	6:37 am
☽	△	♂	1:07 pm	10:07 am
☽	⊼	♀	4:55 pm	1:55 pm
♀	⊼	♆	4:57 pm	1:57 pm
☽	∟	♆	5:30 pm	2:30 pm
☿	□	♃	7:39 pm	4:39 pm
☽	△	♆	11:20 pm	8:20 pm ☽ v/c
☽	⊻	♀	11:59 pm	8:59 pm

4 WEDNESDAY

4th ♊

New Moon   **11:04 pm**

☽	∟	♄	4:34 am	1:34 am
☽	☍	♇	6:55 am	3:55 am
☽	⊻	♅	8:43 am	5:43 am
☽	△	♀	10:33 am	7:33 am
☽	△	♅	2:57 pm	11:57 am
☽	□	✶	7:19 pm	4:19 pm
☽	⊡	♀	7:28 pm	4:28 pm
☽	✶	♆	8:56 pm	5:56 pm
☉	⊡	♆		10:52 pm
☽	⊡	♆		11:03 pm
☽	☌	☉		11:04 pm

5 THURSDAY

1st ♊

New Moon   2:04 am

☉	⊡	♆	1:52 am	
☽	⊡	♆	2:03 am	
☽	☌	☉	2:04 am	
♀	⊡	♀	5:54 am	2:54 am
☽	✶	♄	7:36 am	4:36 am
☿	△	♂	12:42 pm	9:42 am
☽	⊡	♀	1:22 pm	10:22 am
☽	△	♃	3:12 pm	12:12 pm
☽	⊡	♅	6:00 pm	3:00 pm
☽	□	♂	8:16 pm	5:16 pm ☽ v/c
☽	⊻	♀	9:05 pm	6:05 pm
☽	△	♀	10:36 pm	7:36 pm
♀	⊼	✶	11:46 pm	8:46 pm

6 FRIDAY

☽	⊼	♆	5:22 am	**2:22 am**
☿	⊼	⚷	8:57 am	**5:57 am**
☽	♂	♀	11:45 am	**8:45 am**
☽	⊼	♇	1:16 pm	**10:16 am**
☽	⊼	♀	4:47 pm	**1:47 pm**
☽	♂	⚸	5:41 pm	**2:41 pm**
☽	⊡	♃	6:55 pm	**3:55 pm**
☽	⊼	♅	9:43 pm	**6:43 pm**

1st ♊

☽ enters ♋ 6:03 am **3:03 am**

7 SATURDAY

☽	△	?	3:06 am	**12:06 am**
♀	⊼	♇	3:24 am	**12:24 am**
☽	∟	☿	5:05 am	**2:05 am**
☽	□	⚸	5:48 am	**2:48 am**
☿	∟	⚸	11:53 am	**8:53 am**
☽	⊻	☉	2:02 pm	**11:02 am**
☽	□	♄	3:42 pm	**12:42 pm**
☽	⊡	♇	5:29 pm	**2:29 pm**
♃	⊡	⚸	10:44 pm	**7:44 pm**
☽	⊼	♃	11:22 pm	**8:22 pm**

1st ♋

8 SUNDAY

☽	⚹	♂	6:23 am	**3:23 am**	
☽	□	⚷	6:59 am	**3:59 am**	
☽	⊡	?	8:08 am	**5:08 am**	
☿	△	♆	12:49 pm	**9:49 am**	
♀	⊼	♀	1:04 pm	**10:04 am**	
☉	⚹	♄	1:51 pm	**10:51 am**	
☽	♂	♆	2:11 pm	**11:11 am**	
☽	⚹	☿	2:25 pm	**11:25 am**	☽ v/c
☽	∟	☉	9:26 pm	**6:26 pm**	
☽	△	♇	10:28 pm	**7:28 pm**	
♂	⊻	⚷		**9:43 pm**	
☽	♂	☿		**10:49 pm**	

1st ♋

☽ enters ♌ 2:59 pm **11:59 am**
☿ enters ♊ 6:25 pm **3:25 pm**

JUNE

S	M	T	W	T	F	S
1	2	3	4	5	6	7
8	9	10	11	12	13	14
15	16	17	18	19	20	21
22	23	24	25	26	27	28
29	30					

9 MONDAY

1st ♌

♂	⊼	⚷	12:43 am		
☽	☍	♀	1:49 am		
☽	⊼	♀	3:22 am	12:22 am	
☽	⊼	♇	5:59 am	2:59 am	
☽	☍	♅	7:25 am	4:25 am	
☽	∟	♂	12:43 pm	9:43 am	
☽	⊼	♃	1:57 pm	10:57 am	
♀	⊡	♃	3:32 pm	12:32 pm	
☽	△	♆	5:54 pm	2:54 pm	
☽	△	♄		11:49 pm	

♃ Rx   6:28 pm   **3:28 pm**

10 TUESDAY

1st ♌

☽	△	♄	2:49 am		
☽	✶	☉	5:45 am	2:45 am	
☽	☍	♃	10:28 am	7:28 am	☽ v/c
☽	∟	♀	12:38 pm	9:38 am	
♅	⊼	♇	12:39 pm	9:39 am	
☿	∟	♄	12:58 pm	9:58 am	
☽	∟	♇	1:20 pm	10:20 am	
☽	✶	⚷	6:17 pm	3:17 pm	
♀	⊼	♅	7:07 pm	4:07 pm	
☽	⊻	♂	7:46 pm	4:46 pm	
☿	☍	♇	9:04 pm	6:04 pm	
☉	⊡	♀	11:29 pm	8:29 pm	
♀	☌	♇		9:37 pm	
☽	⊡	♆		10:01 pm	
☽	⊼	♆		10:49 pm	

☽ enters ♍   **11:44 pm**

11 WEDNESDAY

1st ♍

♀	☌	♇	12:37 am		
☽	⊡	♆	1:01 am		
☽	⊼	♆	1:49 am		
☽	⊡	♄	9:17 am	6:17 am	
☽	□	♇	10:22 am	7:22 am	
☽	□	☿	12:52 pm	9:52 am	
☽	⊼	♀	1:19 pm	10:19 am	
☿	△	♀	3:37 pm	12:37 pm	
☽	⊼	♅	7:37 pm	4:37 pm	
☽	✶	♇	9:11 pm	6:11 pm	
☽	✶	♀	10:30 pm	7:30 pm	
☽	∟	⚷		9:39 pm	

☽ enters ♍   2:44 am

12 THURSDAY

1st ♍

☽	∟	⚷	12:39 am		
☽	☍	♃	3:11 am	12:11 am	
☽	⊡	♆	8:13 am	5:13 am	
☽	⊼	♆	8:28 am	5:28 am	
☽	⊼	♄	3:58 pm	12:58 pm	
☉	△	♃	4:22 pm	1:22 pm	
☽	⊡	♀	7:28 pm	4:28 pm	
☽	⊼	♃	11:16 pm	8:16 pm	
☽	□	☉	11:52 pm	8:52 pm	
☽	⊡	♅		11:02 pm	

2nd Quarter   11:52 pm   **8:52 pm**

13 FRIDAY

2nd ♍

☽ enters ♎   3:36 pm   **12:36 pm**

☽	⊡	♅	2:02 am		
☿	△	♅	6:30 am	**3:30 am**	
☽	⊻	⚸	7:03 am	**4:03 am**	
☽	♂	♂	10:46 am	**7:46 am**	
☽	△	♆	2:35 pm	**11:35 am**	☽ v/c
☽	⚹	♇	11:03 pm	**8:03 pm**	
♀	△	♃		**9:50 pm**	
☽	△	☿		**10:24 pm**	
☉	⊡	♅		**11:04 pm**	

14 SATURDAY

2nd ♎

♀	△	♃	12:50 am		
☽	△	☿	1:24 am		
☉	⊡	♅	2:04 am		
☽	⊡	♃	5:29 am	**2:29 am**	
☽	△	♅	8:11 am	**5:11 am**	
☿	⊻	⚹	9:11 am	**6:11 am**	
☿	⊡	⚸	12:42 pm	**9:42 am**	
☽	□	⚹	12:44 pm	**9:44 am**	
☽	△	☿	1:14 pm	**10:14 am**	
☽	⊼	♃	4:24 pm	**1:24 pm**	
☽	□	♀	5:58 pm	**2:58 pm**	
☽	☍	⚷	10:45 pm	**7:45 pm**	

15 SUNDAY

2nd ♎

☽ enters ♏   **11:51 pm**

☽	☍	♄	4:32 am	**1:32 am**	
☽	∟	♇	4:49 am	**1:49 am**	
☿	□	♃	9:24 am	**6:24 am**	
☽	△	♃	11:08 am	**8:08 am**	
☽	△	☉	4:49 pm	**1:49 pm**	
☽	♂	⚸	6:37 pm	**3:37 pm**	
☽	⊡	♃	10:06 pm	**7:06 pm**	
☽	⊻	♂		**9:17 pm**	
☽	⊡	☿		**9:25 pm**	
☽	□	♆		**10:47 pm**	☽ v/c

FATHER'S DAY

JUNE

S	M	T	W	T	F	S
1	2	3	4	5	6	7
8	9	10	11	12	13	14
15	16	17	18	19	20	21
22	23	24	25	26	27	28
29	30					

16 MONDAY

2nd ♏

☽	⊻	♂	12:17 am		
☽	⊡	☿	12:25 am		
☽	□	♆	1:47 am		☽ v/c
☿	⊡	♆	8:41 am	5:41 am	
☽	⊻	♇	9:49 am	6:49 am	
☽	□	♀	11:27 am	8:27 am	
☉	△	⚷	3:41 pm	12:41 pm	
♄	⊡	♇	4:47 pm	1:47 pm	
☽	□	♅	6:29 pm	3:29 pm	
☽	⊡	☉	11:50 pm	8:50 pm	
☽	△	⚵		10:29 pm	
☽	△	☋		11:54 pm	

☽ enters ♏   2:51 am

17 TUESDAY

2nd ♏

☽	△	⚵	1:29 am		
☽	△	☋	2:54 am		
☿	⊻	♀	4:42 am	1:42 am	
☽	⊾	♂	5:42 am	2:42 am	
☿	✶	♆	8:10 am	5:10 am	
☽	△	♀	9:51 am	6:51 am	
☽	⊼	♆	9:58 am	6:58 am	
☽	⊼	☿	10:15 am	7:15 am	
♀	□	♆	11:36 am	8:36 am	
☽	⊼	♄	2:04 pm	11:04 am	
♂	△	♆	6:33 pm	3:33 pm	
☽	□	♃	7:50 pm	4:50 pm	
☽	⊻	⚷		11:53 pm	

18 WEDNESDAY

2nd ♏

☽	⊻	⚷	2:53 am		
☽	⊼	☉	5:39 am	2:39 am	
☽	⊡	⚵	6:17 am	3:17 am	
☽	✶	♆	9:34 am	6:34 am	
☽	✶	♂	10:05 am	7:05 am	☽ v/c
☿	✶	♄	10:35 am	7:35 am	
☽	⊡	♀	2:03 pm	11:03 am	
☿	⊡	♀	2:52 pm	11:52 am	
☿	⊡	♀	3:56 pm	12:56 pm	
☽	♂	♇	5:04 pm	2:04 pm	
☽	⊡	♄	5:25 pm	2:25 pm	
☽	✶	♀	6:00 pm	3:00 pm	
☋	△	⚵	7:17 pm	4:17 pm	
☽	✶	♅		10:10 pm	

☽ enters ♐   10:39 am   **7:39 am**

19 THURSDAY

2nd ♐

☽	✶	♅	1:10 am		
♀	⊡	♇	4:16 am	1:16 am	
☽	⊾	⚷	5:40 am	2:40 am	
♀	□	♄	9:12 am	6:12 am	
☽	□	☋	9:35 am	6:35 am	
☽	⊼	⚵	10:04 am	7:04 am	
☽	⊾	♆	12:06 pm	9:06 am	
☽	△	♀	5:12 pm	2:12 pm	
☽	△	♄	7:54 pm	4:54 pm	
☽	⊾	♀	8:01 pm	5:01 pm	
☿	△	♃	8:45 pm	5:45 pm	
☽	⊼	♀	8:53 pm	5:53 pm	
☽	✶	♃		9:57 pm	
☽	☍	☿		10:43 pm	

♂ enters ♎   3:30 am   **12:30 am**

20 FRIDAY

☽	✳	♃	12:57 am		
☽	☍	☿	1:43 am		
☽	⊥	♅	3:15 am	12:15 am	
☽	✳	♆	7:40 am	4:40 am	
☉	⊼	♆	10:57 am	7:57 am	
☿	⊡	♅	11:32 am	8:32 am	
☽	⊻	♆	1:56 pm	10:56 am	
☽	☍	☉	2:09 pm	11:09 am	☽ v/c
☽	□	♂	4:11 pm	1:11 pm	
☽	⊻	♇	9:02 pm	6:02 pm	
☽	⊻	♀	9:21 pm	6:21 pm	
☽	⊥	♃		11:28 pm	

2nd ♐

Full Moon   2:09 pm   **11:09 am**
☽ enters ♑   3:02 pm   **12:02 pm**

MIDSUMMER'S EVE

21 SATURDAY

☽	⊥	♃	2:28 am		
☽	⊻	♅	4:44 am	1:44 am	
☽	✳	♀	1:14 pm	10:14 am	
☽	☍	♆	3:21 pm	12:21 pm	
☿	△	♅	4:10 pm	1:10 pm	
♀	⊼	♃	6:11 pm	3:11 pm	
☽	□	⚷	9:27 pm	6:27 pm	
☽	⊥	♇	10:13 pm	7:13 pm	
☽	□	♄	11:01 pm	8:01 pm	
♇	✳	♀	11:45 pm	8:45 pm	

3rd ♑

☉ enters ♋   3:20 am   **12:20 am**

SUMMER SOLSTICE • SUN ENTERS CANCER

22 SUNDAY

☽	⊻	♃	3:32 am	12:32 am	
☽	☍	♀	4:26 am	1:26 am	
☽	□	♅	10:10 am	7:10 am	
☽	⊼	☿	1:22 pm	10:22 am	
☽	⊥	♃	2:25 pm	11:25 am	
☽	☌	♆	4:11 pm	1:11 pm	☽ v/c
☽	⊼	☉	8:02 pm	5:02 pm	
☽	△	♂	8:03 pm	5:03 pm	
☉	□	♂	8:49 pm	5:49 pm	
☽	☌	♀	10:51 pm	7:51 pm	
☽	✳	♇	11:07 pm	8:07 pm	
♇	⊡	⚷		11:59 pm	

3rd ♑

☽ enters ♒   5:21 pm   **2:21 pm**

JUNE

S	M	T	W	T	F	S
1	2	3	4	5	6	7
8	9	10	11	12	13	14
15	16	17	18	19	20	21
22	23	24	25	26	27	28
29	30					

23 MONDAY

3rd ♒

⚷ D	9:26 am	**6:26 am**	
☿ enters ♋	3:40 pm	**12:40 pm**	
♇ ⚼ ⚶	2:59 am		
☽ ☌ ♅	6:39 am	**3:39 am**	
☿ ⚻ ♆	7:49 am	**4:49 am**	
♂ △ ⚴	2:37 pm	**11:37 am**	
☽ ⚺ ⚳	3:27 pm	**12:27 pm**	
☽ ⚼ ☿	6:40 pm	**3:40 pm**	
☽ ⚻ ⚵	7:10 pm	**4:10 pm**	
☽ ⚼ ♂	9:44 pm	**6:44 pm**	
☽ ⚼ ☉	10:40 pm	**7:40 pm**	
☽ ⚹ ⚶		**9:30 pm**	
☽ ⚹ ♄		**10:04 pm**	

24 TUESDAY

3rd ♒

☽ enters ♓	7:09 pm	**4:09 pm**	
☽ ⚹ ⚶	12:30 am		
☽ ⚹ ♄	1:04 am		
☽ ☌ ♃	5:12 am	**2:12 am**	☽ v/c
☉ ⚻ ⚴	7:44 am	**4:44 am**	
☽ ⚻ ♀	10:49 am	**7:49 am**	
☽ △ ⚷	11:57 am	**8:57 am**	
☽ ⚺ ♆	5:54 pm	**2:54 pm**	
☉ ⚻ ♇	5:55 pm	**2:55 pm**	
☿ □ ♂	7:26 pm	**4:26 pm**	
☽ ⚼ ⚵	9:05 pm	**6:05 pm**	
☿ ⚻ ⚴	11:26 pm	**8:26 pm**	
☽ ⚻ ♂	11:30 pm	**8:30 pm**	
☽ ⚺ ⚴	11:59 pm	**8:59 pm**	
☽ △ ☿		**9:05 pm**	
⚴ □ ⚷		**9:23 pm**	
☽ □ ♇		**9:53 pm**	
☽ △ ☉		**10:23 pm**	
☽ ∟ ⚶		**11:04 pm**	
☽ ∟ ♄		**11:09 pm**	

25 WEDNESDAY

3rd ♓

☽ △ ☿	12:05 am		
⚴ □ ⚷	12:23 am		
☽ □ ♇	12:53 am		
☽ △ ☉	1:23 am		
☽ ∟ ⚶	2:04 am		
☽ ∟ ♄	2:09 am		
☿ ⚻ ♇	5:16 am	**2:16 am**	
♄ ☌ ⚶	6:21 am	**3:21 am**	
☽ ⚺ ♅	8:27 am	**5:27 am**	
♂ ⚹ ⚴	9:43 am	**6:43 am**	
☽ ⚼ ⚷	1:01 pm	**10:01 am**	
☽ ⚼ ♀	2:11 pm	**11:11 am**	
☿ ☌ ☉	2:14 pm	**11:14 am**	
☽ ☌ ⚳	5:44 pm	**2:44 pm**	
☽ ∟ ♆	6:58 pm	**3:58 pm**	
☽ △ ⚵	11:12 pm	**8:12 pm**	
☽ ∟ ⚴		**9:46 pm**	

26 THURSDAY

3rd ♓

☽ enters ♈	9:39 pm	**6:39 pm**	
☽ ∟ ⚴	12:46 am		
☽ ⚺ ♄	3:26 am	**12:26 am**	
☽ ⚺ ⚶	3:51 am	**12:51 am**	
☽ ⚺ ♃	7:15 am	**4:15 am**	
☽ ∟ ♅	9:38 am	**6:38 am**	
☽ ⚻ ⚷	2:19 pm	**11:19 am**	
☿ ⚼ ♃	2:54 pm	**11:54 am**	
♂ ⚹ ♇	4:09 pm	**1:09 pm**	
☽ △ ♀	5:53 pm	**2:53 pm**	
☽ ⚹ ♆	8:17 pm	**5:17 pm**	☽ v/c
☽ ⚹ ⚴		**10:49 pm**	

27 FRIDAY

☽	⚹	♀	1:49 am	
☽	△	♇	3:25 am	**12:25 am**
☽	☍	♂	3:50 am	**12:50 am**
☿	⊼	♅	6:23 am	**3:23 am**
☽	□	☉	7:43 am	**4:43 am**
☽	⌲	♃	8:40 am	**5:40 am**
♀	⌑	♃	10:11 am	**7:11 am**
☽	⚹	♅	11:08 am	**8:08 am**
☽	□	☿	12:01 pm	**9:01 am**
☽	⌴	♃	9:00 pm	**6:00 pm**
☉	⌑	♃	9:03 pm	**6:03 pm**
♀	☍	♆	9:21 pm	**6:21 pm**

3rd ♈

4th Quarter   7:43 am   **4:43 am**

28 SATURDAY

☽	□	✶	4:25 am	**1:25 am**
☽	⌑	♇	5:10 am	**2:10 am**
☽	♂	♄	6:55 am	**3:55 am**
☽	♂	⚷	8:22 am	**5:22 am**
☽	⚹	♃	10:25 am	**7:25 am**
☽	☍	♅	5:54 pm	**2:54 pm**
♇	⌑	✶	10:52 pm	**7:52 pm**
☽	⌴	♃	11:08 pm	**8:08 pm**
☽	□	♆	11:54 pm	**8:54 pm** ☽ v/c
☽	□	♀		**11:32 pm**

4th ♈

♀ enters ♌   1:38 pm   **10:38 am**
☽ enters ♉   **10:24 pm**

29 SUNDAY

☽	□	♀	2:32 am	
☽	□	♀	4:50 am	**1:50 am**
☽	⊼	♇	7:15 am	**4:15 am**
☉	⊼	♅	8:25 am	**5:25 am**
☽	⊼	♂	9:37 am	**6:37 am**
☽	□	♅	3:07 pm	**12:07 pm**
☽	⚹	☉	3:38 pm	**12:38 pm**
☿	△	♃	11:39 pm	**8:39 pm**
♀	☍	♀		**9:35 pm**
☽	⚹	♃		**10:36 pm**
☽	⚹	☿		**10:57 pm**

4th ♉

☽ enters ♉   1:24 am

JUNE

S	M	T	W	T	F	S
1	2	3	4	5	6	7
8	9	10	11	12	13	14
15	16	17	18	19	20	21
22	23	24	25	26	27	28
29	30					

30 MONDAY

4th ♉

♀	☍	♀	12:35 am		
☽	✶	♄	1:36 am		
☽	✶	☿	1:57 am		
☽	✶	✶	11:11 am	8:11	am
☽	⊻	♄	11:48 am	8:48	am
☽	⊡	♂	1:07 pm	10:07	am
☽	⊻	♇	2:22 pm	11:22	am
☽	□	♃	2:56 pm	11:56	am
☽	∟	☉	8:17 pm	5:17	pm
☽	⊼	⚷	10:56 pm	7:56	pm

♋ CANCER ♋

Cardinal • Water
Rules 4th House
Ruled by Moon
Rules the stomach
Keyword: Sympathy
Keynote: I FEEL

1 TUESDAY

4th ♉
☽ enters Ⅱ   6:36 am   **3:36 am**

♄	□	✶	3:59 am	12:59 am		
☽	△	♆	4:58 am	1:58 am	☽ v/c
♀	△	♇	6:47 am	3:47 am	
☽	△	♀	9:12 am	6:12 am	
☽	∟	☿	9:46 am	6:46 am	
♃	✶	♆	10:12 am	7:12 am	
☽	☍	♇	12:32 pm	9:32 am	
☽	✶	♀	1:08 pm	10:08 am	
☽	∟	♄	2:49 pm	11:49 am	
☽	∟	✶	3:14 pm	12:14 pm	
☽	△	♂	5:05 pm	2:05 pm	
☽	∟	♆	5:59 pm	2:59 pm	
☽	△	♅	8:36 pm	5:36 pm	
☽	⊻	☉		10:27 pm	
☽	⊡	⚷		11:03 pm	

2 WEDNESDAY

4th Ⅱ

☽	⊻	☉	1:27 am		
☽	⊡	⚷	2:03 am		
☿	⊡	♇	3:18 am	12:18 am	
☽	□	♄	7:44 am	4:44 am	
☽	⊡	♆	8:07 am	5:07 am	
♂	⊡	♃	9:29 am	6:29 am	
☽	⊡	♀	11:59 am	8:59 am	
☽	⊻	☿	6:13 pm	3:13 pm	
☽	✶	♄	6:18 pm	3:18 pm	
☿	□	♄	6:46 pm	3:46 pm	
☽	∟	✶	7:17 pm	4:17 pm	
☽	⊻	♅	7:47 pm	4:47 pm	
☽	△	♃	9:03 pm	6:03 pm	☽ v/c
☽	✶	♆	10:06 pm	7:06 pm	
☽	⊡	♅		9:01 pm	

3 THURSDAY

4th ♊

☽	⊡	♅	12:01 am		
☽	△	♀	5:40 am	**2:40**	**am**
☿	♂	⚹	7:07 am	**4:07**	**am**
☿	⊼	♃	11:43 am	**8:43**	**am**
☽	⊼	♆	11:45 am	**8:45**	**am**
☽	⊼	♀	3:14 pm	**12:14**	**pm**
☽	⊼	♇	7:38 pm	**4:38**	**pm**
☿	□	⚷	10:41 pm	**7:41**	**pm**
♃	⊼	⚹	11:11 pm	**8:11**	**pm**
☽	⊡	♃		**9:50**	**pm**
☽	⊻	♀		**11:08**	**pm**
☽	□	♂		**11:40**	**pm**

☽ enters ♋   1:33 pm   **10:33 am**

4 FRIDAY

4th ♋

☽	⊡	♃	12:50 am		
☽	⊻	♀	2:08 am		
☽	□	♂	2:40 am		
☽	⊼	♅	3:57 am	**12:57**	**am**
♀	⚹	♂	11:11 am	**8:11**	**am**
☽	♂	☉	1:40 pm	**10:40**	**am**
☽	△	♃	3:48 pm	**12:48**	**pm**
♀	♂	♅	8:40 pm	**5:40**	**pm**
☽	⊡	♇		**9:00**	**pm**
☽	□	♄		**11:53**	**pm**

New Moon   1:40 pm   **10:40 am**

INDEPENDENCE DAY

5 SATURDAY

1st ♋

☽	⊡	♇	12:00 am			
☽	□	♄	2:53 am			
☽	⊼	♃	5:12 am	**2:12**	**am**	
☽	♂	⚹	6:44 am	**3:44**	**am**	
☽	□	⚷	8:03 am	**5:03**	**am**	
♂	△	♅	9:17 am	**6:17**	**am**	
☽	♂	☿	1:30 pm	**10:30**	**am**	
☽	□	♀	2:37 pm	**11:37**	**am**	
☉	△	♃	6:16 pm	**3:16**	**pm**	
☿	□	♀	8:38 pm	**5:38**	**pm**	
☽	⊡	♃	8:42 pm	**5:42**	**pm**	
☽	♂	♆	8:45 pm	**5:45**	**pm**	☽ v/c
☽	♂	♀	11:21 pm	**8:21**	**pm**	

☽ enters ♌   10:45 pm   **7:45 pm**

6 SUNDAY

1st ♌

☽	△	♇	5:00 am	**2:00**	**am**
☽	♂	♅	1:37 pm	**10:37**	**am**
♆	∟	♃	2:04 pm	**11:04**	**am**
☽	⚹	♂	2:55 pm	**11:55**	**am**
☽	♂	♀	6:17 pm	**3:17**	**pm**
☽	⊼	♃		**11:13**	**pm**

7 MONDAY

1st ♌

☽	⊼	♄	2:13 am		
☽	⊻	☉	4:56 am	1:56 am	
☿	☍	♆	11:04 am	8:04 am	
☿	⊡	♃	11:27 am	8:27 am	
☽	△	♄	1:55 pm	10:55 am	
☽	☍	♃	3:44 pm	12:44 pm	☽ v/c
☽	⊻	♅	8:27 pm	5:27 pm	
☽	△	♇	8:36 pm	5:36 pm	
☿	☍	♀	9:58 pm	6:58 pm	
☽	∟	♂	10:06 pm	7:06 pm	
☽	✳	♀		11:03 pm	

♀ enters ♒   3:42 am   **12:42 am**
☿ enters ♌   **9:28 pm**

8 TUESDAY

1st ♌

☽	✳	♀	2:03 am		
✳	⊡	♇	3:33 am	12:33 am	
☽	⊼	♆	8:10 am	5:10 am	
☽	⊼	♀	9:42 am	6:42 am	
☽	⊻	☿	12:15 pm	9:15 am	
☽	∟	☉	1:38 pm	10:38 am	
☽	☐	♇	4:45 pm	1:45 pm	
☽	⊡	♄	8:15 pm	5:15 pm	
☽	⊼	♅		10:32 pm	

☿ enters ♌   12:28 am
☽ enters ♍   10:22 am   **7:22 am**
♃ Rℷ   1:56 pm   **10:56 am**

9 WEDNESDAY

1st ♍

☽	⊼	♅	1:32 am		
☽	⊡	♇	3:40 am	12:40 am	
☽	∟	✳	4:11 am	1:11 am	
☽	⊻	♂	5:48 am	2:48 am	
☽	∟	♀	8:29 am	5:29 am	
☽	⊻	♀	1:26 pm	10:26 am	
☽	⊡	♆	2:31 pm	11:31 am	
☽	☍	♃	2:42 pm	11:42 am	
☽	⊡	♀	3:29 pm	12:29 pm	
☿	△	♇	4:39 pm	1:39 pm	
☽	✳	☉	10:48 pm	7:48 pm	
☽	∟	☿		9:25 pm	
♀	⊼	♃		10:40 pm	
☽	⊼	♄		11:51 pm	

10 THURSDAY

1st ♍

☽	∟	☿	12:25 am		
♀	⊼	♃	1:40 am		
☽	⊼	♄	2:51 am		
☉	⊡	♇	3:38 am	12:38 am	
☽	⊼	♃	4:03 am	1:03 am	
☽	⊡	♅	7:59 am	4:59 am	
☽	⊼	♇	10:58 am	7:58 am	
☽	✳	✳	12:09 pm	9:09 am	
☽	⊻	♀	3:06 pm	12:06 pm	
☽	△	♆	8:59 pm	5:59 pm	☽ v/c
☽	△	♀	9:21 pm	6:21 pm	
☽	∟	♀	11:28 pm	8:28 pm	

☽ enters ♎   11:21 pm   **8:21 pm**

11 FRIDAY

1st ♎

?	∟	♀	3:20 am	**12:20**	**am**
☽	⚹	♇	5:40 am	**2:40**	**am**
☽	⊡	♃	10:18 am	**7:18**	**am**
☽	⚹	☿	12:26 pm	**9:26**	**am**
☽	△	♅	2:20 pm	**11:20**	**am**
♆	☌	♀	2:27 pm	**11:27**	**am**
☽	☌	♂	9:32 pm	**6:32**	**pm**
☿	☍	♅		**9:55**	**pm**
☉	□	♄		**11:48**	**pm**

12 SATURDAY

1st ♎

2nd Quarter   4:44 pm   **1:44 pm**

☿	☍	♅	12:55 am		
☉	□	♄	2:48 am		
☽	⊼	?	3:29 am	**12:29**	**am**
☽	⚹	♀	9:09 am	**6:09**	**am**
☉	⊼	♃	10:23 am	**7:23**	**am**
☽	∟	♇	11:49 am	**8:49**	**am**
☽	☍	♄	3:40 pm	**12:40**	**pm**
☽	△	♃	4:11 pm	**1:11**	**pm**
☽	□	☉	4:44 pm	**1:44**	**pm**
☽	☍	⚹		**9:48**	**pm**

13 SUNDAY

2nd ♎

☽ enters ♏   11:20 am   **8:20 am**

☽	☍	⚹	12:48 am			
☽	□	⚹	3:16 am	**12:16**	**am**	
☽	☌	⚷	3:33 am	**12:33**	**am**	
☽	□	♀	8:07 am	**5:07**	**am**	
☽	□	♆	8:57 am	**5:57**	**am**	☽ v/c
☽	⊡	♃	9:11 am	**6:11**	**am**	
⚹	□	⚷	10:38 am	**7:38**	**am**	
☽	⊻	♇	5:20 pm	**2:20**	**pm**	
☽	□	♅		**10:31**	**pm**	

JULY

S	M	T	W	T	F	S
		1	2	3	4	5
6	7	8	9	10	11	12
13	14	15	16	17	18	19
20	21	22	23	24	25	26
27	28	29	30	31		

14 MONDAY

2nd ♏

☽	□	♅	1:31 am	
☽	□	☿	9:29 am	**6:29 am**
☽	⊻	♂	11:07 am	**8:07 am**
☽	△	⚷	2:02 pm	**11:02 am**
♃	✶	♄	3:58 pm	**12:58 pm**
☽	□	♀		**10:37 pm**
☽	□	♃		**10:41 pm**
☽	⊼	♄		**10:47 pm**
♀	☍	♃		**11:19 pm**
☿	✶	♂		**11:38 pm**

15 TUESDAY

☽ enters ♐   8:03 pm   **5:03 pm**

2nd ♏

☽	□	♀	1:37 am	
☽	□	♃	1:41 am	
☽	⊼	♄	1:47 am	
♀	☍	♃	2:19 am	
☿	✶	♂	2:38 am	
♀	△	♄	3:28 am	**12:28 am**
☽	△	☉	7:15 am	**4:15 am**
☽	⊼	⚷	11:24 am	**8:24 am**
☽	⊻	♅	12:57 pm	**9:57 am**
☽	△	⚳	2:54 pm	**11:54 am**
☽	✶	♀	3:53 pm	**12:53 pm**
☽	∟	♂	4:21 pm	**1:21 pm**
☽	✶	♆	5:42 pm	**2:42 pm** ☽ v/c
☿	⊼	⚷	7:06 pm	**4:06 pm**
☽	☌	♇		**10:33 pm**

16 WEDNESDAY

2nd ♐

☽	☌	♇	1:33 am	
☽	⊡	♄	5:20 am	**2:20 am**
♀	☍	⚷	7:26 am	**4:26 am**
☽	✶	♅	9:05 am	**6:05 am**
☽	⊡	☉	12:38 pm	**9:38 am**
☽	⊡	⚷	3:05 pm	**12:05 pm**
☽	∟	⚳	4:07 pm	**1:07 pm**
☽	∟	♀	6:20 pm	**3:20 pm**
☽	⊡	⚷	6:59 pm	**3:59 pm**
☽	✶	♂	8:25 pm	**5:25 pm**
☽	∟	♆	8:33 pm	**5:33 pm**
☽	□	⚷	8:42 pm	**5:42 pm**
☽	△	☿		**9:16 pm**
♂	⊼	⚷		**11:43 pm**

17 THURSDAY

☽ enters ♑

2nd ♐

9:46 pm

☽	△	☿	12:16 am	
♂	⊼	⚷	2:43 am	
☽	✶	♃	7:17 am	**4:17 am**
☽	△	♄	7:53 am	**4:53 am**
☽	∟	♅	11:22 am	**8:22 am**
☽	△	♀	12:46 pm	**9:46 am** ☽ v/c
☽	⊼	☉	4:48 pm	**1:48 pm**
☽	△	⚳	5:43 pm	**2:43 pm**
☽	✶	♇	6:19 pm	**3:19 pm**
☽	⊻	♀	7:53 pm	**4:53 pm**
☽	⊼	⚷	10:01 pm	**7:01 pm**
☽	⊻	♆	10:28 pm	**7:28 pm**

18   FRIDAY

2nd ♑

☽	⊡	☿	5:23 am	**2:23**	**am**
☽	⌄	♇	5:51 am	**2:51**	**am**
☽	∟	♃	8:43 am	**5:43**	**am**
♆	☍	⚹	9:39 am	**6:39**	**am**
☉	□	⚷	10:53 am	**7:53**	**am**
⚵	⊡	⚹	11:19 am	**8:19**	**am**
☽	⌄	♅	12:48 pm	**9:48**	**am**
☉	□	⚷	4:09 pm	**1:09**	**pm**
☽	⊡	♀	4:34 pm	**1:34**	**pm**
☽	⚹	⚵	11:39 pm	**8:39**	**pm**
☽	□	♂		**10:35**	**pm**

☽ enters ♑   12:46 am

19   SATURDAY

2nd ♑

☽	□	♂	1:35 am		
☉	☍	♀	4:46 am	**1:46**	**am**
☽	∟	♇	6:50 am	**3:50**	**am**
☽	⊼	☿	9:23 am	**6:23**	**am**
☽	⌄	♃	9:28 am	**6:28**	**am**
☿	☍	♃	10:12 am	**7:12**	**am**
⚹	☍	⚵	10:30 am	**7:30**	**am**
☽	□	♄	10:30 am	**7:30**	**am**
♆	∟	⚵	1:15 pm	**10:15**	**am**
☽	⊼	♀	7:33 pm	**4:33**	**pm**
☿	△	♄	8:13 pm	**5:13**	**pm**
☽	□	⚵	8:29 pm	**5:29**	**pm**
☽	□	⚹	8:37 pm	**5:37**	**pm**
☽	♂	♀	8:55 pm	**5:55**	**pm**
☽	☍	☉	10:21 pm	**7:21**	**pm**
☽	∟	⚵		**9:11**	**pm**

Full Moon   10:21 pm   **7:21 pm**
☽ enters ≈   **11:29 pm**

☽ ♂ ♆   9:12 pm   ☽ v/c
☽ ☍ ⚹   10:41 pm

20   SUNDAY

3rd ≈

☽	∟	⚵	12:11 am		
☽	♂	♆	12:12 am		
☽	☍	⚹	1:41 am		
♀	□	⚵	5:10 am	**2:10**	**am**
♀	⚹	⚵	7:19 am	**4:19**	**am**
☽	⚹	♇	7:20 am	**4:20**	**am**
♀	⊼	♀	9:20 am	**6:20**	**am**
☽	△	⚵	11:33 am	**8:33**	**am**
☽	♂	♅	1:56 pm	**10:56**	**am**
♀	□	⚵	4:39 pm	**1:39**	**pm**
☽	⌄	⚵		**9:22**	**pm**
☉	⊡	⚵		**9:44**	**pm**
☉	☍	♆		**11:15**	**pm**

☽ v/c

☽ enters ≈   2:29 am
⚹ enters ♌   **9:19 pm**

JULY

S	M	T	W	T	F	S
		1	2	3	4	5
6	7	8	9	10	11	12
13	14	15	16	17	18	19
20	21	22	23	24	25	26
27	28	29	30	31		

Eastern Standard Time in medium type
Pacific Standard Time in bold type

21 MONDAY

3rd ♒

⚵ enters ♌ 12:19 am

☽	⚺	⚳	12:22 am		
☉	⚼	⚳	12:44 am		
☉	☍	♆	2:15 am		
☽	△	♂	4:22 am	**1:22 am**	
☽	☌	♃	9:50 am	**6:50 am**	
☽	⚹	♄	11:16 am	**8:16 am**	
☽	☍	☿	3:33 pm	**12:33 pm**	
☽	⚺	⚴	8:36 pm	**5:36 pm**	
☽	△	⚷	9:13 pm	**6:13 pm**	
☽	⚹	⚶	9:59 pm	**6:59 pm**	
☽	☍	♀		**9:25 pm**	☽ v/c
☽	⚺	♆		**9:39 pm**	
☽	⚻	☉		**11:14 pm**	

22 TUESDAY

3rd ♒

☽ enters ♓ 3:00 am **12:00 am**
☉ enters ♌ 2:15 pm **11:15 am**

☽	☍	♀	12:25 am		☽ v/c
☽	⚺	♆	12:39 am		
☽	⚻	☉	2:14 am		
♀	⚻	♆	3:12 am	**12:12 am**	
☽	⚻	⚵	3:58 am	**12:58 am**	
☽	⚼	♂	5:32 am	**2:32 am**	
☽	□	♇	7:47 am	**4:47 am**	
☽	∠	♄	11:33 am	**8:33 am**	
☽	⚺	♅	2:18 pm	**11:18 am**	
☽	∠	⚴	8:29 pm	**5:29 pm**	
☽	⚼	⚷	9:37 pm	**6:37 pm**	
☽	∠	⚶	10:41 pm	**7:41 pm**	
☽	☌	⚳		**9:41 pm**	
☽	∠	♆		**9:57 pm**	

SUN ENTERS LEO

23 WEDNESDAY

3rd ♓

♀ enters ♍ 8:16 am **5:16 am**

☽	☌	⚳	12:41 am		
☽	∠	♆	12:57 am		
☽	⚼	☉	4:17 am	**1:17 am**	
☽	⚼	⚵	5:14 am	**2:14 am**	
☽	⚻	♂	6:53 am	**3:53 am**	
☽	⚺	♃	10:08 am	**7:08 am**	
☽	⚺	♄	12:02 pm	**9:02 am**	
☿	⚻	⚴	12:37 pm	**9:37 am**	
☽	∠	♅	2:44 pm	**11:44 am**	
☽	⚹	⚴	8:37 pm	**5:37 pm**	
☽	⚻	☿	9:37 pm	**6:37 pm**	
☽	⚻	⚷	10:18 pm	**7:18 pm**	
☽	⚺	⚶	11:42 pm	**8:42 pm**	
☽	⚹	♆		**10:33 pm**	☽ v/c

24 THURSDAY

3rd ♓

☽ enters ♈ 4:04 am **1:04 am**

☽	⚹	♆	1:33 am		☽ v/c
☿	⚹	⚷	5:02 am	**2:02 am**	
☽	⚻	♀	5:52 am	**2:52 am**	
☽	△	☉	6:44 am	**3:44 am**	
☽	△	⚵	6:53 am	**3:53 am**	
☽	△	♇	8:56 am	**5:56 am**	
☽	∠	♃	10:44 am	**7:44 am**	
☉	☌	⚵	11:13 am	**8:13 am**	
☽	⚹	♅	3:33 pm	**12:33 pm**	
♂	∠	♇	4:20 pm	**1:20 pm**	
☿	△	⚶	11:36 pm	**8:36 pm**	
☽	⚼	☿		**10:17 pm**	
☽	⚺	⚳		**11:06 pm**	
♀	⚺	⚵		**11:26 pm**	

Eastern Standard Time in medium type
Pacific Standard Time in bold type

25 FRIDAY

3rd ♈

☽	⊡	☿	1:17 am	
☽	⊻	♄	2:06 am	
♀	⊻	⚷	2:26 am	
☽	⊡	♀	9:23 am	**6:23 am**
☽	⊡	♇	10:10 am	**7:10 am**
☽	☍	♂	10:55 am	**7:55 am**
☽	✶	♃	11:49 am	**8:49 am**
☽	♂	♄	2:15 pm	**11:15 am**
☿	⊼	♆	3:02 pm	**12:02 pm**
☉	△	♇	3:40 pm	**12:40 pm**
♀	□	♇	6:27 pm	**3:27 pm**
☽	□	♀	10:11 pm	**7:11 pm**
☽	♂	⚷		**10:06 pm**

26 SATURDAY

3rd ♈

☽	♂	⚷	1:06 am	
☽	♂	⚷	3:10 am	**12:10 am**
☽	∟	♄	3:32 am	**12:32 am**
☽	□	♆	4:11 am	**1:11 am**
♂	△	♃	5:16 am	**2:16 am**
♀	⊻	☉	5:20 am	**2:20 am**
☽	△	☿	5:35 am	**2:35 am** ☽ v/c
☽	□	✶	11:49 am	**8:49 am**
☽	⊼	♇	11:57 am	**8:57 am**
☽	□	☉	1:29 pm	**10:29 am**
☽	△	♀	1:38 pm	**10:38 am**
♇	∟	✶	3:26 pm	**12:26 pm**
♀	∟	♂	6:04 pm	**3:04 pm**
☽	□	♅	6:45 pm	**3:45 pm**
♄	∟	⚷	7:25 pm	**4:25 pm**

☽ enters ♉	6:54 am	**3:54 am**
4th Quarter	1:29 pm	**10:29 am**
☿ enters ♍	7:42 pm	**4:42 pm**

27 SUNDAY

4th ♉

☽	✶	♄	5:32 am	**2:32 am**
☽	□	♃	3:38 pm	**12:38 pm**
☽	⊼	♂	5:28 pm	**2:28 pm**
☽	⊻	♄	6:41 pm	**3:41 pm**
♀	⊡	♄	6:47 pm	**3:47 pm**
☽	△	♀		**10:57 pm**

JULY

S	M	T	W	T	F	S
		1	2	3	4	5
6	7	8	9	10	11	12
13	14	15	16	17	18	19
20	21	22	23	24	25	26
27	28	29	30	31		

Eastern Standard Time in medium type
Pacific Standard Time in bold type

28 MONDAY

☽	△	♀	1:57 am	
☽	⊼	⚷	6:14 am	3:14 am
☽	⊻	⚸	9:01 am	6:01 am
☽	△	♆	9:08 am	6:08 am ☽ v/c
♆	⊡	⚸	3:41 pm	12:41 pm
☽	□	☿	4:17 pm	1:17 pm
☽	☍	♇	5:20 pm	2:20 pm
☽	✶	⚷	7:23 pm	4:23 pm
☽	⊡	♂	9:47 pm	6:47 pm
☽	∟	♄	9:49 pm	6:49 pm
♀	⊼	♅	10:22 pm	7:22 pm
♂	☍	♄	10:25 pm	7:25 pm
☽	✶	☉	11:09 pm	8:09 pm
☽	△	♅		9:19 pm
☽	□	♀		9:31 pm

4th ♉

☽ enters ♊   12:04 pm   **9:04 am**

29 TUESDAY

☽	△	♅	12:19 am	
☽	□	♀	12:31 am	
☿	□	♇	3:47 am	12:47 am
☽	⊡	♀	4:42 am	1:42 am
☽	⊡	⚷	9:44 am	6:44 am
☽	□	☊	11:16 am	8:16 am
☽	⊡	♆	12:30 pm	9:30 am
☽	∟	⚸	12:52 pm	9:52 am
☉	☍	♅	2:29 pm	11:29 am
☽	△	♃	9:47 pm	6:47 pm
☽	∟	✶		9:11 pm
☽	✶	♄		10:31 pm
☽	△	♂		11:47 pm ☽ v/c

4th ♊

30 WEDNESDAY

☽	∟	✶	12:11 am	
☽	✶	♄	1:31 am	
☽	△	♂	2:47 am	☽ v/c
☽	⊡	♅	3:59 am	12:59 am
☽	∟	☉	5:07 am	2:07 am
☽	⊼	♀	7:59 am	4:59 am
☽	△	⚷	1:50 pm	10:50 am
♀	⊡	♀	2:48 pm	11:48 am
☽	⊼	♆	4:27 pm	1:27 pm
☽	✶	⚸	5:19 pm	2:19 pm
☽	⊼	♇		10:05 pm
☽	⊡	♃		10:42 pm

4th ♊

☽ enters ♋   7:38 pm   **4:38 pm**

31 THURSDAY

☽	⊼	♇	1:05 am	
☽	⊡	♃	1:42 am	
☿	⊻	✶	5:02 am	2:02 am
☽	⊻	✶	5:37 am	2:37 am
☽	✶	☿	5:39 am	2:39 am
☿	⊡	♄	7:23 am	4:23 am
☽	⊼	♅	8:13 am	5:13 am
☽	⊻	☉	11:48 am	8:48 am
☽	✶	♀	2:33 pm	11:33 am
☽	△	☊	7:14 pm	4:14 pm

4th ♋

♌ **LEO** ♌
Fixed • Fire
Rules 5th House
Ruled by Sun
Rules heart and back
Keyword: Faith
Keynote: I WILL

1 FRIDAY

☽	⊡	♇	5:48 am	**2:48 am**
☽	⊼	♃	6:09 am	**3:09 am**
☿	⊼	♅	10:32 am	**7:32 am**
☽	□	♄	10:38 am	**7:38 am**
☽	∟	☿	1:14 pm	**10:14 am**
☽	□	♂	2:45 pm	**11:45 am**
☽	☍	♀	4:14 pm	**1:14 pm**
☽	∟	♀	10:40 pm	**7:40 pm**
☽	□	⚷	11:44 pm	**8:44 pm**
☽	⊡	☊	11:59 pm	**8:59 pm**
☽	☍	♆		**11:00 pm** ☽ v/c

4th ♋
♄ ℞   10:01 am   **7:01 am**

LAMMAS

2 SATURDAY

☽	☍	♆	2:00 am	☽ v/c
☽	□	⚳	3:55 am	**12:55 am**
♀	∟	⚷	10:04 am	**7:04 am**
♀	☍	☊	10:48 am	**7:48 am**
☽	△	♇	11:04 am	**8:04 am**
♂	□	♀	1:09 pm	**10:09 am**
☊	⊡	⚷	2:40 pm	**11:40 am**
♅	☍	✳	5:23 pm	**2:23 pm**
☽	☍	♅	6:18 pm	**3:18 pm**
☽	♂	✳	6:21 pm	**3:21 pm**
☿	⊡	♀	6:58 pm	**3:58 pm**
☽	⊻	☿	9:21 pm	**6:21 pm**

4th ♋
☽ enters ♌   5:27 am   **2:27 am**

3 SUNDAY

☽	♂	☉	3:14 am	**12:14 am**
☽	⊼	☊	5:14 am	**2:14 am**
☿	∟	♂	7:03 am	**4:03 am**
☽	⊻	♀	7:30 am	**4:30 am**
♀	⊡	♆	8:06 am	**5:06 am**
☽	☍	♃	4:35 pm	**1:35 pm**
☽	△	♄	9:50 pm	**6:50 pm**
☉	⊼	☊		**10:16 pm**
☽	⊼	♀		**11:28 pm**

1st ♌
New Moon   3:14 am   **12:14 am**

4 MONDAY

1st ♌

			EST		PST	
☉	⊼	♃	1:16	am		
☽	⊼	☿	2:28	am		
☽	✶	♂	5:10	am	2:10 am	☽ v/c
☽	✶	⚷	11:43	am	8:43 am	
♀	⚼	⚸	12:21	pm	9:21 am	
☽	⊼	♆	1:35	pm	10:35 am	
☽	△	⚸	4:33	pm	1:33 pm	
☽	□	♇	11:00	pm	8:00 pm	

☽ enters ♍   5:15 pm   **2:15 pm**

5 TUESDAY

1st ♍

			EST		PST	
☽	⚼	♄	4:05	am	1:05 am	
☽	⊼	♅	6:16	am	3:16 am	
☽	⚼	♀	8:11	am	5:11 am	
☽	⊻	⚷	9:13	am	6:13 am	
☽	⊔	♂	1:07	pm	10:07 am	
☽	♂	☿	2:43	pm	11:43 am	
☽	☍	♃	4:53	pm	1:53 pm	
☽	⊔	⚸	6:18	pm	3:18 pm	
☽	⚼	♆	7:55	pm	4:55 pm	
☽	⊻	☉	8:57	pm	5:57 pm	
☽	⚼	⚸	11:24	pm	8:24 pm	
☽	♂	♀			11:50 pm	

6 WEDNESDAY

1st ♍

			EST		PST	
☽	♂	♀	2:50	am		
☽	⊼	♃	4:37	am	1:37 am	
☽	⊼	♄	10:35	am	7:35 am	
☽	⚼	♅	12:42	pm	9:42 am	
☽	△	♀	2:09	pm	11:09 am	
☿	☍	♃	4:49	pm	1:49 pm	
☽	⊔	⚷	5:08	pm	2:08 pm	
♀	⊼	♃	6:43	pm	3:43 pm	
☽	⊻	♂	9:18	pm	6:18 pm	
☽	⊻	⚸			10:05 pm	
☽	△	♆			11:26 pm	☽ v/c

⚸ enters ♉   9:28 pm   **6:28 pm**

7 THURSDAY

1st ♍

			EST		PST	
☽	⊻	⚸	1:05	am		
☽	△	♆	2:26	am		☽ v/c
☽	⊔	☉	6:15	am	3:15 am	
☽	⊼	⚸	6:24	am	3:24 am	
☽	⚼	♃	10:52	am	7:52 am	
☽	✶	♇	12:03	pm	9:03 am	
☽	△	♅	7:10	pm	4:10 pm	
♂	⚼	♃			9:23 pm	
☽	✶	⚸			10:03 pm	
☿	⊔	⚸			10:31 pm	

☽ enters ♎   6:17 am   **3:17 am**

8 FRIDAY

1st ♎

♂	⊐	♀	12:23	am		
☽	⚹	♇	1:03	am		
☿	∟	♅	1:31	am		
☽	⊼	♀	5:09	am	**2:09**	**am**
☽	⋁	☿	8:09	am	**5:09**	**am**
☽	⚹	☉	3:24	pm	**12:24**	**pm**
☽	△	♃	4:58	pm	**1:58**	**pm**
☽	∟	♇	6:29	pm	**3:29**	**pm**
☿	⊐	♆	8:07	pm	**5:07**	**pm**
☽	⋁	♀	10:42	pm	**7:42**	**pm**
☽	☍	♄	11:28	pm	**8:28**	**pm**
☽	□	♀			**10:58**	**pm**

9 SATURDAY

1st ♎   ☽ enters ♏   6:50 pm   **3:50 pm**

☽	□	♀	1:58	am			
♀	⊼	♄	6:22	am	**3:22**	**am**	
☉	☍	♃	8:39	am	**5:39**	**am**	
☽	⊐	♀	10:55	am	**7:55**	**am**	
☽	♂	♂	1:16	pm	**10:16**	**am**	
☽	♂	♀	2:10	pm	**11:10**	**am**	
☽	□	♆	2:58	pm	**11:58**	**am**	☽ v/c
☽	∟	☿	4:05	pm	**1:05**	**pm**	
☽	☍	♦	7:40	pm	**4:40**	**pm**	
☽	⋁	♇			**9:27**	**pm**	
♀	⊐	♅			**10:08**	**pm**	

10 SUNDAY

1st ♏

☽	⋁	♇	12:27	am		
♀	⊐	♅	1:08	am		
♀	△	♀	3:02	am	**12:02**	**am**
☽	□	♅	7:09	am	**4:09**	**am**
☽	∟	♀	7:50	am	**4:50**	**am**
♂	♂	♀	9:55	am	**6:55**	**am**
☽	□	⚹	3:34	pm	**12:34**	**pm**
☽	△	♀	4:06	pm	**1:06**	**pm**
♂	□	♆	9:50	pm	**6:50**	**pm**
☽	⚹	☿	11:00	pm	**8:00**	**pm**
♀	⊼	⚹			**10:23**	**pm**

AUGUST

S	M	T	W	T	F	S
					1	2
3	4	5	6	7	8	9
10	11	12	13	14	15	16
17	18	19	20	21	22	23
24	25	26	27	28	29	30
31						

Eastern Standard Time in medium type
Pacific Standard Time in bold type

11　MONDAY

☽	⊼	⚹	1:23 am	
☽	□	♃	3:39 am	**12:39 am**
☽	□	☉	7:43 am	**4:43 am**
☽	⊼	♄	10:23 am	**7:23 am**
☽	⚹	♀	11:53 am	**8:53 am**
☽	⚹	♀	3:54 pm	**12:54 pm**
☽	⊻	⚷		**9:44 pm**
☽	⚹	♆		**9:59 pm** ☽ v/c
☽	⊻	♂		**11:25 pm**

1st ♏

2nd Quarter　　7:43 am　　**4:43 am**

12　TUESDAY

☽	⊻	⚷	12:44 am		
☽	⚹	♆	12:59 am		☽ v/c
☽	⊻	♂	2:25 am		
☽	⊼	♅	6:06 am	**3:06 am**	
☽	♂	♇	10:01 am	**7:01 am**	
☽	⊡	♄	2:31 pm	**11:31 am**	
☽	∟	♀	3:35 pm	**12:35 pm**	
☽	⚹	♅	4:09 pm	**1:09 pm**	
☉	△	♄	5:59 pm	**2:59 pm**	
☽	□	☿	11:53 pm	**8:53 pm**	
☽	△	♅		**11:24 pm**	

2nd ♏

☽ enters ♐　　4:46 am　　**1:46 am**
♇ D　　　　　　　　　　　**10:34 pm**

13　WEDNESDAY

☽	△	♅	2:24 am	
☽	∟	⚷	4:34 am	**1:34 am**
☽	∟	♆	4:35 am	**1:35 am**
☉	⊼	♀	5:49 am	**2:49 am**
♆	□	⚷	7:15 am	**4:15 am**
☽	∟	♂	7:19 am	**4:19 am**
☽	□	☿	9:03 am	**6:03 am**
☽	⊡	♅	9:47 am	**6:47 am**
☽	⚹	♃	10:53 am	**7:53 am**
☽	△	♄	5:36 pm	**2:36 pm**
☽	⊻	♀	6:18 pm	**3:18 pm**
☽	∟	♅	7:08 pm	**4:08 pm**
☽	△	☉	7:26 pm	**4:26 pm**

2nd ♐

♇ D　　1:34 am

14　THURSDAY

☽	□	♀	4:02 am	**1:02 am**	☽ v/c
☽	⊡	⚹	6:05 am	**3:05 am**	
☽	⊻	♆	7:08 am	**4:08 am**	
☽	⚹	⚷	7:20 am	**4:20 am**	
☽	⚹	♂	11:02 am	**8:02 am**	
☽	△	♅	12:24 pm	**9:24 am**	
☽	∟	♃	1:00 pm	**10:00 am**	
☽	⊻	♇	3:36 pm	**12:36 pm**	
☽	⊻	♅	9:08 pm	**6:08 pm**	
☽	⊡	☉	11:24 pm	**8:24 pm**	

2nd ♐

♂ enters ♏　　3:42 am　　**12:42 am**
☽ enters ♑　　10:43 am　　**7:43 am**

15 FRIDAY

2nd ♑

☽	⚹	⚳	3:45 am	**12:45 am**
☽	⊼	♅	8:41 am	**5:41 am**
☽	△	☿	1:59 pm	**10:59 am**
☽	⋎	♃	2:14 pm	**11:14 am**
♀	△	♆	3:13 pm	**12:13 pm**
☽	∠	♇	4:57 pm	**1:57 pm**
♀	∠	♅	7:03 pm	**4:03 pm**
☽	□	♄	8:52 pm	**5:52 pm**
♀	⋎	⚷	8:53 pm	**5:53 pm**
☽	☌	♀	8:58 pm	**5:58 pm**
☿	∠	♂	10:48 pm	**7:48 pm**
♂	☍	♆	11:09 pm	**8:09 pm**
☿	⊼	♃	11:11 pm	
☿	⊼	☉	11:17 pm	
☿	∠	♆	11:30 pm	

16 SATURDAY

2nd ♑

☽ enters ≈   12:59 pm   **9:59 am**

☿	⊼	♃	2:11 am	
☽	⊼	☉	2:17 am	
☿	⊡	♆	2:30 am	
☽	∠	⚳	4:24 am	**1:24 am**
♄	□	♀	7:46 am	**4:46 am**
☽	☌	♆	9:32 am	**6:32 am**
☽	□	⚷	10:06 am	**7:06 am**
☽	△	♀	11:11 am	**8:11 am** ☽ v/c
☽	⊡	♆	2:54 pm	**11:54 am**
☽	⊡	☿	2:55 pm	**11:55 am**
☽	□	♂	3:29 pm	**12:29 pm**
☽	⚹	♇	5:35 pm	**2:35 pm**
☽	☌	♅	10:41 pm	**7:41 pm**

17 SUNDAY

2nd ≈

♀ enters ♎   9:31 am   **6:31 am**
☿ R   2:42 pm   **11:42 am**

☿	⊡	♆	3:20 am	**12:20 am**
☽	⋎	⚳	4:25 am	**1:25 am**
☽	☍	♅	11:27 am	**8:27 am**
☽	⊡	♀	1:29 pm	**10:29 am**
☽	☌	♃	2:39 pm	**11:39 am**
☽	⊼	☿	3:08 pm	**12:08 pm**
☽	⋎	♀	9:00 pm	**6:00 pm**
☽	⚹	♄	9:21 pm	**6:21 pm**

AUGUST

S	M	T	W	T	F	S
					1	2
3	4	5	6	7	8	9
10	11	12	13	14	15	16
17	18	19	20	21	22	23
24	25	26	27	28	29	30
31						

Eastern Standard Time in medium type
Pacific Standard Time in bold type

18 MONDAY

2nd ≈

♀	⊓	♃	3:01 am	**12:01 am**		
☽	☍	☉	5:56 am	**2:56 am**	☽ v/c	
☽	⊻	♆	9:36 am	**6:36 am**		
☽	△	♅	10:31 am	**7:31 am**		
♀	⊼	⚵	12:27 pm	**9:27 am**		
☽	✶	⚵	3:09 pm	**12:09 pm**		
☽	⊼	♀	3:22 pm	**12:22 pm**		
☽	△	♂	5:31 pm	**2:31 pm**		
☽	□	♇	5:31 pm	**2:31 pm**		
♂	⊻	♇	5:40 pm	**2:40 pm**		
☽	∟	♀	8:34 pm	**5:34 pm**		
☽	∟	♄	9:07 pm	**6:07 pm**		
☽	⊻	♅	10:23 pm	**7:23 pm**		

Full Moon   5:56 am   **2:56 am**
☽ enters ♓   1:02 pm   **10:02 am**

19 TUESDAY

3rd ♓

☽	♂	♃	3:31 am	**12:31 am**
☽	∟	♆	9:21 am	**6:21 am**
☽	⊓	⚵	10:27 am	**7:27 am**
☽	⊼	♅	12:43 pm	**9:43 am**
☽	⊻	♃	1:54 pm	**10:54 am**
☽	☍	☿	2:28 pm	**11:28 am**
☽	∟	⚵	3:03 pm	**12:03 pm**
☽	⊓	♂	6:20 pm	**3:20 pm**
♀	✶	♇	6:54 pm	**3:54 pm**
☽	✶	♀	8:08 pm	**5:08 pm**
☽	⊻	♄	8:53 pm	**5:53 pm**
☽	∟	♅	10:09 pm	**7:09 pm**

20 WEDNESDAY

3rd ♓

☽	⊼	☉	8:52 am	**5:52 am**		
☽	✶	♆	9:13 am	**6:13 am**	☽ v/c	
☽	⊼	⚵	10:31 am	**7:31 am**		
☽	⊓	♅	1:28 pm	**10:28 am**		
☽	∟	♃	1:39 pm	**10:39 am**		
☉	⊼	♆	2:13 pm	**11:13 am**		
☽	⊻	⚵	3:08 pm	**12:08 pm**		
☽	△	♇	5:20 pm	**2:20 pm**		
♃	☍	♅	5:57 pm	**2:57 pm**		
☽	☍	♀	7:16 pm	**4:16 pm**		
☽	⊼	♂	7:24 pm	**4:24 pm**		
☽	✶	♅	10:09 pm	**7:09 pm**		
♀	⊻	♂	10:56 pm	**7:56 pm**		
☿	⊻	♅		**9:58 pm**		
☽	⊻	♃		**11:51 pm**		

☽ enters ♈   12:45 pm   **9:45 am**

21 THURSDAY

3rd ♈

☿	⊻	♅	12:58 am		
☽	⊻	♃	2:51 am		
☽	⊓	☉	10:48 am	**7:48 am**
☉	✶	⚵	1:16 pm	**10:16 am**
☽	✶	♃	1:47 pm	**10:47 am**
☽	⊼	☿	1:53 pm	**10:53 am**
☽	△	♅	2:39 pm	**11:39 am**
☽	⊓	♇	5:45 pm	**2:45 pm**
☿	⊼	♃	7:03 pm	**4:03 pm**
☽	□	♀	8:11 pm	**5:11 pm**
☽	♂	♄	9:19 pm	**6:19 pm**

22 FRIDAY

3rd ♈

☽	⊥	♃	3:07 am	**12:07 am**	
♀	△	♅	6:34 am	**3:34 am**	
☽	□	♆	10:11 am	**7:11 am**	
☽	☍	⚷	11:57 am	**8:57 am**	
☽	△	☉	1:26 pm	**10:26 am**	☽ v/c
☽	⊡	☿	2:04 pm	**11:04 am**	
☽	☌	⯓	4:39 pm	**1:39 pm**	
☽	⊼	♇	6:46 pm	**3:46 pm**	
☽	☍	♂	11:15 pm	**8:15 pm**	
☽	□	♅	11:42 pm	**8:42 pm**	
☽	⊼	♀		**10:19 pm**	

☽ enters ♉	1:57 pm	**10:57 am**
☉ enters ♍	9:19 pm	**6:19 pm**

SUN ENTERS VIRGO

23 SATURDAY

3rd ♉

☽	⊼	♀	1:19 am		
☽	✳	♃	3:59 am	**12:59 am**	
♂	□	♅	8:53 am	**5:53 am**	
☽	△	☿	2:44 pm	**11:44 am**	
☽	□	♃	3:52 pm	**12:52 pm**	
☽	□	✳	7:04 pm	**4:04 pm**	
☽	△	♀	10:35 pm	**7:35 pm**	
☽	⋎	♄		**9:08 pm**	

24 SUNDAY

3rd ♉

☽	⋎	♄	12:08 am		
♀	⊼	♃	4:41 am	**1:41 am**	
☽	⊡	♀	5:43 am	**2:43 am**	
⚷	⊥	⚷	11:38 am	**8:38 am**	
☽	△	♆	1:50 pm	**10:50 am**	☽ v/c
☉	△	⯓	3:02 pm	**12:02 pm**	
☽	⊼	⚷	4:11 pm	**1:11 pm**	
☽	⋎	⯓	8:57 pm	**5:57 pm**	
☽	□	☉	9:24 pm	**6:24 pm**	
☽	☍	♇	11:04 pm	**8:04 pm**	
☽	⊡	♀		**9:57 pm**	
☽	⊥	♄		**11:43 pm**	

4th Quarter	9:24 pm	**6:24 pm**
☽ enters ♊	5:56 pm	**2:56 pm**

AUGUST

S	M	T	W	T	F	S
					1	2
3	4	5	6	7	8	9
10	11	12	13	14	15	16
17	18	19	20	21	22	23
24	25	26	27	28	29	30
31						

25 MONDAY

4th ♊

		EST		PST	
☽	⊼	♀	12:57 am		
☽	⊥	♄	2:43 am		
☽	△	♅	4:09 am	1:09 am	
☽	⊼	♂	6:27 am	3:27 am	
☽	□	☊	8:00 am	5:00 am	
☽	△	♀	11:12 am	8:12 am	
☽	⊼	♆	4:53 pm	1:53 pm	
☽	□	☿	5:43 pm	2:43 pm	
☽	⊼	⚷	7:34 pm	4:34 pm	
☉	□	♇	8:47 pm	5:47 pm	
☽	△	♃	8:59 pm	5:59 pm	
☽	⊥	⚸		9:19 pm	
☽	✳	⚵		11:59 pm	

26 TUESDAY

☽ enters ♋   10:10 pm

4th ♊

		EST		PST	
☽	⊥	⚸	12:19 am		
☽	✳	⚵	2:59 am		
☽	⊼	♀	4:09 am	1:09 am	
☽	✳	♄	6:07 am	3:07 am	☽ v/c
♂	△	☊	6:48 am	3:48 am	
☽	⊼	♅	7:36 am	4:36 am	
☿	⊼	♆	8:27 am	5:27 am	
☽	⊼	♂	11:29 am	8:29 am	
☉	⊼	♀	5:56 pm	2:56 pm	
☽	⊼	♆	8:44 pm	5:44 pm	
☽	△	⚷	11:46 pm	8:46 pm	
☽	⊼	♃		9:45 pm	

27 WEDNESDAY

☽ enters ♋   1:10 am

4th ♋

		EST		PST	
☽	⊼	♃	12:45 am		
☽	✳	⚸	4:28 am	1:28 am	
♀	⊼	⚵	4:34 am	1:34 am	
☽	⊼	♇	6:39 am	3:39 am	
☽	⊥	⚵	8:18 am	5:18 am	
☿	⊼	♀	9:08 am	6:08 am	
☽	✳	☉	9:26 am	6:26 am	
☽	⊼	♅	11:50 am	8:50 am	
☽	△	☊	3:05 pm	12:05 pm	
☽	△	♂	5:26 pm	2:26 pm	
☉	⊼	♄	8:09 pm	5:09 pm	
☽	✳	☿	10:50 pm	7:50 pm	
☽	□	♀		10:19 pm	

28 THURSDAY

4th ♋

		EST		PST	
☽	□	♀	1:19 am		
☽	⊼	♃	5:14 am	2:14 am	
☽	⊼	♇	11:33 am	8:33 am	
☽	☍	♀	12:49 pm	9:49 am	
☽	⊥	⚵	2:24 pm	11:24 am	
☽	□	♄	3:09 pm	12:09 pm	
☉	⊼	♅	3:48 pm	12:48 pm	
☽	⊥	☉	4:51 pm	1:51 pm	
☽	⊼	☊	7:39 pm	4:39 pm	
☽	⊥	☿		11:04 pm	

Eastern Standard Time in medium type
Pacific Standard Time in bold type

29 FRIDAY

4th ♋

☽ ⊥ ☿	2:04 am				
☽ ☍ ♆	6:35 am	3:35 am	☽ v/c		
♄ △ ⚷	8:05 am	5:05 am			
☽ □ ⚷	10:21 am	7:21 am			
☽ □ ♇	2:47 pm	11:47 am			
♀ △ ♃	3:16 pm	12:16 pm			
☿ ✶ ♂	3:58 pm	12:58 pm			
☽ △ ♇	5:03 pm	2:03 pm			
☉ ☍ ♃	10:12 pm	7:12 pm			
☽ ☍ ♅	10:16 pm	7:16 pm			
☽ ⊼ ♃		9:44 pm			
☽ ⊻ ☉		10:01 pm			

⚸ ℞   5:18 am   **2:18 am**
☽ enters ♌   11:19 am   **8:19 am**

30 SATURDAY

4th ♌

☽ ⊼ ♃	12:44 am			
☽ ⊻ ☉	1:01 am			
☽ ⊻ ☿	5:40 am	2:40 am		
☽ □ ♂	7:34 am	4:34 am		
☽ ☍ ♃	3:56 pm	12:56 pm		
☽ ✶ ♀	6:53 pm	3:53 pm		
☽ ⊼ ♀	11:52 pm	8:52 pm		
☽ △ ♄		11:30 pm	☽ v/c	

31 SUNDAY

4th ♌

☽ △ ♄	2:30 am		☽ v/c	
☽ ♂ ⚷	4:27 am	1:27 am		
☿ ♂ ☉	8:42 am	5:42 am		
☽ ⊼ ♆	6:30 pm	3:30 pm		
☽ ✶ ⚷	11:01 pm	8:01 pm		
☽ △ ⚷		11:57 pm		

☽ enters ♍   11:27 pm   **8:27 pm**

♍ VIRGO ♍

Mutable • Earth
Rules 6th House
Ruled by Mercury
Rules intestines
Keyword: Service
Keynote: I ANALYZE

1 MONDAY

☽	△	⚷	2:57 am	
☽	⎿	♀	4:29 am	**1:29 am**
☽	□	♇	5:23 am	**2:23 am**
☽	⊓	♀	6:00 am	**3:00 am**
☽	⊓	♄	8:43 am	**5:43 am**
☽	⊼	♅	10:30 am	**7:30 am**
☽	☍	?	12:04 pm	**9:04 am**
♀	⎿	♇	1:36 pm	**10:36 am**
☽	♂	☿	1:48 pm	**10:48 am**
☽	♂	☉	6:52 pm	**3:52 pm**
♀	□	♀	6:57 pm	**3:57 pm**
☽	⚹	♂	11:41 pm	**8:41 pm**
☽	⊓	♆		**9:55 pm**

4th ♍

New Moon   6:52 pm   **3:52 pm**

PARTIAL ECLIPSE OF THE SUN 9° ♍ 34'

LABOR DAY

2 TUESDAY

☽	⊓	♆	12:55 am	
☽	⊼	♃	4:06 am	**1:06 am**
☽	⎿	⚷	5:47 am	**2:47 am**
☽	⊓	⚷	9:23 am	**6:23 am**
☽	△	♀	12:21 pm	**9:21 am**
☽	⊻	♀	2:23 pm	**11:23 am**
☽	⊼	♄	3:07 pm	**12:07 pm**
☽	⊓	♅	4:57 pm	**1:57 pm**
☽	⊻	⚷	7:55 pm	**4:55 pm**
♀	♂	♄	9:26 pm	**6:26 pm**
☿	♂	?	10:05 pm	**7:05 pm**

1st ♍

⚷ enters ♏   10:11 pm   **7:11 pm**

3 WEDNESDAY

☽	△	♆	7:26 am	**4:26 am**	☽ v/c
☽	⎿	♂	8:03 am	**5:03 am**
☽	⊓	♃	10:24 am	**7:24 am**
☽	⊻	⚷	12:38 pm	**9:38 am**
☿	⊼	♅	1:43 pm	**10:43 am**
☿	⎿	♀	2:55 pm	**11:55 am**
☽	⊼	⚷	3:51 pm	**12:51 pm**
☽	⚹	♇	6:31 pm	**3:31 pm**
♀	⊓	?	9:56 pm	**6:56 pm**
☽	⊻	☿	10:52 pm	**7:52 pm**
☽	△	♅	11:26 pm	**8:26 pm**
☽	⊼	?		**9:02 pm**

1st ♍

☽ enters ♎   12:30 pm   **9:30 am**

4 THURSDAY

☽	⊼	?	12:02 am	
☽	⎿	⚹	3:45 am	**12:45 am**
☽	⊻	☉	1:24 pm	**10:24 am**
☽	⊻	♂	4:20 pm	**1:20 pm**
☽	△	♃	4:38 pm	**1:38 pm**
☉	⊓	♆	7:17 pm	**4:17 pm**
♂	□	♃	9:05 pm	**6:05 pm**
☿	⊓	♄	11:24 pm	**8:24 pm**
☽	⎿	♇		**9:59 pm**
☽	□	♀		**10:03 pm**

1st ♎

Eastern Standard Time in medium type
Pacific Standard Time in bold type

5 FRIDAY

☽	⊥	♇	12:59	am		
☽	□	♀	1:03	am		
☽	⊥	☿	3:36	am	**12:36**	**am**
☽	☍	♄	3:48	am	**12:48**	**am**
☽	⊓	♃	5:53	am	**2:53**	**am**
☽	♂	♀	10:01	am	**7:01**	**am**
☽	⚹	♆	11:21	am	**8:21**	**am**
♅	⊻	♃	1:57	pm	**10:57**	**am**
♇	⊥	♀	2:13	pm	**11:13**	**am**
☽	□	♆	8:06	pm	**5:06**	**pm** ☽ v/c
☽	⊥	☉	10:20	pm	**7:20**	**pm**
☉	⊼	♃			**10:33**	**pm**
☽	♂	⚷			**10:53**	**pm**

☽ enters ♏   1st ♎   **10:10 pm**

6 SATURDAY

☉	⊼	♃	1:33	am		
☽	♂	⚷	1:53	am		
☽	☍	♅	4:12	am	**1:12**	**am**
☽	⊻	♇	7:08	am	**4:08**	**am**
♀	⚹	♆	8:01	am	**5:01**	**am**
☽	⚹	☿	8:20	am	**5:20**	**am**
☽	△	♃	11:24	am	**8:24**	**am**
☽	□	♅	11:44	am	**8:44**	**am**

☽ enters ♏   1:10 am   1st ♏

7 SUNDAY

☽	□	♃	4:08	am	**1:08**	**am**
☽	⚹	☉	6:39	am	**3:39**	**am**
☽	♂	♂	7:44	am	**4:44**	**am**
☽	⚹	♀	12:34	pm	**9:34**	**am**
☽	⊼	♄	3:09	pm	**12:09**	**pm**
☿	□	♇	7:37	pm	**4:37**	**pm**
☉	⊥	⚷	11:41	pm	**8:41**	**pm**
☽	□	♆			**10:02**	**pm**

1st ♏

SEPTEMBER

S	M	T	W	T	F	S
	1	2	3	4	5	6
7	8	9	10	11	12	13
14	15	16	17	18	19	20
21	22	23	24	25	26	27
28	29	30				

8 MONDAY

1st ♏

☽ enters ♐ 11:55 am **8:55 am**

☽ □ ⚵	1:02 am		
☽ ⚺ ♀	3:34 am	**12:34 am**	
☽ ⚹ ♆	6:59 am	**3:59 am**	☽ v/c
☿ ⚼ ♀	7:10 am	**4:10 am**	
☽ ⚺ ⚷	1:08 pm	**10:08 am**	
☽ ⚻ ⚶	2:29 pm	**11:29 am**	
☽ □ ☿	5:15 pm	**2:15 pm**	
☽ ∠ ♀	5:23 pm	**2:23 pm**	
☽ ☌ ♇	5:40 pm	**2:40 pm**	
☉ ⚼ ⚶	6:28 pm	**3:28 pm**	
☽ ⚼ ♄	7:50 pm	**4:50 pm**	
☽ □ ⚳	8:42 pm	**5:42 pm**	
☽ ⚹ ♅	9:51 pm	**6:51 pm**	
☉ ⚹ ♂	11:26 pm	**8:26 pm**	

9 TUESDAY

1st ♐

2nd Quarter 8:32 pm **5:32 pm**

☿ D 8:33 pm **5:33 pm**

☽ ∠ ♀	10:52 am	**7:52 am**	
☽ ∠ ♆	11:19 am	**8:19 am**	
☽ ⚹ ♃	1:08 pm	**10:08 am**	
♀ □ ♆	3:51 pm	**12:51 pm**	
☽ ∠ ⚷	5:34 pm	**2:34 pm**	
☽ ⚼ ⚶	6:26 pm	**3:26 pm**	
☽ ⚺ ♂	8:01 pm	**5:01 pm**	
☽ □ ☉	8:32 pm	**5:32 pm**	
☽ ⚺ ♀	9:22 pm	**6:22 pm**	
☽ △ ♄	11:39 pm	**8:39 pm**	
☽ ∠ ♅		**10:41 pm**	

10 WEDNESDAY

2nd ♐

☽ enters ♑ 7:24 pm **4:24 pm**

☽ ∠ ♅	1:41 am		
☉ △ ♀	7:38 am	**4:38 am**	
☽ △ ⚵	11:15 am	**8:15 am**	
☽ ⚺ ♆	2:44 pm	**11:44 am**	
☽ ∠ ♃	4:20 pm	**1:20 pm**	
☽ ⚹ ♀	4:56 pm	**1:56 pm**	☽ v/c
☽ ⚹ ⚷	9:02 pm	**6:02 pm**	
☽ △ ⚶	9:27 pm	**6:27 pm**	
♂ ⚹ ♀	10:04 pm	**7:04 pm**	
☽ △ ☿		**9:23 pm**	
☽ ∠ ♂		**9:34 pm**	
☽ ⚺ ♇		**9:50 pm**	
☽ ⚹ ⚳		**11:47 pm**	

11 THURSDAY

2nd ♑

♀ enters ♏ 9:17 pm **6:17 pm**

☽ △ ☿	12:23 am		
☽ ∠ ♂	12:34 am		
☽ ⚺ ♇	12:50 am		
☽ ⚹ ⚳	2:47 am		
☿ ⚼ ♀	3:58 am	**12:58 am**	
☽ ⚺ ♅	4:35 am	**1:35 am**	
☉ ⚻ ♄	12:09 pm	**9:09 am**	
☽ ⚼ ⚵	2:47 pm	**11:47 am**	
☽ ⚺ ♃	6:37 pm	**3:37 pm**	
⚶ ☍ ⚷	10:54 pm	**7:54 pm**	
♄ ∠ ⚳		**10:41 pm**	
☿ □ ♇		**11:00 pm**	
☽ ☌ ♀		**11:35 pm**	

12 FRIDAY

2nd ♑

♄	∟	♃	1:41 am			♀ D	7:40 pm	**4:40 pm**
☿	□	♇	2:00 am			☽ enters ♒	11:10 pm	**8:10 pm**
☽	♂	♀	2:35 am				
☽	∟	♇	3:01 am	12:01 am			
☽	⊡	☿	3:02 am	12:02 am			
☽	✶	♂	4:02 am	1:02 am			
☽	∟	♃	4:29 am	1:29 am			
☽	□	♄	4:31 am	1:31 am			
☽	△	☉	5:48 am	2:48 am			
♂	⊼	♄	1:22 pm	10:22 am			
☉	⊡	♅	4:18 pm	1:18 pm			
♀	☍	⚷	5:06 pm	2:06 pm			
☽	⊼	✶	5:20 pm	2:20 pm			
☽	♂	♆	6:45 pm	3:45 pm	☽ v/c		
♀	♂	⚷	9:05 pm	6:05 pm		☽ □ ⚷	10:08 pm
♀	□	⚷		9:43 pm		☽ □ ♀	10:27 pm

13 SATURDAY

2nd ♒

☽	□	⚷	12:43 am	
☽	□	⚷	1:08 am	
☽	□	♀	1:27 am	
☽	✶	♇	4:19 am	1:19 am
☽	⊼	☿	5:05 am	2:05 am
☽	⌄	♃	5:22 am	2:22 am
☽	♂	♅	7:41 am	4:41 am
☽	⊡	☉	8:49 am	5:49 am
☿	♂	♃	10:59 am	7:59 am
☿	⊡	♄	6:16 pm	3:16 pm
☽	♂	♃	8:40 pm	5:40 pm

14 SUNDAY

2nd ♒

☽	⌄	♀	4:27 am	1:27 am		☽ enters ♓	11:59 pm	**8:59 pm**
☽	✶	♄	6:03 am	3:03 am			
☽	□	♂	8:10 am	5:10 am	☽ v/c		
☽	⊼	☉	10:58 am	7:58 am			
♆	⊼	✶	12:25 pm	9:25 am			
♀	⌄	♇	1:42 pm	10:42 am			
☽	⌄	♆	7:44 pm	4:44 pm			
♀	△	♃	7:50 pm	4:50 pm			
☽	♂	✶	7:59 pm	4:59 pm			
☽	✶	⚷		10:05 pm			
☽	△	⚷		11:15 pm			

SEPTEMBER

S	M	T	W	T	F	S
	1	2	3	4	5	6
7	8	9	10	11	12	13
14	15	16	17	18	19	20
21	22	23	24	25	26	27
28	29	30				

15 MONDAY

2nd ♓

☽	✶	⚷	1:05	am		
☽	△	♋	2:15	am		
☽	⊾	♀	4:30	am	1:30	am
☽	□	♇	4:58	am	1:58	am
☽	♂	?	5:18	am	2:18	am
☽	⊾	♄	5:58	am	2:58	am
☽	△	♀	6:13	am	3:13	am
☽	♂	☿	7:51	am	4:51	am
☽	⊻	♅	8:03	am	5:03	am
☿	⊼	♅	11:32	am	8:32	am
☽	⊾	♆	7:32	pm	4:32	pm
☽	⊻	♃	8:26	pm	5:26	pm
☽	⊾	⚷			9:38	pm
☽	⊡	♋			11:12	pm

16 TUESDAY

2nd ♓

Full Moon   1:51 pm   **10:51 am**
☽ enters ♈   11:25 pm   **8:25 pm**

☽	⊾	⚷	12:38	am			
☽	⊡	♋	2:12	am			
☽	✶	♀	4:16	am	1:16	am	
♇	□	?	5:27	am	2:27	am	
☽	⊻	♄	5:35	am	2:35	am	
♀	□	♅	5:50	am	2:50	am	
☽	⊾	♅	7:44	am	4:44	am	
☽	⊡	♀	7:53	am	4:53	am	
☽	△	♂	10:04	am	7:04	am	
☽	♂	☉	1:51	pm	10:51	am	
☽	✶	♆	7:10	pm	4:10	pm	☽ v/c
☽	⊾	♃	7:59	pm	4:59	pm	
☽	⊼	⚹	8:56	pm	5:56	pm	
☽	⊻	⚷			9:05	pm	
☽	⊼	⚷			11:03	pm	

TOTAL ECLIPSE OF THE MOON 23° ♓ 56'

17 WEDNESDAY

3rd ♈

☽	⊻	⚷	12:05	am		
☽	⊼	⚷	2:03	am		
☽	⊻	?	4:06	am	1:06	am
☽	△	♇	4:25	am	1:25	am
☽	✶	♅	7:22	am	4:22	am
☽	⊼	♀	9:31	am	6:31	am
☽	⊼	☿	10:22	am	7:22	am
☽	⊡	♂	10:51	am	7:51	am
?	⊾	♀	2:59	pm	11:59	am
☽	✶	♃	7:37	pm	4:37	pm
☽	⊡	⚹	9:26	pm	6:26	pm

18 THURSDAY

3rd ♈

☽ enters ♉   11:21 pm   **8:21 pm**

☽	⊾	?	3:40	am	12:40	am	
☽	□	♀	3:50	am	12:50	am	
☽	⊡	♇	4:17	am	1:17	am	
☽	♂	♄	4:53	am	1:53	am	
☽	⊼	♂	11:56	am	8:56	am	
☽	⊡	☿	12:16	pm	9:16	am	
☽	⊼	☉	4:52	pm	1:52	pm	
☽	□	♆	6:57	pm	3:57	pm	☽ v/c
☽	△	⚹	10:19	pm	7:19	pm	
☽	♂	⚷	11:34	pm	8:34	pm	
☽	♂	⚷			11:29	pm	

19 FRIDAY

☽ ☍ ⚷	2:29 am		
☽ ✶ ♆	3:37 am	12:37 am	
☽ ⚻ ♇	4:35 am	1:35 am	
☽ □ ♅	7:30 am	4:30 am	
☽ ☍ ♀	1:58 pm	10:58 am	
☽ △ ☿	3:01 pm	12:01 pm	
☽ ⊡ ☉	7:13 pm	4:13 pm	
☽ □ ♃	8:09 pm	5:09 pm	
☉ △ ♆		9:06 pm	

3rd ♉

♇ enters ♉   7:28 pm   **4:28 pm**

20 SATURDAY

☉ △ ♆	12:06 am		
✶ △ ♇	4:37 am	1:37 am	
☽ △ ♀	5:06 am	2:06 am	
☽ ⚺ ♄	5:50 am	2:50 am	
☉ ⊡ ♃	8:09 am	5:09 am	
☽ ☍ ♂	4:03 pm	1:03 pm	
☽ △ ♆	8:55 pm	5:55 pm	
☽ △ ☉	10:31 pm	7:31 pm	☽ v/c
☽ ⚺ ♇		10:17 pm	
☽ □ ✶		11:14 pm	

3rd ♉

✶ enters ♍   7:53 am   **4:53 am**
☽ enters ♊   **10:38 pm**

21 SUNDAY

☽ ⚺ ♇	1:17 am		
☽ □ ✶	2:14 am		
☽ ⚻ ⚷	5:26 am	2:26 am	
☽ □ ♇	5:34 am	2:34 am	
☽ ⊡ ♀	6:54 am	3:54 am	
☽ ☍ ♇	7:17 am	4:17 am	
☽ ∟ ♄	7:26 am	4:26 am	
☽ △ ♅	10:16 am	7:16 am	
♇ △ ⚷	11:28 am	8:28 am	
☿ ⊡ ♆	1:51 pm	10:51 am	
☿ ⚻ ♃	6:10 pm	3:10 pm	
☽ ⚻ ♀	10:01 pm	7:01 pm	
☽ ⊡ ♆	11:12 pm	8:12 pm	
☽ △ ♃	11:39 pm	8:39 pm	
☽ □ ☿		9:22 pm	

3rd ♊

☽ enters ♊   1:38 am

SEPTEMBER

S	M	T	W	T	F	S
		1	2	3	4	5	6
7	8	9	10	11	12	13
14	15	16	17	18	19	20
21	22	23	24	25	26	27
28	29	30				

22 MONDAY

3rd ♊

☽	□	☿	12:22 am	
☽	∟	♆	3:24 am	**12:24 am**
♄	⊼	♇	5:50 am	**2:50 am**
☽	⊼	♀	8:18 am	**5:18 am**
☉	⊼	♆	8:30 am	**5:30 am**
☽	∧	♀	9:40 am	**6:40 am**
☽	✶	♄	9:59 am	**6:59 am** ☽ v/c
☽	⊼	♅	1:01 pm	**10:01 am**
♀	□	♃	4:29 pm	**1:29 pm**
☽	⊼	♂		**9:12 pm**
☿	⊼	♆		**9:29 pm**
☽	⊼	♆		**11:27 pm**
☽	⊼	♃		**11:50 pm**

☉ enters ♎ 6:56 pm **3:56 pm**

FALL EQUINOX • SUN ENTERS LIBRA

23 TUESDAY

3rd ♊

☽	⊼	♂	12:12 am	
☿	⊼	♀	12:29 am	
☽	⊼	♆	2:27 am	
☽	⊼	♃	2:50 am	
☽	⊼	♀	3:53 am	**12:53 am**
☽	✶	♆	6:27 am	**3:27 am**
☽	□	☉	8:35 am	**5:35 am**
☽	✶	♅	10:09 am	**7:09 am**
☽	△	♃	11:06 am	**8:06 am**
☽	△	♂	12:11 pm	**9:11 am**
☽	⊼	♇	1:43 pm	**10:43 am**
☽	⊼	♅	4:45 pm	**1:45 pm**
♄	□	♀	5:14 pm	**2:14 pm**

☽ enters ♋ 7:33 am **4:33 am**
4th Quarter 8:35 am **5:35 am**

24 WEDNESDAY

4th ♋

☽	⊼	♂	6:00 am	**3:00 am**
♃	☍	♅	6:23 am	**3:23 am**
☽	⊼	♃	6:59 am	**3:59 am**
☽	△	♀	11:01 am	**8:01 am**
☉	⊼	♃	1:22 pm	**10:22 am**
☽	⊼	♃	3:16 pm	**12:16 pm**
☽	∟	♅	3:43 pm	**12:43 pm**
☽	✶	☿	4:02 pm	**1:02 pm**
♂	✶	♆	5:52 pm	**2:52 pm**
☽	□	♄	5:55 pm	**2:55 pm**
☽	☍	♀	6:11 pm	**3:11 pm**
☽	⊼	♇	6:23 pm	**3:23 pm**
☉	⊻	♅	9:13 pm	**6:13 pm**
☿	∟	♃		**9:09 pm**

25 THURSDAY

4th ♋

☿	∟	♃	12:09 am	
☿	⊼	♄	5:34 am	**2:34 am**
☿	△	♀	8:43 am	**5:43 am**
☽	☍	♆	11:45 am	**8:45 am**
☽	△	♂	12:51 pm	**9:51 am** ☽ v/c
☉	⊻	♃	2:16 pm	**11:16 am**
☽	□	♆	3:10 pm	**12:10 pm**
☽	⊼	♃	8:16 pm	**5:16 pm**
☽	⊻	♅	10:12 pm	**7:12 pm**
☽	□	♃	10:45 pm	**7:45 pm**
☽	✶	☉	11:23 pm	**8:23 pm**
☽	△	♇	11:51 pm	**8:51 pm**
☽	∟	☿		**11:08 pm**
☽	☍	♅		**11:52 pm**

☽ enters ♌ 5:13 pm **2:13 pm**

26 FRIDAY

4th ♌

☽	∟	☿	2:08 am		
☽	☍	♅	2:52 am		
☉	⚹	♇	5:12 am	2:12 am	
☿	⊡	♅	7:19 am	4:19 am	
☽	☍	♃	5:43 pm	2:43 pm	
♇	∟	♀	5:53 pm	2:53 pm	
⚹	⚹	♋	7:05 pm	4:05 pm	
♄	⊡	⚹	8:22 pm	5:22 pm	
♂	⊼	⚷	9:01 pm	6:01 pm	

27 SATURDAY

4th ♌

☽	□	♀	4:24 am	1:24 am	
☽	△	♄	4:58 am	1:58 am	
☽	⊼	♀	5:59 am	2:59 am	
☽	∟	☉	8:07 am	5:07 am	
♀	⊼	♄	9:57 am	6:57 am	
☽	⊻	☿	1:19 pm	10:19 am	
☉	△	♅	5:40 pm	2:40 pm	
♇	□	⚹	9:48 pm	6:48 pm	
♀	⚹	♀	10:10 pm	7:10 pm	
☽	⊼	♆	11:49 pm	8:49 pm	
♀	⊡	⚹		11:10 pm	
☽	△	⚷		11:20 pm	

28 SUNDAY

4th ♌

♀	⊡	⚹	2:10 am		
☽	△	⚷	2:20 am		
☽	□	♂	4:43 am	1:43 am	☽ v/c
☽	☍	♃	7:54 am	4:54 am	
☽	⊡	♄	11:10 am	8:10 am	
☽	⚹	⚷	11:50 am	8:50 am	
☽	□	♇	12:25 pm	9:25 am	
☽	⊡	♀	12:37 pm	9:37 am	
☽	☌	⚹	12:57 pm	9:57 am	
☽	⊼	♅	3:18 pm	12:18 pm	
☽	⊻	☉	5:18 pm	2:18 pm	

☽ enters ♍	5:28 am	2:28 am
♂ enters ♐	5:22 pm	2:22 pm

SEPTEMBER

S	M	T	W	T	F	S
	1	2	3	4	5	6
7	8	9	10	11	12	13
14	15	16	17	18	19	20
21	22	23	24	25	26	27
28	29	30				

29 MONDAY

4th ♍

☽	⊼ ♇	6:19 am	**3:19 am**	
☽	⊼ ♃	6:21 am	**3:21 am**	
☽	⊼ ⚷	8:20 am	**5:20 am**	
☽	⊼ ♄	5:32 pm	**2:32 pm**	
☽	∟ ♅	6:44 pm	**3:44 pm**	
☽	△ ♀	7:25 pm	**4:25 pm**	
☽	⊼ ♅	9:50 pm	**6:50 pm**	
☽	✳ ♀	11:52 pm	**8:52 pm**	
♂	□ ♇		**11:49 pm**	

30 TUESDAY

4th ♍

☽ enters ♎   6:33 pm   **3:33 pm**

♂	□ ♇	2:49 am		
☿	⊼ ♃	11:02 am	**8:02 am**	
☿	△ ♇	11:13 am	**8:13 am**	
☽	⊼ ♃	12:50 pm	**9:50 am**	
☽	△ ♇	12:52 pm	**9:52 am**	
☽	♂ ☿	1:09 pm	**10:09 am**	☽ v/c
☽	⊼ ⚷	2:19 pm	**11:19 am**	
☿	⊼ ⚷	8:06 pm	**5:06 pm**	
☽	⊼ ♇	8:21 pm	**5:21 pm**	
☽	✳ ♂	9:39 pm	**6:39 pm**	
☽	⊻ ♅		**10:36 pm**	
☽	✳ ♇		**10:37 pm**	
♅	⊼ ✳		**11:37 pm**	

♎ LIBRA ♎
Cardinal • Air
Rules 7th House
Ruled by Venus
Rules the kidneys
Keyword: Harmony
Keynote: WE ARE

1 WEDNESDAY

1st ♎

New Moon   11:53 am   **8:53 am**
☿ enters ♎   **9:38 pm**

☽	⊻ ♅	1:36 am		
☽	<✳ ♇	1:37 am		
♅	⊼ ✳	2:38 am		
♇	⊻ ♅	3:34 am	**12:34 am**	
☽	△ ♅	4:19 am	**1:19 am**	
☽	⊻ ✳	4:22 am	**1:22 am**	
☽	∟ ♀	9:35 am	**6:35 am**	
☽	♂ ☉	11:53 am	**8:53 am**	
☽	△ ♃	7:11 pm	**4:11 pm**	
☽	⊼ ♇		**11:25 pm**	

ROSH HASHANAH BEGINS

2 THURSDAY
1st ♎

☿ enters ♎ 12:38 am

☽	⊓	♃	2:25 am	
☽	∟	♂	5:53 am	**2:53 am**
☽	☍	♄	5:59 am	**2:59 am**
♂	⊓	♄	7:21 am	**4:21 am**
☽	∟	♇	7:59 am	**4:59 am**
☽	□	♀	8:44 am	**5:44 am**
☿	⊼	♃	10:07 am	**7:07 am**
☽	∟	★	11:48 am	**8:48 am**
☽	⊻	♀	6:58 am	**3:58 am**
☽	□	♆		**10:22 pm**	☽ v/c
☽	☍	⚷		**10:41 pm**

3 FRIDAY
1st ♎

☽ enters ♏ 6:58 am **3:58 am**

☽	□	♆	1:22 am		☽ v/c
☽	☍	⚷	1:41 am	
☽	△	♃	8:11 am	**5:11 am**
☽	⊻	☿	12:17 pm	**9:17 am**
☽	⊻	♂	1:44 pm	**10:44 am**
☽	⊻	♇	2:01 pm	**11:01 am**
☽	☌	⚷	2:32 pm	**11:32 am**
☽	□	♅	4:28 pm	**1:28 pm**
♆	□	⚷	6:27 pm	**3:27 pm**
♂	☌	♇	6:44 pm	**3:44 pm**
☽	✶	★	6:50 pm	**3:50 pm**
☿	✶	♇		**9:03 pm**

ROSH HASHANAH ENDS

4 SATURDAY
1st ♏

☿	✶	♇	12:03 am	
☿	✶	♂	3:22 am	**12:22 am**
☿	⊻	⚷	4:29 am	**1:29 am**
☽	⊻	☉	5:11 am	**2:11 am**
♂	⊻	⚷	6:38 am	**3:38 am**
☽	□	♃	6:56 am	**3:56 am**
♂	∟	♀	2:26 pm	**11:26 am**
☿	△	♅	4:21 pm	**1:21 pm**
☽	⊼	♄	5:09 pm	**2:09 pm**
☽	✶	♀	8:44 pm	**5:44 pm**
☽	∟	☿	10:53 pm	**7:53 pm**
☉	△	♃		**11:41 pm**

5 SUNDAY
1st ♏

☽ enters ♐ 5:43 pm **2:43 pm**

☉	△	♃	2:41 am	
♀	⊼	⚷	7:20 am	**4:20 am**
☽	⊼	⚷	11:31 am	**8:31 am**
☽	☌	♀	12:01 pm	**9:01 am**
♂	✶	♅	12:08 pm	**9:08 am**
☽	✶	♆	12:18 pm	**9:18 am**	☽ v/c
☽	∟	☉	12:58 pm	**9:58 am**
♀	✶	♆	3:05 pm	**12:05 pm**
☽	□	♃	6:27 pm	**3:27 pm**
☿	⊻	★	8:22 pm	**5:22 pm**
☽	⊓	♄	9:59 pm	**6:59 pm**
☽	☌	♇		**9:38 pm**
☽	⊻	★		**10:39 pm**
☽	∟	♀		**10:58 pm**
☽	✶	♅		**11:51 pm**

6 MONDAY

1st ♐

		EST		PST	
☽	☌	♇	12:38 am		
☽	⊻	⚷	1:39 am		
☽	⊥	♀	1:58 am		
☽	✶	♅	2:51 am		
☽	☌	♂	3:44 am	12:44 am	
☽	□	⚷	7:13 am	4:13 am	
☽	✶	☿	8:35 am	5:35 am	
☽	⊡	⚸	3:37 pm	12:37 pm	
☽	✶	♃	4:46 pm	1:46 pm	
☽	⊥	♆	4:56 pm	1:56 pm	
☽	✶	☉	7:59 pm	4:59 pm	
☽	△	♄		11:14 pm	☽ v/c

7 TUESDAY

1st ♐

		EST		PST	
☽	△	♄	2:14 am		☽ v/c
☽	⊥	⚷	6:18 am	3:18 am	
☽	⊻	♀	6:34 am	3:34 am	
☽	⊥	♅	7:08 am	4:08 am	
☽	△	⚸	7:06 am	4:06 am	
☽	⊥	♃	8:44 pm	5:44 pm	
☽	⊻	♆	8:53 pm	5:53 pm	
☽	⊻	♀		10:56 pm	
☽	✶	♄		11:25 pm	

♃ D   11:21 pm   **8:21 pm**
☽ enters ♑   **11:04 pm**

8 WEDNESDAY

1st ♑

		EST		PST	
☽	⊻	♀	1:56 am		
☽	✶	♄	2:25 am		
☉	⊡	♄	5:36 am	2:36 am	
♀	□	♃	7:18 am	4:18 am	
☽	⊻	♇	8:46 am	5:46 am	
☽	✶	⚷	10:12 am	7:12 am	
☽	⊻	♅	10:43 am	7:43 am	
☽	⊻	♂	2:46 pm	11:46 am	
☽	△	⚷	4:46 pm	1:46 pm	
☿	△	♃	7:01 pm	4:01 pm	
♀	⊥	☉	9:16 pm	6:16 pm	
☽	⊻	♃	11:58 pm	8:58 pm	
☽	□	☿		9:43 pm	

☽ enters ♑   2:04 am
♀ enters ♐   3:25 am   **12:25 am**
♆ D   6:22 pm   **3:22 pm**

9 THURSDAY

1st ♑

		EST		PST	
☽	□	☿	12:43 am		
☽	⊥	♃	5:22 am	2:22 am	
☽	□	☉	7:22 am	4:22 am	
☽	⊥	♀	7:28 am	4:28 am	
☽	□	♄	8:38 am	5:38 am	
☽	⊥	♇	11:44 am	8:44 am	
☽	☌	☿	1:35 pm	10:35 am	
☽	⊥	♂	6:58 pm	3:58 pm	
☽	⊡	⚷	8:17 pm	5:17 pm	
♀	⊡	♄	8:39 pm	5:39 pm	
☉	☍	♄	11:26 pm	8:26 pm	
☽	□	⚸	11:55 pm	8:55 pm	
☽	☌	♆		11:35 pm	☽ v/c

2nd Quarter   7:22 am   **4:22 am**

10 FRIDAY

☽	☌	♆	2:35 am		☽ v/c
☽	⊻	♃	7:34 am	4:34 am	
♅	□	♅	11:09 am	8:09 am	
☿	⊓	♃	11:19 am	8:19 am	
☽	✶	♀	12:01 pm	9:01 am	
☽	✶	♇	1:56 pm	10:56 am	
☽	☌	♅	3:39 pm	12:39 pm	
☽	□	♅	3:41 pm	12:41 pm	
☽	✶	♂	10:17 pm	7:17 pm	
☽	⊼	♃	10:59 pm	7:59 pm	

2nd ♑

☽ enters ≈   7:29 am   **4:29 am**

YOM KIPPUR BEGINS

11 SATURDAY

☽	☌	♃	4:11 am	1:11 am	
☿	☍	♄	11:28 am	8:28 am	
☽	✶	♄	12:04 pm	9:04 am	
☽	△	☿	12:09 pm	9:09 am	
♀	☌	♇	12:41 pm	9:41 am	
☽	△	☉	2:59 pm	11:59 am	☽ v/c
☽	⊻	♀	5:33 pm	2:33 pm	
☉	∟	♇	8:53 pm	5:53 pm	
☽	✶	♆		10:57 pm	

2nd ≈

♃ enters ♓   3:51 am   **12:51 am**

YOM KIPPUR ENDS

12 SUNDAY

☽	✶	♆	1:57 am		
☽	⊻	♆	5:21 am	2:21 am	
♂	□	♆	6:38 am	3:38 am	
♀	✶	♅	9:40 am	6:40 am	
☽	☌	♃	9:53 am	6:53 am	
☽	∟	♄	12:47 pm	9:47 am	
☿	∟	♇	3:27 pm	12:27 pm	
☽	□	♇	4:13 pm	1:13 pm	
☽	⊓	☿	4:19 pm	1:19 pm	
♀	⊻	♅	4:25 pm	1:25 pm	
☽	⊓	☉	5:34 pm	2:34 pm	
☽	⊻	♅	5:45 pm	2:45 pm	
♂	⊓	♆	6:14 pm	3:14 pm	
☽	△	♅	6:16 pm	3:16 pm	
☽	□	♀	6:24 pm	3:24 pm	

☽	∟	♀	6:32 pm	3:32 pm
♀	∟	♀	8:20 pm	5:20 pm
♆	⊓	♆	11:23 pm	8:23 pm
☽	∟	♆		11:04 pm
☽	☍	♆		11:12 pm

OCTOBER

S	M	T	W	T	F	S
			1	2	3	4
5	6	7	8	9	10	11
12	13	14	15	16	17	18
19	20	21	22	23	24	25
26	27	28	29	30	31	

13 MONDAY

2nd ♓

☽	∟	♆	2:04 am	
☽	☍	⚷	2:12 am	
☽	□	♂	2:37 am	
☽	⊻	♃	5:46 am	2:46 am
☽	∟	♇	5:50 am	2:50 am
☉	□	♀	10:09 am	7:09 am
☿	□	♀	12:52 pm	9:52 am
☽	⊻	♄	1:00 pm	10:00 am
☿	♂	☉	4:02 pm	1:02 pm
☽	∟	♅	6:00 pm	3:00 pm
☽	⊡	⚷	6:45 pm	3:45 pm
☽	⚹	♀	7:01 pm	4:01 pm
☽	⊼	☉	7:33 pm	4:33 pm
☽	⊼	☿	7:45 pm	4:45 pm
☽	⊻	♆		10:48 pm

COLUMBUS DAY, OBSERVED

14 TUESDAY

2nd ♓

♅ D	3:06 am	**12:06 am**
☽ enters ♈	10:25 am	**7:25 am**

☽	⊻	♆	1:48 am		
☽	∟	♃	5:53 am	2:53 am	
☽	⚹	♆	5:56 am	2:56 am	☽ v/c
☽	⊻	♇	10:11 am	7:11 am	
☿	∟	♀	2:59 pm	11:59 am	
☽	△	♇	4:35 pm	1:35 pm	
☽	⚹	♅	5:58 pm	2:58 pm	
☽	⊼	⚷	6:55 pm	3:55 pm	
☽	△	♀	10:24 pm	7:24 pm	

15 WEDNESDAY

2nd ♈

Full Moon	10:46 pm	**7:46 pm**

☽	⊼	⚷	3:36 am	12:36 am
☽	△	♂	5:03 am	2:03 am
☽	⚹	♃	5:48 am	2:48 am
☽	∟	♇	10:01 am	7:01 am
☽	♂	♄	12:38 pm	9:38 am
☽	⊡	♇	4:30 pm	1:30 pm
☿	☍	♆	6:56 pm	3:56 pm
☽	□	♀	7:22 pm	4:22 pm
♂	∟	♆	9:12 pm	6:12 pm
♂	⚹	♃	9:16 pm	6:16 pm
☽	☍	☉	10:46 pm	7:46 pm
☽	⊡	♀		9:11 pm
☽	♂	♆		9:48 pm
☽	☍	☿		10:40 pm

SUKKOT BEGINS

16 THURSDAY

3rd ♈

☽ enters ♉	10:16 am	**7:16 am**

☽	⊡	♀	12:11 am		
☽	♂	♆	12:48 am		
☽	☍	☿	1:40 am		
☽	⊡	⚷	4:12 am	1:12 am	
☽	□	♆	5:46 am	2:46 am	☽ v/c
☽	⊡	♂	6:12 am	3:12 am	
♀	⊡	♆	7:10 am	4:10 am	
☽	⚹	♃	9:56 am	6:56 am	
☽	⊼	♇	4:35 pm	1:35 pm	
☽	□	♅	5:54 pm	2:54 pm	
☽	☍	⚷	7:19 pm	4:19 pm	
☉	♂	♆	11:39 pm	8:39 pm	
☽	⊼	♀		11:14 pm	

17 FRIDAY

3rd ♉

☽	⚻	♀	2:14 am	
☽	△	♅	5:05 am	**2:05 am**
☽	□	♃	6:03 am	**3:03 am**
☿	⊥	♅	6:59 am	**3:59 am**
☽	⚻	♂	7:41 am	**4:41 am**
☽	⚺	♄	12:43 pm	**9:43 am**
☿	□	♆	2:34 pm	**11:34 am**
☽	△	♀	8:29 pm	**5:29 pm**
☽	⚺	♇		**9:42 pm**

SUKKOT ENDS

18 SATURDAY

3rd ♉

☽ enters ♊   11:27 am   **8:27 am**

☽	⚺	♇	12:42 am		
☽	⚻	☉	3:02 am	**12:02 am**	
☽	△	♆	6:45 am	**3:45 am**	☽ v/c
☽	⚻	☿	8:52 am	**5:52 am**	
☽	□	♃	11:03 am	**8:03 am**	
☽	⊥	♄	1:31 pm	**10:31 am**	
♆	⚼	♅	2:08 pm	**11:08 am**	
☽	☍	♇	6:12 pm	**3:12 pm**	
♃	⚻	♅	6:46 pm	**3:46 pm**	
☽	△	♅	7:28 pm	**4:28 pm**	
☽	⚻	⚷	9:27 pm	**6:27 pm**	
☽	⚼	♀	9:58 pm	**6:58 pm**	
☿	⊥	♂	10:29 pm	**7:29 pm**	
☽	⊥	♇		**10:33 pm**	

19 SUNDAY

3rd ♊

☿ enters ♏   7:08 am   **4:08 am**
♃ D   **10:29 pm**

☽	⊥	♇	1:33 am	
☿	△	♃	3:36 am	**12:36 am**
♀	⊥	♆	5:19 am	**2:19 am**
☽	⚼	☉	6:22 am	**3:22 am**
♀	⚹	♃	7:24 am	**4:24 am**
☽	⚼	♆	8:17 am	**5:17 am**
☽	△	♃	8:26 am	**5:26 am**
☽	☍	♀	8:32 am	**5:32 am**
☽	□	♅	8:49 am	**5:49 am**
☽	☍	♂	12:50 pm	**9:50 am**
☽	⚼	☿	1:56 pm	**10:56 am**
♀	□	♅	2:18 pm	**11:18 am**
☽	⚹	♄	3:08 pm	**12:08 pm**
☽	⚼	♅	9:27 pm	**6:27 pm**
☽	⚼	⚷	11:46 pm	**8:46 pm**
☽	⊥	♀		**9:23 pm**

OCTOBER

S	M	T	W	T	F	S
			1	2	3	4
5	6	7	8	9	10	11
12	13	14	15	16	17	18
19	20	21	22	23	24	25
26	27	28	29	30	31	

Eastern Standard Time in medium type
Pacific Standard Time in bold type

20 MONDAY

☽	⊼	☿	12:23 am	
☽	⚹	⚷	3:15 am	**12:15 am**
☉	□	♆	9:07 am	**6:07 am**
☽	⊼	♆	10:44 am	**7:44 am**
☽	△	☉	10:52 am	**7:52 am** ☽ v/c
☽	⛢	♃	10:59 am	**7:59 am**
☽	△	⚸	3:19 pm	**12:19 pm**
☽	△	☿	8:23 pm	**5:23 pm**
☽	⊼	♇	11:10 pm	**8:10 pm**
☽	⊼	♅		**9:26 pm**

3rd ♊

♃ D   1:29 am
☽ enters ♋   3:46 pm   **12:46 pm**

21 TUESDAY

☽	⊼	♅	12:26 am	
☽	△	☿	3:08 am	**12:08 am**
♂	△	♄	4:08 am	**1:08 am**
☉	⚼	⚷	2:11 pm	**11:11 am**
☽	⊼	♃	2:35 pm	**11:35 am**
☽	⚹	⚷	4:34 pm	**1:34 pm**
☽	⛢	⚸	7:01 pm	**4:01 pm**
☿	⚹	♇	7:21 pm	**4:21 pm**
☽	⊼	♀	7:28 pm	**4:28 pm**
☽	□	♄	9:18 pm	**6:18 pm**
☽	⊼	♂	10:27 pm	**7:27 pm**

3rd ♋

22 WEDNESDAY

☽	⛢	♇	3:13 am	**12:13 am**
☿	□	♅	5:14 am	**2:14 am**
☽	☍	♀	8:25 am	**5:25 am**
☽	□	⚷	9:37 am	**6:37 am**
♀	△	♄	3:51 pm	**12:51 pm**
☽	☍	♆	6:49 pm	**3:49 pm**
☽	⚼	⚷	10:09 pm	**7:09 pm**
☉	△	⚸	10:56 pm	**7:56 pm**
☽	⊼	⚸	11:45 pm	**8:45 pm**
☽	□	☉	11:49 pm	**8:49 pm** ☽ v/c
☽	⛢	♀		**11:56 pm**

3rd ♋

4th Quarter   11:49 pm   **8:49 pm**
☽ enters ♌   **9:11 pm**

23 THURSDAY

☽	⛢	♀	2:56 am	
☽	⛢	♂	5:06 am	**2:06 am**
☿	♂	⚷	7:36 am	**4:36 am**
☽	△	♇	8:17 am	**5:17 am**
☽	☍	♅	9:31 am	**6:31 am**
☽	□	⚷	1:02 pm	**10:02 am**
☽	□	☿	1:47 pm	**10:47 am**
♀	□	⚷	6:57 pm	**3:57 pm**
☽	☍	♃		**9:49 pm**

4th ♌

☽ enters ♌   12:11 am
☉ enters ♏   4:15 am   **1:15 am**

SUN ENTERS SCORPIO

24 FRIDAY

4th ♌

☽	☍	♃	12:49 am		
☽	⊼	⚹	4:42 am	1:42 am	
☽	△	♄	7:22 am	4:22 am	
☽	△	♀	11:31 am	8:31 am	
☽	△	♂	12:46 pm	9:46 am	☽ v/c
☽	△	♆	7:31 pm	4:31 pm	
☽	⊼	☿	8:27 pm	5:27 pm	

25 SATURDAY

4th ♌

☽ enters ♍   12:00 pm   **9:00 am**

☽	⊼	♆	6:26 am	3:26 am
☽	☍	?	11:41 am	8:41 am
☽	⋈	♄	1:26 pm	10:26 am
☽	⚹	☉	5:08 pm	2:08 pm
☽	□	♇	8:36 pm	5:36 pm
☽	⊼	♅	9:45 pm	6:45 pm
☽	⋈	♆		10:19 pm
☽	⚹	♅		11:05 pm

26 SUNDAY

4th ♍

☽	⋈	♆	1:19 am	
☽	⚹	♅	2:05 am	
☽	⋈	♀	3:23 am	12:23 am
♀	☌	♂	6:34 am	3:34 am
♀	∟	♅	7:12 am	4:12 am
♂	∟	♅	7:29 am	4:29 am
☽	⚹	☿	11:33 am	8:33 am
☽	⋈	♆	12:58 pm	9:58 am
☽	⊼	♃	1:46 pm	10:46 am
☽	☌	⚹	7:33 pm	4:33 pm
☽	⊼	♄	7:47 pm	4:47 pm
♄	⊼	⚹		10:41 pm
☽	∟	☉		11:32 pm

DAYLIGHT SAVINGS TIME ENDS 2:00 AM
(Aspect times *not* adjusted for Daylight Savings)

OCTOBER

S	M	T	W	T	F	S
			1	2	3	4
5	6	7	8	9	10	11
12	13	14	15	16	17	18
19	20	21	22	23	24	25
26	27	28	29	30	31	

Eastern Standard Time in medium type
Pacific Standard Time in bold type

27 MONDAY

4th ♍
☽ enters ♎ **10:05 pm**

	EST	PST	
♄ ⚻ ⚵	1:41 am		
☽ ∠ ☉	2:32 am		
☽ ⚼ ♅	4:21 am	**1:21 am**	
☿ □ ♃	4:46 am	**1:46 am**	
☽ □ ♂	5:43 am	**2:43 am**	
☽ □ ♀	6:25 am	**3:25 am**	
☽ ⚻ ⚶	7:17 am	**4:17 am**	
☽ ∠ ⚷	9:02 am	**6:02 am**	
☽ △ ⚴	10:30 am	**7:30 am**	
☉ ⚺ ♇	11:33 am	**8:33 am**	
♀ △ ⚶	2:29 pm	**11:29 am**	
☽ △ ♆	7:34 pm	**4:34 pm**	☽ v/c
☽ ⚼ ♃	8:30 pm	**5:30 pm**	
☽ ∠ ☿	10:49 pm	**7:49 pm**	
☉ □ ♅		**9:11 pm**	
♂ △ ⚶		**9:56 pm**	
☽ ⚻ ⚳		**9:59 pm**	

28 TUESDAY

4th ♎
☽ enters ♎ 1:05 am

	EST	PST
☉ □ ♅	12:11 am	
♂ △ ⚶	12:56 am	
☽ ⚻ ⚳	12:59 am	
☽ ⚹ ♇	9:52 am	**6:52 am**
☽ △ ♅	10:52 am	**7:52 am**
☽ ⚺ ☉	11:50 am	**8:50 am**
☽ ⚺ ⚷	3:51 pm	**12:51 pm**
♀ ∠ ⚷	3:56 pm	**12:56 pm**
☿ ⚻ ♄	11:06 pm	**8:06 pm**

29 WEDNESDAY

4th ♎
⚳ enters ♓ 3:15 am **12:15 am**

	EST	PST
☽ △ ♃	3:01 am	**12:01 am**
☽ ⚼ ⚳	7:24 am	**4:24 am**
☽ ☍ ♄	8:15 am	**5:15 am**
☽ ⚺ ☿	9:41 am	**6:41 am**
☽ ⚺ ⚵	10:25 am	**7:25 am**
♀ ⚺ ⚴	2:33 pm	**11:33 am**
☽ ∠ ♇	4:08 pm	**1:08 pm**
☿ ⚹ ⚵	5:01 pm	**2:01 pm**
☽ ☍ ⚶	6:44 pm	**3:44 pm**
♂ ∠ ⚷	10:12 pm	**7:12 pm**
☽ ⚹ ♂	10:19 pm	**7:19 pm**
☽ □ ⚴		**9:05 pm**
☽ ⚹ ♀		**9:49 pm**

30 THURSDAY

4th ♎
☽ enters ♏ 1:16 pm **10:16 am**

	EST	PST	
☽ □ ⚴	12:05 am		
☽ ⚹ ♀	12:49 am		
☽ □ ♆	7:56 am	**4:56 am**	☽ v/c
☽ △ ⚳	1:26 pm	**10:26 am**	
☽ ∠ ⚵	5:13 pm	**2:13 pm**	
☉ ☌ ⚷	6:40 pm	**3:40 pm**	
☽ ⚺ ♇	9:57 pm	**6:57 pm**	
☽ □ ♅	10:49 pm	**7:49 pm**	

31 FRIDAY

☽	♂	♅	4:17 am	**1:17**	**am**
☽	♂	☉	5:01 am	**2:01**	**am**
☽	∟	♂	5:51 am	**2:51**	**am**
☽	∟	☿	9:07 am	**6:07**	**am**
♂	⊻	♀	1:58 pm	**10:58**	**am**
☽	□	♃	2:45 pm	**11:45**	**am**
☽	⊼	♄	7:07 pm	**4:07**	**pm**
☽	✶	♇	11:26 pm	**8:26**	**pm**
☿	⊼	♆		**9:17**	**pm**

4th ♏

New Moon   5:01 am   **2:01 am**

SAMHAIN • HALLOWEEN

♏ SCORPIO ♏
Fixed • Water
Rules 8th House
Ruled by Pluto
Rules genitals
Keyword: Determined
Keynote: I DESIRE

1 SATURDAY

☿	⊼	♆	12:17 am			
☽	⊼	♆	4:32 am	**1:32**	**am**	
☽	♂	☿	5:13 am	**2:13**	**am**	
♄	∟	♃	11:17 am	**8:17**	**am**	
☽	✶	♀	11:46 am	**8:46**	**am**	
☽	⊻	♂	12:45 pm	**9:45**	**am**	
☽	⊻	♀	4:43 pm	**1:43**	**pm**	
☉	∟	♂	6:12 pm	**3:12**	**pm**	
☽	✶	♆	6:22 pm	**3:22**	**pm**	☽ v/c
☽	⊡	♄	11:47 pm	**8:47**	**pm**	
☽	□	♃	11:55 pm	**8:55**	**pm**	

1st ♏

☽ enters ♐   11:27 pm   **8:27 pm**

ALL SAINTS DAY

2 SUNDAY

☽	♂	♇	7:59 am	**4:59**	**am**
☽	⊡	♆	8:42 am	**5:42**	**am**
☽	✶	♅	8:44 am	**5:44**	**am**
♀	⊻	♆	1:13 pm	**10:13**	**am**
☽	⊻	♅	2:34 pm	**11:34**	**am**
☽	∟	♀	4:47 pm	**1:47**	**pm**
☽	⊻	☉	7:32 pm	**4:32**	**pm**
☽	∟	♆	10:47 pm	**7:47**	**pm**
☽	✶	♃		**9:21**	**pm**

1st ♐

3 MONDAY
1st ♐

			EST	PST
☽	✶	♃	12:21 am	
☽	△	♄	3:55 am	**12:55 am**
♀	∟	♃	9:51 am	**6:51 am**
☽	□	⚷	10:05 am	**7:05 am**
☽	△	⚸	12:22 pm	**9:22 am**
☽	∟	♅	12:53 pm	**9:53 am**
☽	∟	⚴	6:54 pm	**3:54 pm**
☿	✶	♀	7:04 pm	**4:04 pm**
☽	⊻	♀	9:15 pm	**6:15 pm**
♇	⚼	⚸	9:29 pm	**6:29 pm**
☽	⊻	☿	9:29 pm	**6:29 pm**
☽	☌	♂		**9:38 pm**
☽	∟	☉		**10:47 pm**
☽	⊻	♆		**11:41 pm**

4 TUESDAY
1st ♐

			EST	PST
☽	☌	♂	12:38 am	
☽	∟	☉	1:47 am	
☽	⊻	♆	2:41 am	
☽	∟	♃	4:23 am	**1:23 am**
☽	☌	♀	5:48 am	**2:48 am** ☽ v/c
☽	✶	⚴	8:20 am	**5:20 am**
☽	⊻	♇	3:54 pm	**12:54 pm**
☽	⊻	♅	4:32 pm	**1:32 pm**
☽	✶	⚸	10:41 pm	**7:41 pm**

☽ enters ♑   7:31 am   **4:31 am**

GENERAL ELECTION DAY

5 WEDNESDAY
1st ♑

			EST	PST
☽	∟	☿	4:28 am	**1:28 am**
☽	✶	☉	7:24 am	**4:24 am**
☽	⊻	♃	7:53 am	**4:53 am**
☽	□	♄	10:42 am	**7:42 am**
☽	∟	⚴	11:47 am	**8:47 am**
♂	⊻	♆	1:07 pm	**10:07 am**
☉	□	♃	2:27 pm	**11:27 am**
✶	⊼	⚸	2:49 pm	**11:49 am**
♀	✶	⚴	5:30 pm	**2:30 pm**
☽	□	⚸	6:19 pm	**3:19 pm**
☽	△	⚷	6:28 pm	**3:28 pm**
☿	✶	♆	6:49 pm	**3:49 pm**
☽	∟	♇	7:06 pm	**4:06 pm**
☿	⊻	♂		**9:23 pm**

♀ enters ♑   3:50 am   **12:50 am**

6 THURSDAY
1st ♑

			EST	PST
☿	⊻	♂	12:23 am	
☽	☌	♀	4:36 am	**1:36 am**
☽	☌	♆	8:58 am	**5:58 am**
☽	⊻	♂	10:06 am	**7:06 am**
☽	✶	☿	10:42 am	**7:42 am** ☽ v/c
☽	⊻	⚴	2:43 pm	**11:43 am**
☽	⊻	♀	4:15 pm	**1:15 pm**
☽	✶	♇	9:48 pm	**6:48 pm**
☽	⚼	⚷	9:50 pm	**6:50 pm**
☽	☌	♅	10:19 pm	**7:19 pm**
☉	⊼	♄		**9:37 pm**
♂	∟	♃		**11:29 pm**

☽ enters ♒   1:33 pm   **10:33 am**

7 FRIDAY

1st ≈

☉	⊼	♄	12:37	am		
♂	⦣	♃	2:29	am		
☽	□	⚷	4:44	am	1:44	am
☿	⊡	♄	9:52	am	6:52	am
☽	☌	♃	1:24	pm	10:24	am
☽	⦣	♂	1:57	pm	10:57	am
☽	⚹	♄	3:29	pm	12:29	pm
☽	□	☉	4:44	pm	1:44	pm
♅	⊡	⚵	5:31	pm	2:31	pm
☽	⦣	♀	8:29	pm	5:29	pm
☽	⚹	♆	10:22	pm	7:22	pm
☽	⊼	⚵			9:38	pm
☿	□	⚷			10:53	pm

2nd Quarter   4:44 pm   **1:44 pm**
☿ enters ♐   12:42 pm   **9:42 am**

8 SATURDAY

2nd ≈

☽	⊼	⚵	12:38	am			
☿	□	⚷	1:53	am			
☽	⋎	♀	9:51	am	6:51	am	
☽	⋎	♆	1:13	pm	10:13	am	
☽	⦣	♄	5:09	pm	2:09	pm	
☽	⚹	♂	5:11	pm	2:11	pm	☽ v/c
☽	☌	⚷	7:06	pm	4:06	pm	
☽	□	☿	8:57	pm	5:57	pm	
☽	⦣	♆	11:41	pm	8:41	pm	
☽	⚹	♀			9:04	pm	
☽	□	♇			10:38	pm	
☽	⋎	♅			11:05	pm	

☽ enters ♓   5:35 pm   **2:35 pm**
♂ enters ♑   **9:33 pm**

9 SUNDAY

2nd ♓

☽	⚹	♀	12:04	am		
☽	□	♇	1:38	am		
☽	⋎	♅	2:05	am		
☽	△	⚷	8:42	am	5:42	am
☽	⦣	♀	11:42	am	8:42	am
☽	⦣	♆	2:37	pm	11:37	am
☽	⋎	♃	4:53	pm	1:53	pm
☽	⋎	♄	6:20	pm	3:20	pm
☿	⊡	♆	8:48	pm	5:48	pm
☽	△	☉	11:34	pm	8:34	pm
♀	⋎	♇	11:39	pm	8:39	pm
☽	⋎	♆			9:34	pm

♂ enters ♑   12:33 am

NOVEMBER

S	M	T	W	T	F	S
						1
2	3	4	5	6	7	8
9	10	11	12	13	14	15
16	17	18	19	20	21	22
23	24	25	26	27	28	29
30						

10 MONDAY

2nd ♓

☽	⚹	⚷	12:34 am		
☽	⊥	♅	3:16 am	12:16 am	
☽	☍	⚷	4:39 am	1:39 am	
♀	⚺	♅	5:59 am	2:59 am	
☽	⊓	♂	9:58 am	6:58 am	
♂	⚹	♄	11:21 am	8:21 am	
☉	⊼	⚷	12:09 pm	9:09 am	
☽	⚹	♀	1:07 pm	10:07 am	
☽	⚹	♆	3:35 pm	12:35 pm	☽ v/c
☽	⊥	♃	5:58 pm	2:58 pm	
☿	♂	♇	7:17 pm	4:17 pm	
☽	⚺	♄	9:37 pm	6:37 pm	
☽	☐	♂	10:05 pm	7:05 pm	
☿	⚹	♅	11:17 pm	8:17 pm	
☽	⊓	☉		11:12 pm	

☽ enters ♈   7:44 pm   **4:44 pm**

11 TUESDAY

2nd ♈

☽	⊓	☉	2:12 am		
☽	△	♇	3:41 am	12:41 am	
☽	⚹	♅	4:04 am	1:04 am	
☽	△	☿	4:35 am	1:35 am	
☽	☐	♀	5:36 am	2:36 am	
☽	⊼	♄	10:53 am	7:53 am	
☽	⚹	♃	6:44 pm	3:44 pm	
☽	♂	♄	7:36 pm	4:36 pm	
☽	⊥	♄	10:24 pm	7:24 pm	
☽	♂	⚷		10:22 pm	

VETERANS' DAY

12 WEDNESDAY

2nd ♈

☽	♂	⚷	1:22 am		
☽	⊓	♇	4:16 am	1:16 am	
☽	⊼	☉	4:32 am	1:32 am	
☽	⊼	⚹	7:07 am	4:07 am	
☽	⊓	☿	7:46 am	4:46 am	
☿	⚺	♀	8:53 am	5:53 am	
☽	☐	♀	3:03 pm	12:03 pm	
☽	☐	♆	4:43 pm	1:43 pm	☽ v/c
☽	⚹	♃	11:03 pm	8:03 pm	
☽	△	♂		10:44 pm	

☽ enters ♉   8:46 pm   **5:46 pm**

13 THURSDAY

2nd ♉

☽	△	♂	1:44 am		
☽	⊼	♇	4:46 am	1:46 am	
☽	☐	♅	5:06 am	2:06 am	
☽	⊓	⚹	8:10 am	5:10 am	
☽	△	♀	9:57 am	6:57 am	
☽	⊼	☿	10:53 am	7:53 am	
☽	☍	♄	12:17 pm	9:17 am	
☽	☐	♃	8:04 pm	5:04 pm	
☽	⚺	♄	8:23 pm	5:23 pm	
☽	⚺	⚷		10:53 pm	
☿	⚺	♄		11:47 pm	

14 FRIDAY

2nd ♉

| Full Moon | 9:13 am | **6:13 am** |
| ☽ enters ♊ | 10:05 pm | **7:05 pm** |

☽	⊻	♇	1:53 am		
☿	⊻	♃	2:47 am		
☽	⊡	♂	3:38 am	12:38 am	
☽	☍	☉	9:13 am	6:13 am	
☽	△	♅	9:23 am	6:23 am	
☽	⊡	♀	12:19 pm	9:19 am	
☉	⚹	♅	1:04 pm	10:04 am	
☽	△	☿	5:07 pm	2:07 pm	
☽	△	♆	6:01 pm	3:01 pm	☽ v/c
☽	∟	♄	9:05 pm	6:05 pm	
♃	⚹	♄	10:56 pm	7:56 pm	
☽	□	⚷		9:56 pm	
☽	∟	♇		11:33 pm	

15 SATURDAY

3rd ♊

☽	□	⚷	12:56 am		
☽	∟	♇	2:33 am		
♀	⚹	♃	4:15 am	1:15 am	
☽	⊼	♂	5:58 am	2:58 am	
☽	☍	♇	6:27 am	3:27 am	
☽	△	♅	6:45 am	3:45 am	
☽	⊼	♃	2:35 pm	11:35 am	
☽	⊼	♀	3:12 pm	12:12 pm	
♂	⊻	♇	3:44 pm	12:44 pm	
☽	☍	☿	6:11 pm	3:11 pm	
☽	⊡	♀	6:49 pm	3:49 pm	
☽	⊡	♆	7:18 pm	4:18 pm	
♂	⊻	♅	9:27 pm	6:27 pm	
☽	⚹	♄	10:19 pm	7:19 pm	
☽	△	♃	10:36 pm	7:36 pm	☽ v/c
☿	∟	♀		10:42 pm	

16 SUNDAY

3rd ♊

☽ enters ♋	**10:33 pm**

☿	∟	♀	1:42 am		
☽	⚹	♇	3:48 am	12:48 am	
☿	∟	♆	5:31 am	2:31 am	
☽	⊡	♅	8:23 am	5:23 am	
☽	□	♅	1:25 pm	10:25 am	
☽	⊼	☉	3:57 pm	12:57 pm	
☽	⊡	♇	4:40 pm	1:40 pm	
☽	⊼	♀	9:16 pm	6:16 pm	
☽	⊼	♆	9:19 pm	6:19 pm	
♆	☌	♀		9:06 pm	
☽	⊡	♃		9:55 pm	

NOVEMBER						
S	M	T	W	T	F	S
						1
2	3	4	5	6	7	8
9	10	11	12	13	14	15
16	17	18	19	20	21	22
23	24	25	26	27	28	29
30						

17 MONDAY

3rd ♋

Ψ	♂	♀	12:06 am	
☽	⬓	♃	12:55 am	
☽	△	?	5:08 am	**2:08 am**
☿	△	♄	10:29 am	**7:29 am**
☽	⊼	♇	10:35 am	**7:35 am**
☽	⊼	♅	10:52 am	**7:52 am**
☽	☍	♂	1:02 pm	**10:02 am**
☿	✶	♃	6:35 pm	**3:35 pm**
☽	△	⚷	7:39 pm	**4:39 pm**
☽	⬓	☉	8:50 pm	**5:50 pm**
☽	☍	♀	11:42 pm	**8:42 pm**

☽ enters ♋   1:33 am

18 TUESDAY

3rd ♋

☽	□	♄	3:10 am	**12:10 am**
☽	⊼	♃	4:11 am	**1:11 am**
☽	⊼	☿	5:12 am	**2:12 am**
☽	⬓	?	8:38 am	**5:38 am**
☽	□	♆	8:47 am	**5:47 am**
☽	⬓	♇	2:03 pm	**11:03 am**
?	∟	♆	4:03 pm	**1:03 pm**
☽	✶	⚷	9:04 pm	**6:04 pm**
☽	△	☉		**11:59 pm**

19 WEDNESDAY

3rd ♋

☽	△	☉	2:59 am	
☽	☍	Ψ	4:10 am	**1:10 am**	☽ v/c
☽	☍	♀	5:11 am	**2:11 am**
☽	⬓	☿	12:41 pm	**9:41 am**
☽	⊼	?	1:13 pm	**10:13 am**
☿	△	♆	1:22 pm	**10:22 am**
☉	✶	Ψ	6:14 pm	**3:14 pm**
☽	△	♇	6:32 pm	**3:32 pm**
☽	☍	♅	6:47 pm	**3:47 pm**
♀	□	♄		**9:22 pm**
☽	⊼	♂		**9:39 pm**
☽	∟	⚷		**11:30 pm**

☽ enters ♌   8:38 am   **5:38 am**

20 THURSDAY

3rd ♌

♀	□	♄	12:22 am	
☽	⊼	♂	12:39 am	
☽	∟	⚷	2:30 am	
☽	□	⚷	4:45 am	**1:45 am**
☽	△	♄	11:58 am	**8:58 am**
☽	⊼	♀	12:55 pm	**9:55 am**
☽	☍	♃	1:51 pm	**10:51 am**
☉	✶	♀	3:27 pm	**12:27 pm**
☽	△	♆	5:43 pm	**2:43 pm**
☽	△	☿	9:28 pm	**6:28 pm**

21 FRIDAY

☉	⚹	♄	4:15 am	**1:15 am**		
♀	⚺	♃	4:19 am	**1:19 am**		
☽	⚹	♂	8:11 am	**5:11 am**		
☽	⚺	⚳	8:55 am	**5:55 am**		
☽	⊼	♆	2:56 pm	**11:56 am**		
☽	⊼	♀	5:13 pm	**2:13 pm**		
☽	⚼	♄	5:41 pm	**2:41 pm**		
☽	□	☉	6:58 pm	**3:58 pm**	☽ v/c	
☽	⚼	♀	9:06 pm	**6:06 pm**		
☽	⚼	♅	11:28 pm	**8:28 pm**		
☿	⊥	♅	11:39 pm	**8:39 pm**		
☽	☍	⚷		**10:14 pm**		

		3rd ♌
4th Quarter	6:58 pm	**3:58 pm**
☽ enters ♍	7:33 pm	**4:33 pm**
☉ enters ♐		**10:47 pm**

SUN ENTERS SAGITTARIUS-PST

22 SATURDAY

☽	☍	⚷	1:14 am		
☽	□	♇	6:10 am	**3:10 am**	
☽	⊼	♅	6:24 am	**3:24 am**	
☽	△	♂	4:30 pm	**1:30 pm**	
☽	⚹	⚷	5:21 pm	**2:21 pm**	
☽	⚼	♆	9:20 pm	**6:20 pm**	
☽	⊼	♄	11:56 pm	**8:56 pm**	
☽	⚼	♀		**9:17 pm**	
☽	⊼	♃		**11:49 pm**	

	4th ♍
☉ enters ♐	1:47 am

SUN ENTERS SAGITTARIUS-EST

23 SUNDAY

☽	⚼	♀	12:17 am		
☽	⊼	♃	2:49 am		
♀	□	♅	3:26 am	**12:26 am**	
☽	⊼	♅	5:42 am	**2:42 am**	
☽	△	♀	5:54 am	**2:54 am**	
♂	⚹	⚷	8:22 am	**5:22 am**	
☽	⚼	♅	12:58 pm	**9:58 am**	
☽	□	☿	5:21 pm	**2:21 pm**	
☉	⚼	♅	8:43 pm	**5:43 pm**	
☽	♂	⚳	11:24 pm	**8:24 pm**	
☽	⊥	⚷		**9:15 pm**	

	4th ♍

NOVEMBER

S	M	T	W	T	F	S
						1
2	3	4	5	6	7	8
9	10	11	12	13	14	15
16	17	18	19	20	21	22
23	24	25	26	27	28	29
30						

Eastern Standard Time in medium type
Pacific Standard Time in bold type

24 MONDAY

4th ♍

☽	⊥	♅	12:15 am		
☽	△	♆	3:56 am	**12:56 am**	☽ v/c
☽	△	♀	7:34 am	**4:34 am**	
☽	⊓	♃	9:43 am	**6:43 am**	
☽	✳	☉	1:37 pm	**10:37 am**	
☽	⊼	♄	3:10 pm	**12:10 pm**	
☽	✳	♇	7:23 pm	**4:23 pm**	
☽	△	♅	7:34 pm	**4:34 pm**	
♀	⊥	♄	9:58 pm	**6:58 pm**	

☽ enters ♎   8:29 am   **5:29 am**

25 TUESDAY

4th ♎

☽	∨	♅	7:02 am	**4:02 am**	
☽	□	♂	9:41 am	**6:41 am**	
☉	□	♄	11:42 am	**8:42 am**	
☽	☍	♄	12:40 pm	**9:40 am**	
☽	△	♃	4:26 pm	**1:26 pm**	
☽	☍	♆	6:15 pm	**3:15 pm**	
☽	⊓	♃	9:56 pm	**6:56 pm**	
☽	⊥	☉	10:42 pm	**7:42 pm**	
☽	□	♀	11:17 pm	**8:17 pm**	
☽	⊥	♇		**10:41 pm**	

♀ enters ≈   11:26 pm   **8:26 pm**

26 WEDNESDAY

4th ♎

☽	⊥	♇	1:41 am		
✳	⊥	♅	7:13 am	**4:13 am**	
☽	✳	☿	12:36 pm	**9:36 am**	
☽	∨	✳	1:29 pm	**10:29 am**	
☽	□	♆	4:26 pm	**1:26 pm**	☽ v/c
☽	□	♀	9:13 pm	**6:13 pm**	
☿	⊥	♅	10:19 pm	**7:19 pm**	
☿	□	✳		**10:38 pm**	

☽ enters ♏   8:43 pm   **5:43 pm**

27 THURSDAY

4th ♏

☿	□	✳	1:38 am		
☽	△	♃	4:09 am	**1:09 am**	
♀	⊥	☉	6:01 am	**3:01 am**	
♂	□	♄	6:05 am	**3:05 am**	
☽	∨	☉	7:05 am	**4:05 am**	
☽	∨	♇	7:26 am	**4:26 am**	
☽	□	♅	7:36 am	**4:36 am**	
☉	☌	♇	11:34 am	**8:34 am**	
♀	⊥	♇	1:11 pm	**10:11 am**	
☉	✳	♅	1:34 pm	**10:34 am**	
☽	☌	♅	7:07 pm	**4:07 pm**	
☽	⊥	✳	7:38 pm	**4:38 pm**	
☽	⊥	☿	8:51 pm	**5:51 pm**	
☽	⊼	♄	11:42 pm	**8:42 pm**	
☽	✶	♂		**9:54 pm**	

THANKSGIVING DAY

28 FRIDAY

4th ♏

☽	⚹	♂	12:54 am	
☽	□	♃	4:10 am	1:10 am
☽	⊼	♆	5:01 am	2:01 am
☿	⊻	♆	8:34 am	5:34 am
☽	⚹	♀	1:58 pm	10:58 am
☽	⚹	⚷		10:00 pm
☽	⚹	♆		11:30 pm ☽ v/c

29 SATURDAY

4th ♏

☽	⚹	⚷	1:00 am	
☽	⚹	♆	2:30 am	☽ v/c
☽	⊻	☿	3:59 am	12:59 am
☽	⊡	♄	4:13 am	1:13 am
☽	⊥	♂	7:17 am	4:17 am
☽	⚹	♀	8:14 am	5:14 am
☽	⊡	♆	9:24 am	6:24 am
☽	□	♇	2:28 pm	11:28 am
☽	♂	♇	4:52 pm	1:52 pm
☽	⚹	♅	5:01 pm	2:01 pm
☽	⊥	♀	7:59 pm	4:59 pm
☽	♂	☉	9:14 pm	6:14 pm

☽ enters ♐   6:28 am   **3:28 am**
New Moon   9:14 pm   **6:14 pm**

30 SUNDAY

1st ♐

☽	⊻	⚷	4:24 am	1:24 am
☽	⊥	♆	6:31 am	3:31 am
☽	△	♄	8:04 am	5:04 am
☽	⊥	♀	12:41 pm	9:41 am
☽	⊻	♂	12:53 pm	9:53 am
☽	⚹	♃	1:07 pm	10:07 am ☽ v/c
☽	△	♆	1:10 pm	10:10 am
♃	⚹	♆	4:51 pm	1:51 pm
♂	□	♆	5:35 pm	2:35 pm
♂	⊻	♃	5:47 pm	2:47 pm
☽	⊥	♅	8:44 pm	5:44 pm
☽	⊻	♀		10:14 pm

☿ enters ♑   2:11 pm   **11:11 am**

♐ **SAGITTARIUS** ♐

Mutable • Fire

Rules 9th House

Ruled by Jupiter

Rules thighs

Keyword: Freedom

Keynote: I SEE

1 MONDAY

1st ♐

☽ enters ♑   1:38 pm   **10:38 am**

☽ ⊼ ♀	1:14 am		
☽ ∟ ⚷	8:05 am	**5:05 am**	
☽ □ ✶	9:40 am	**6:40 am**	
☽ ⊼ ♆	9:57 am	**6:57 am**	
☽ ☌ ☿	3:11 pm	**12:11 pm**	
☽ ⊼ ♀	4:32 pm	**1:32 pm**	
☽ ∟ ♃	4:41 pm	**1:41 pm**	
☽ ✶ ♄	10:13 pm	**7:13 pm**	
☽ ⊼ ♇	11:48 pm	**8:48 pm**	
♆ △ ✶	11:55 pm	**8:55 pm**	
☽ ⊼ ♅	11:55 pm	**8:55 pm**	

2 TUESDAY

1st ♑

⚷ D   1:03 pm   **10:03 am**

☽ ⊼ ☉	8:18 am	**5:18 am**	
☽ ✶ ⚷	11:17 am	**8:17 am**	
☽ □ ♄	2:11 pm	**11:11 am**	
☽ □ ✶	7:11 pm	**4:11 pm**	
☽ ⊼ ♃	7:48 pm	**4:48 pm**	
☽ ☌ ♂	10:13 pm	**7:13 pm**	
☽ ∟ ♃		**10:22 pm**	
☽ ∟ ♇		**11:34 pm**	

3 WEDNESDAY

1st ♑

☽ enters ♒   6:58 pm   **3:58 pm**

☽ ∟ ♃	1:22 am		
☽ ∟ ♇	2:34 am		
☿ ∟ ♃	3:31 am	**12:31 am**	
☽ ☌ ♀	9:53 am	**6:53 am**	
☿ ⊼ ♀	11:19 am	**8:19 am**	
☽ ∟ ☉	1:01 pm	**10:01 am**	
☽ ☌ ♆	3:29 pm	**12:29 pm**	☽ v/c
☽ △ ✶	4:15 pm	**1:15 pm**	
☽ ☌ ♀	10:56 pm	**7:56 pm**	
☽ ⊼ ☿	11:10 pm	**8:10 pm**	

4 THURSDAY

1st ♒

☽ ⊼ ♃	4:11 am	**1:11 am**	
☽ ✶ ♇	5:01 am	**2:01 am**	
☽ ☌ ♅	5:09 am	**2:09 am**	
☉ ⊼ ⚷	5:18 am	**2:18 am**	
☽ □ ⚷	4:35 pm	**1:35 pm**	
☽ ✶ ☉	5:22 pm	**2:22 pm**	
☽ ✶ ♄	6:50 pm	**3:50 pm**	
☽ ⚼ ✶	7:02 pm	**4:02 pm**	
☉ ∟ ♆	11:05 pm	**8:05 pm**	
☽ ✶ ⚷	11:52 pm	**8:52 pm**	
☽ ☌ ♃		**10:03 pm**	☽ v/c
☽ ∟ ☿		**11:13 pm**	

5 FRIDAY

1st ≈

☽	☌	♃	1:03 am		☽ v/c
☽	⊥	☿	2:13 am		
☽	⩘	♂	5:54 am	2:54 am	
☉	△	♄	12:53 pm	9:53 am	
☽	⩘	♀	4:52 pm	1:52 pm	
☽	⩘	♆	7:49 pm	4:49 pm	
☽	⊼	⚸	8:46 pm	5:46 pm	
☽	⊼	♅	9:32 pm	6:32 pm	
☽	⊥	⚷		10:50 pm	
♂	⊥	☋		11:58 pm	

☽ enters ♓   11:08 pm   **8:08 pm**

6 SATURDAY

1st ♓

☽	⊥	⚸	1:50 am		
♂	⊥	☋	2:58 am		
☽	⩘	♀	4:08 am	1:08 am	
☽	✶	☿	4:41 am	1:41 am	
♂	⊥	♇	6:24 am	3:24 am	
☽	☌	☋	9:03 am	6:03 am	
☽	□	♇	9:09 am	6:09 am	
☽	⩘	♅	9:16 am	6:16 am	
☽	⊥	♂	9:18 am	6:18 am	
♇	□	☋	4:04 pm	1:04 pm	
☽	⊥	♀	7:54 pm	4:54 pm	
☽	△	⚷	8:50 pm	5:50 pm	
☽	⊥	♆	9:39 pm	6:39 pm	
☽	⩘	♄	10:30 pm	7:30 pm	
☽	□	☉		10:10 pm	
♅	⩘	☋		10:31 pm	

2nd Quarter   **10:10 pm**

7 SUNDAY

2nd ♓

☽	□	☉	1:10 am		
♅	⩘	☋	1:31 am		
☽	⩘	⚸	3:37 am	12:37 am	
☽	⩘	♃	5:18 am	2:18 am	
☽	⊥	♀	6:23 am	3:23 am	
☽	⊥	♅	11:01 am	8:01 am	
☽	✶	♂	12:27 pm	9:27 am	
☿	⩘	♀	5:45 pm	2:45 pm	
☽	✶	⚷	10:38 pm	7:38 pm	
☽	⧖	⚷	10:38 pm	7:38 pm	
☽	✶	♆	11:16 pm	8:16 pm	☽ v/c
☽	☍	⚸		10:50 pm	

2nd Quarter   1:10 am
☿ ℞   11:47 am   **8:47 am**
☽ enters ♈   **11:25 pm**

DECEMBER

S	M	T	W	T	F	S
		1	2	3	4	5	6
7	8	9	10	11	12	13
14	15	16	17	18	19	20
21	22	23	24	25	26	27
28	29	30	31			

8 MONDAY

2nd ♈

☽	☍	⚷	1:50 am	
☽	∟	♃	7:06 am	4:06 am
☽	□	☿	8:01 am	5:01 am
☽	⚹	♀	8:25 am	5:25 am
☉	△	♆	12:12 pm	9:12 am
☽	△	♇	12:24 pm	9:24 am
☽	⚹	♅	12:33 pm	9:33 am
☽	⚺	?	1:02 pm	10:02 am
♀	☌	♆	2:31 pm	11:31 am
☽	⚻	⚷		9:15 pm
☽	☌	♄		10:23 pm

☽ enters ♈   2:25 am

9 TUESDAY

2nd ♈

☽	⚻	⚷	12:15 am	
☽	☌	♄	1:23 am	
☽	☌	♆	6:37 am	3:37 am
☽	△	☉	7:58 am	4:58 am
☽	⚹	♃	8:45 am	5:45 am
☿	∟	♃	11:28 pm	10:28 am
☽	⚶	♇	1:47 pm	10:47 am
☽	∟	?	2:47 pm	11:47 am
☽	□	♂	6:07 pm	3:07 pm
☉	⚹	♃	8:59 pm	5:59 pm
☽	□	♆		10:59 pm

⚷ enters ♎   8:18 am   **5:18 am**

10 WEDNESDAY

2nd ♈

☽	□	♆	1:59 am		
☽	□	♀	3:23 am	12:23 am	☽ v/c
☽	⚻	⚷	5:24 am	2:24 am	
☽	△	☿	9:24 am	6:24 am	
☽	⚶	☉	11:08 am	8:08 am	
☽	□	♀	12:03 pm	9:03 am	
☽	⚻	♇	3:04 pm	12:04 pm	
☽	□	♅	3:14 pm	12:14 pm	
☽	⚹	?	4:26 pm	1:26 pm	

☽ enters ♉   5:01 am   **2:01 am**

11 THURSDAY

2nd ♉

☽	☍	⚷	3:10 am	12:10 am
☽	⚺	♄	3:49 am	12:49 am
☉	∟	♀	4:58 am	1:58 am
☽	⚶	⚹	7:05 am	4:05 am
☽	⚺	♆	9:17 am	6:17 am
☽	⚶	☿	9:34 am	6:34 am
☽	□	♃	11:51 am	8:51 am
☽	⚻	☉	2:19 pm	11:19 am
☽	△	♂	11:33 pm	8:33 pm

♀ enters ♒   11:39 pm   **8:39 pm**

12 FRIDAY

2nd ♉

☽ enters ♊		7:36 am	**4:36 am**	
☽ △ ♆	4:40 am	**1:40 am**		☽ v/c
☽ ∠ ♄	5:08 am	**2:08 am**		
☽ △ ♀	7:53 am	**4:53 am**		
☽ △ ⚵	8:54 am	**5:54 am**		
☽ ⚻ ☿	9:33 am	**6:33 am**		
☽ ∠ ⚶	10:47 am	**7:47 am**		
☽ △ ⚴	3:49 pm	**12:49 pm**		
☿ □ ⚵	5:06 pm	**2:06 pm**		
☽ ☍ ♇	5:56 pm	**2:56 pm**		
☽ △ ♅	6:06 pm	**3:06 pm**		
☽ □ ⚳	8:06 pm	**5:06 pm**		
☉ ∠ ♅	11:05 pm	**8:05 pm**		
☿ ⚺ ♀		**10:18 pm**		
☽ ⚼ ♂		**11:36 pm**		

13 SATURDAY

2nd ♊

☿ enters ♐	1:06 pm	**10:06 am**	
Full Moon	9:38 pm	**6:38 pm**	
☿ ⚺ ♀	1:18 am		
☽ ⚼ ♂	2:36 am		
☽ ⚼ ♆	6:20 am	**3:20 am**	
☽ ⚻ ⚷	6:34 am	**3:34 am**	
☽ ✶ ♄	6:45 am	**3:45 am**	
☽ ⚼ ♀	10:28 am	**7:28 am**	
☽ ✶ ⚶	12:39 pm	**9:39 am**	
☽ △ ♃	3:41 pm	**12:41 pm**	
☽ ⚼ ⚴	6:12 pm	**3:12 pm**	
☽ ⚼ ♅	8:02 pm	**5:02 pm**	
☽ ☍ ☉	9:38 pm	**6:38 pm**	
♄ ⚻ ⚷		**11:38 pm**	

14 SUNDAY

3rd ♊

☽ enters ♋	11:25 am	**8:25 am**	
♄ ⚻ ⚷	2:38 am		
☽ ⚻ ♂	6:11 am	**3:11 am**	
☽ ⚻ ♆	8:30 am	**5:30 am**	
☽ ⚼ ⚷	8:54 am	**5:54 am**	
☽ ☍ ☿	9:40 am	**6:40 am**	☽ v/c
☽ ⚻ ♀	1:32 pm	**10:32 am**	
☽ □ ⚵	1:44 pm	**10:44 am**	
☿ ∠ ⚷	5:26 pm	**2:26 pm**	
☽ ⚼ ♃	6:21 pm	**3:21 pm**	
☽ ⚻ ⚴	9:11 pm	**6:11 pm**	
☿ ⚺ ♆	10:14 pm	**7:14 pm**	
☽ ⚻ ♇	10:20 pm	**7:20 pm**	
☽ ⚻ ♅	10:33 pm	**7:33 pm**	
☽ △ ⚳		**10:29 pm**	

DECEMBER

S	M	T	W	T	F	S
	1	2	3	4	5	6
7	8	9	10	11	12	13
14	15	16	17	18	19	20
21	22	23	24	25	26	27
28	29	30	31			

15 MONDAY

3rd ♋

☽	△	♃	1:29 am	
♀	△	♆	4:20 am	1:20 am
☿	⊼	♂	7:40 am	4:40 am
☽	□	♄	11:37 am	8:37 am
☽	△	⚷	11:55 am	8:55 am
☽	□	♇	6:11 pm	3:11 pm
☽	⊼	♃	9:48 pm	6:48 pm
♂	☌	♆		9:19 pm
☽	⚻	♇		10:36 pm

16 TUESDAY

3rd ♋

♂	☌	♆	12:19 am		
☽	⚻	♇	1:36 am		
☽	⚻	♃	5:20 am	2:20 am	
☽	⊼	☉	7:54 am	4:54 am	
☽	⊼	☿	11:05 am	8:05 am	
☽	☍	♆	2:59 pm	11:59 am	
☽	☍	♂	3:54 pm	12:54 pm	☽ v/c
☽	⚹	⚷	9:27 pm	6:27 pm	
☽	☍	♀	9:57 pm	6:57 pm	
☿	☌	☉		11:53 pm	

♄ D   5:06 am   **2:06 am**
☽ enters ♌   5:58 pm   **2:58 pm**

17 WEDNESDAY

3rd ♌

☿	☌	☉	2:53 am	
☽	☍	♀	5:43 am	2:43 am
☽	△	♇	5:44 am	2:44 am
☽	☍	♅	6:01 am	3:01 am
♇	⚹	♀	6:28 am	3:28 am
☽	⊼	♃	10:07 am	7:07 am
☽	⚻	☿	12:38 pm	9:38 am
☽	⚻	☉	2:40 pm	11:40 am
♅	☌	♀	7:33 pm	4:33 pm
☽	△	♄	7:43 pm	4:43 pm
☽	□	⚷	8:35 pm	5:35 pm
☽	∟	♆		11:41 pm

♂ enters ♒   **10:37 pm**

18 THURSDAY

3rd ♌

☽	∟	♆	2:41 am		
☽	△	♇	3:11 am	12:11 am	
☽	☍	♃	7:26 am	4:26 am	
☽	△	☿	2:51 pm	11:51 am	
☽	△	☉	10:34 pm	7:34 pm	☽ v/c
☽	⊼	♆		10:00 pm	
☽	⚻	♄		10:06 pm	

♂ enters ♒   1:37 am

19 FRIDAY

3rd ♌

☽	⊼	♆	1:00 am	
☽	⊡	♄	1:06 am	
☽	⊼	♂	5:49 am	2:49 am
☽	⊻	♅	8:48 am	5:48 am
☽	⊡	♆	9:02 am	6:02 am
☽	⊼	♀	9:48 am	6:48 am
☿	⊾	♀	4:19 pm	1:19 pm
☽	□	♇	4:38 pm	1:38 pm
☽	⊼	♅	4:58 pm	1:58 pm
☽	⊼	♀	5:59 pm	2:59 pm
☽	☍	♃	10:26 pm	7:26 pm
☿	⊾	♅		10:30 pm

☽ enters ♍   3:59 am   **12:59 am**

20 SATURDAY

3rd ♍

☿	⊾	♅	1:30 am	
☉	⊻	♆	4:35 am	1:35 am
☽	⊡	♆	7:09 am	4:09 am
☽	⊼	♄	7:10 am	4:10 am
☽	✳	♀	8:38 am	5:38 am
☽	⊡	♂	2:06 pm	11:06 am
☽	⊼	♆	3:32 pm	12:32 pm
☽	⊡	♀	4:40 pm	1:40 pm
☽	⊼	♃	8:21 pm	5:21 pm
☽	□	☿	9:23 pm	6:23 pm
☽	⊡	♅	11:25 pm	8:25 pm
☉	⊾	♀	11:44 pm	8:44 pm
☽	⊡	♀		10:08 pm

21 SUNDAY

3rd ♍

☽	⊡	♀	1:08 am		
☿	✳	♃	7:01 am	4:01 am	
☽	△	♆	1:42 pm	10:42 am	☽ v/c
☽	⊾	♀	3:24 pm	12:24 pm	
☽	□	☉	4:43 pm	1:43 pm	
♂	△	♅	7:42 am	4:42 am	
☽	♂	♅	10:36 pm	7:36 pm	
☽	△	♂	10:46 pm	7:46 pm	
☽	△	♀	11:42 pm	8:42 pm	

☉ enters ♑   3:07 pm   **12:07 pm**
☽ enters ♎   4:35 pm   **1:35 pm**
4th Quarter   4:43 pm   **1:43 pm**

WINTER SOLSTICE • SUN ENTERS CAPRICORN

DECEMBER

S	M	T	W	T	F	S
	1	2	3	4	5	6
7	8	9	10	11	12	13
14	15	16	17	18	19	20
21	22	23	24	25	26	27
28	29	30	31			

Eastern Standard Time in medium type
Pacific Standard Time in bold type

22 MONDAY

4th ♎

☽	⚼	♃	3:22 am	**12:22 am**	
☽	✶	♇	5:39 am	**2:39 am**	
☽	△	♅	6:03 am	**3:03 am**	
☽	△	♀	8:29 am	**5:29 am**	
☽	⚼	♄	12:48 pm	**9:48 am**	
♀	☌	♂	4:43 pm	**1:43 pm**	
☽	☍	♄	8:09 pm	**5:09 pm**	
☿	∟	♂	8:14 pm	**5:14 pm**	
☽	⚺	⚸	10:10 pm	**7:10 pm**	
☿	∟	♀	10:39 pm	**7:39 pm**	

23 TUESDAY

4th ♎

☽	☍	♆	5:08 am	**2:08 am**	
☽	✶	☿	5:59 am	**2:59 am**	
☽	△	♃	10:15 am	**7:15 am**	
☽	∟	♇	12:05 pm	**9:05 am**	
☿	△	♆	6:37 pm	**3:37 pm**	
☽	⚼	♄	7:47 pm	**4:47 pm**	
☽	□	♆		**11:29 pm**	☽ v/c

CHANUKKAH BEGINS

24 WEDNESDAY

4th ♎   ☽ enters ♏   5:07 am   **2:07 am**

☽	□	♆	2:29 am		☽ v/c
☽	∟	☿	10:32 am	**7:32 am**	
☽	✶	☉	10:49 am	**7:49 am**	
☽	⚺	✶	12:00 pm	**9:00 am**	
☽	□	♀	12:44 pm	**9:44 am**	
☽	□	♂	3:18 pm	**12:18 pm**	
☽	⚺	♇	5:59 pm	**2:59 pm**	
☽	□	♅	6:27 pm	**3:27 pm**	
☽	□	♀	10:08 pm	**7:08 pm**	
☽	△	♄		**11:08 pm**	

CHRISTMAS EVE

25 THURSDAY

4th ♏

☽	△	♃	2:08 am		
☉	□	✶	3:59 am	**12:59 am**	
☽	⚼	♄	7:51 am	**4:51 am**	
☽	☌	⚸	10:14 am	**7:14 am**	
♀	⚺	☉	11:11 am	**8:11 am**	
☽	⚺	☿	2:57 pm	**11:57 am**	
☽	⚼	♆	5:03 pm	**2:03 pm**	
☽	∟	✶	5:42 pm	**2:42 pm**	
☽	∟	☉	6:41 pm	**3:41 pm**	
☽	□	♃	10:10 pm	**7:10 pm**	

CHRISTMAS DAY

26 FRIDAY

4th ♏

♂	⚹	♇	11:05 am	**8:05 am**		
☽	⊞	♄	12:33 pm	**9:33 am**		
☽	⚹	♆	12:47 pm	**9:47 am**	☽ v/c	
♂	☌	♅	7:39 pm	**4:39 pm**		
☽	⊞	⚷	9:48 pm	**6:48 pm**		
☽	⚹	⚸	10:29 pm	**7:29 pm**		
☽	⚹	♀	10:29 pm	**7:29 pm**		
♀	△	⚷	10:59 pm	**7:59 pm**		
☽	⊻	☉		**10:28 pm**		

☽ enters ♐   3:08 pm   **12:08 pm**
♀ ℞   4:15 pm   **1:15 pm**

BOXING DAY

27 SATURDAY

4th ♐

☽	⊻	☉	1:28 am		
☽	☌	♇	3:26 am	**12:26 am**	
☽	⚹	♅	3:57 am	**12:57 am**	
☽	⚹	♂	4:27 am	**1:27 am**	
☽	⚹	♀	8:36 am	**5:36 am**	
☽	□	♃	12:15 pm	**9:15 am**	
☽	△	♄	4:25 pm	**1:25 pm**	
☽	⊔	♆	4:40 pm	**1:40 pm**	
☽	⊻	⚷	7:03 pm	**4:03 pm**	
☽	☌	☿	10:40 pm	**7:40 pm**	
☉	⊔	♃	11:19 pm	**8:19 pm**	
☉	△	⚸		**10:41 pm**	
☽	⊔	♀		**10:56 pm**	

☿ D   6:39 am   **3:39 am**

28 SUNDAY

4th ♐

☽	△	⚸	1:41 am		
☽	⊔	♀	1:56 am		
☉	⊻	♇	3:25 am	**12:25 am**	
☽	⚹	♃	6:41 am	**3:41 am**	☽ v/c
☽	⊔	♅	7:25 am	**4:25 am**	
☽	⊔	♂	9:30 am	**6:30 am**	
☉	⊻	♅	10:36 am	**7:36 am**	
☽	⊔	♀	12:30 pm	**9:30 am**	
☽	⊻	♆	7:45 pm	**4:45 pm**	
☽	⊔	⚷	10:12 pm	**7:12 pm**	

☽ enters ♑   9:49 pm   **6:49 pm**

DECEMBER

S	M	T	W	T	F	S
		1	2	3	4	5	6
7	8	9	10	11	12	13
14	15	16	17	18	19	20
21	22	23	24	25	26	27
28	29	30	31			

Eastern Standard Time in medium type
Pacific Standard Time in bold type

29 MONDAY

4th ♑

☽ ⊻ ♀	4:33 am	**1:33 am**		
☽ □ ⚹	5:29 am	**2:29 am**		
☽ ⊻ ♇	9:36 am	**6:36 am**		
☽ ∟ ♃	9:44 am	**6:44 am**		
☽ ⊻ ♅	10:09 am	**7:09 am**		
☽ ☌ ☉	11:57 am	**8:57 am**		
☽ ⊻ ♂	1:43 pm	**10:43 am**		
☽ ⊻ ♀	3:39 pm	**12:39 pm**		
☽ ⚹ ☋	7:02 pm	**4:02 pm**		
☽ □ ♄	9:53 pm	**6:53 pm**		
☽ ⚹ ⚷		**9:43 pm**		

New Moon   11:57 am   **8:57 am**

30 TUESDAY

1st ♑

☽ ⚹ ⚷	12:43 am			
☽ ⊻ ☿	4:47 am	**1:47 am**		
☽ □ ♆	7:19 am	**4:19 am**		
☽ ∟ ♇	11:46 am	**8:46 am**		
☽ ⊻ ♃	12:13 pm	**9:13 am**		
☽ ∟ ☋	9:32 pm	**6:32 pm**		
☽ ☌ ♆		**9:08 pm**	☽ v/c	

☽ enters ♒   **10:59 pm**

31 WEDNESDAY

1st ♒

☽ ☌ ♆	12:08 am		☽ v/c	
☽ ∟ ☿	7:28 am	**4:28 am**		
☽ ☌ ♀	7:57 am	**4:57 am**		
☽ △ ⚹	10:00 am	**7:00 am**		
☽ ⚹ ♇	1:31 pm	**10:31 am**		
☽ ☌ ♅	2:07 pm	**11:07 am**		
☿ ∟ ♀	4:39 pm	**1:39 pm**		
☽ ⊻ ☉	7:42 pm	**4:42 pm**		
☽ ☌ ♂	8:25 pm	**5:25 pm**		
☽ ☌ ♀	8:28 pm	**5:28 pm**		
☽ ⊻ ☋	11:41 pm	**8:41 pm**		
☽ ⚹ ♄		**10:26 pm**		

☽ enters ♒   1:59 am

CHANUKKAH ENDS • NEW YEAR'S EVE

♑ **CAPRICORN** ♑

Cardinal • Earth

Rules 10th House

Ruled by Saturn

Rules knees and bones

Keyword: Ambition

Keynote: I USE

Eastern Standard Time in medium type
Pacific Standard Time in bold type

1 THURSDAY

1st ♒

☽	✶	♄	1:26 am		
☽	□	⚷	4:29 am	1:29	am
☽	✶	☿	10:05 am	7:05	am
☉	⊼	♀	10:44 am	7:44	am
☽	✶	♆	11:14 am	8:14	am
☽	⊡	✶	11:47 am	8:47	am
☽	☌	♃	4:08 am	1:08	pm	☽ v/c
☽	∠	☉	11:06 am	8:06	pm
☽	∠	♄		11:54	pm

NEW YEAR'S DAY

2 FRIDAY

1st ♒

☽ enters ♓   4:56 am   **1:56 am**

☽	∠	♄	2:54 am		
☽	⊼	♆	3:14 am	12:14	am
☽	⊼	♀	10:01 am	7:01	am
☽	∠	♆	12:58 pm	9:58	am
☉	⊼	♂	1:16 pm	10:16	am
☽	⊼	✶	1:26 pm	10:26	am
☽	□	♇	4:29 pm	1:29	pm
☽	⊼	♅	5:09 pm	2:09	pm
☿	△	♆	5:19 pm	2:19	pm
☽	⊼	♀		9:27	pm
☽	⊼	♂		11:13	pm
☽	✶	☉		11:26	pm

3 SATURDAY

1st ♓

☽	⊼	♀	12:27 am		
☽	⊼	♂	2:13 am		
☽	✶	☉	2:26 am		
☽	☌	♃	3:36 am	12:36	am
☽	⊼	♄	4:20 am	1:20	am
☽	∠	♆	4:40 am	1:40	am
☽	△	⚷	7:37 am	4:37	am
☽	∠	♀	10:52 am	7:52	am
☽	⊼	♆	2:42 pm	11:42	am
☽	□	☿	3:40 pm	12:40	pm
☽	∠	♅	6:38 pm	3:38	pm
☽	⊼	♃	7:40 pm	4:40	pm
☉	✶	♃		10:17	pm
☽	∠	♀		11:26	pm

4 SUNDAY

1st ♓

☽ enters ♈   7:44 am   **4:44 am**

☉	✶	♃	1:17 am		
☽	∠	♀	2:26 am		
☽	∠	♂	5:07 am	2:07	am
☉	□	♄	5:34 am	2:34	am
☽	✶	♆	6:09 am	3:09	am	☽ v/c
☽	⊡	⚷	9:13 am	6:13	am
☽	✶	♀	11:42 am	8:42	am
♄	⊼	♃	4:21 pm	1:21	pm
☽	☍	✶	4:46 pm	1:46	pm
♂	✶	♄	5:58 pm	2:58	pm
♂	⊼	♃	6:56 pm	3:56	pm
☽	△	♇	7:27 pm	4:27	pm
☽	✶	♅	8:12 pm	5:12	pm
☽	∠	♃	9:31 pm	6:31	pm

Eastern Standard Time in medium type
Pacific Standard Time in bold type

JANUARY 1997

DAY	SID.TIME	SUN	MOON	NODE	MERCURY	VENUS	MARS	JUPITER	SATURN	URANUS	NEPTUNE	PLUTO	CERES	PALLAS	JUNO	VESTA	CHIRON
W 1	6:42:44	10 ♑ 36 27 37	28 ♍ 44	02 ♎ R 27	13 ♑ 51	18 ♐ 27	29 ♍ 14	25 ♑ 10	01 ♈ 20	03 ≈ 16	26 ♑ 50	04 ♐ 24	18 ♑ 52	27 ♐ 30	14 ♈ 40	27 ♑ 09	00 ♏ 13
T 2	6:46:41	11 37	10 ♎ 48	02 27	11 46	19 42	29 34	25 25	01 23	03 19	26 52	04 26	19 16	27 55	15 02	27 40	00 18
F 3	6:50:37	12 38 46	23 09	02 26	10 09	20 57	29 53	25 38	01 26	03 23	26 54	04 28	19 40	28 20	15 24	28 11	00 22
S 4	6:54:34	13 39 57	05 ♏ 51	02 23	09 05	22 12	00 ♎ 12	25 52	01 30	03 26	26 57	04 30	20 06	28 44	15 45	28 43	00 27
S 5	6:58:31	14 41 07	18 59	02 19	07 50	23 27	00 31	26 06	01 33	03 29	26 59	04 32	20 27	29 09	16 07	29 14	00 32
M 6	7:02:27	15 42 17	02 ♐ 37	02 11	06 41	24 42	00 49	26 20	01 36	03 33	27 01	04 34	20 51	29 33	16 30	29 45	00 36
T 7	7:06:24	16 43 28	16 44	02 02	05 41	25 57	01 07	26 34	01 40	03 36	27 03	04 36	21 15	29 58	16 53	00 ≈ 17	00 41
W 8	7:10:20	17 44 38	01 ♑ 17	01 51	04 49	27 12	01 25	26 48	01 44	03 40	27 06	04 38	21 39	00 ♑ 22	17 16	00 48	00 45
T 9	7:14:17	18 45 49	16 11	01 40	04 05	28 28	01 41	27 02	01 47	03 43	27 08	04 40	22 03	00 47	17 39	01 19	00 49
F 10	7:18:13	19 46 59	01 ≈ 16	01 29	03 35	29 43	01 58	27 16	01 51	03 47	27 10	04 41	22 27	01 11	18 03	01 51	00 53
S 11	7:22:10	20 48 09	16 22	01 21	03 14	00 ♑ 58	02 14	27 30	01 55	03 50	27 12	04 43	22 51	01 35	18 27	02 22	00 57
S 12	7:26:06	21 49 19	01 ♓ 20	01 15	03 01	02 13	02 29	27 44	01 59	03 53	27 15	04 45	23 15	02 00	18 51	02 53	01 01
M 13	7:30:03	22 50 28	16 02	01 11	02 58 D	03 28	02 44	27 58	02 03	03 57	27 17	04 47	23 39	02 24	19 15	03 25	01 05
T 14	7:34:00	23 51 36	00 ♈ 23	01 10	03 03	04 43	02 59	28 12	02 07	04 00	27 19	04 49	24 03	02 48	19 40	03 56	01 08
W 15	7:37:56	24 52 44	14 21	01 R 09	03 17	05 58	03 13	28 26	02 11	04 04	27 21	04 50	24 27	03 12	20 05	04 27	01 12
T 16	7:41:53	25 53 51	27 57	01 09	03 37	07 13	03 27	28 40	02 16	04 07	27 24	04 52	24 51	03 36	20 30	04 58	01 15
F 17	7:45:49	26 54 57	11 ♉ 13	01 09	04 01	08 29	03 40	28 55	02 20	04 11	27 26	04 54	25 15	04 00	20 55	05 30	01 19
S 18	7:49:46	27 56 02	24 12	01 06	04 37	09 44	03 52	29 09	02 25	04 14	27 28	04 55	25 39	04 24	21 21	06 01	01 22
S 19	7:53:42	28 57 07	06 ♊ 55	01 01	05 15	10 59	04 04	29 23	02 29	04 18	27 31	04 57	26 02	04 48	21 47	06 32	01 25
M 20	7:57:39	29 58 11	19 27	00 53	05 59	12 14	04 16	29 37	02 34	04 21	27 33	04 58	26 26	05 12	22 13	07 04	01 28
T 21	8:01:35	00 ≈ 59 14	01 ♋ 48	00 43	06 46	13 29	04 27	29 51	02 39	04 25	27 35	05 00	26 50	05 35	22 39	07 35	01 31
W 22	8:05:32	02 00 16	14 06	00 32	07 38	14 44	04 37	00 ≈ 05	02 44	04 28	27 37	05 02	27 14	05 59	23 05	08 06	01 34
T 23	8:09:29	03 01 17	26 05	00 20	08 33	15 59	04 47	00 19	02 48	04 32	27 40	05 03	27 38	06 23	23 32	08 37	01 36
F 24	8:13:25	04 02 18	08 ♌ 03	00 10	09 32	17 15	04 56	00 33	02 53	04 36	27 42	05 05	28 02	06 46	23 59	09 08	01 39
S 25	8:17:22	05 03 18	19 56	00 01	10 33	18 30	05 04	00 48	02 59	04 39	27 44	05 06	28 26	07 10	24 26	09 40	01 41
S 26	8:21:18	06 04 17	01 ♍ 45	29 ♍ 54	11 37	19 45	05 12	01 02	03 04	04 43	27 46	05 07	28 49	07 33	24 53	10 11	01 44
M 27	8:25:15	07 05 15	13 33	29 50	12 44	21 00	05 19	01 16	03 09	04 46	27 49	05 09	29 13	07 57	25 20	10 42	01 46
T 28	8:29:11	08 06 13	25 22	29 49	13 52	22 15	05 26	01 30	03 14	04 50	27 51	05 10	29 37	08 20	25 48	11 13	01 48
W 29	8:33:08	09 07 10	07 ♎ 17	29 49	15 03	23 30	05 32	01 44	03 19	04 53	27 53	05 12	00 ≈ 01	08 43	26 16	11 44	01 50
T 30	8:37:04	10 08 06	19 21	29 50	16 15	24 45	05 37	01 58	03 25	04 57	27 55	05 13	00 24	09 06	26 44	12 15	01 52
F 31	8:41:01	11 09 01	01 ♏ 40	29 51	17 30	26 01	05 42	02 12	03 30	05 00	27 58	05 14	00 48	09 29	27 12	12 47	01 53

EPHEMERIS IS CALCULATED FOR MIDNIGHT GREENWICH MEAN TIME.

FEBRUARY 1997

DAY	SID.TIME	SUN	MOON	NODE	MERCURY	VENUS	MARS	JUPITER	SATURN	URANUS	NEPTUNE	PLUTO	CERES	PALLAS	JUNO	VESTA	CHIRON
S 1	8:44:58	12 ≈ 09 56	14 ♏ 17	29 ♍℞ 51	18 ♑ 46	27 ♑ 16	05 ♎ 46	02 ≈ 26	03 ♈ 36	05 ≈ 04	28 ♑ 00	05 ♐ 15	01 ≈ 12	09 ♑ 52	27 ♈ 40	13 ≈ 18	01 ♏ 55
S 2	8:48:54	13 10 50	27 19	29 49	20 03	28 31	05 49	02 40	03 42	05 07	28 02	05 16	01 36	10 15	28 09	13 49	01 57
M 3	8:52:51	14 11 43	10 ♐ 48	29 46	21 22	29 46	05 52	02 54	03 47	05 11	28 04	05 18	01 59	10 38	28 37	14 20	01 58
T 4	8:56:47	15 12 36	24 47	29 40	22 42	01 ≈ 01	05 54	03 08	03 53	05 14	28 07	05 19	02 23	11 01	29 06	14 51	01 59
W 5	9:00:44	16 13 27	09 ♑ 15	29 34	24 03	02 16	05 55	03 22	03 59	05 18	28 09	05 20	02 47	11 23	29 35	15 22	02 00
T 6	9:04:40	17 14 18	24 07	29 27	25 25	03 31	05 ℞ 55	03 36	04 05	05 21	28 11	05 21	03 10	11 46	00 ♉ 04	15 53	02 01
F 7	9:08:37	18 15 07	09 ≈ 17	29 21	26 49	04 47	05 55	03 50	04 11	05 25	28 13	05 22	03 34	12 09	00 34	16 24	02 02
S 8	9:12:33	19 15 55	24 33	29 16	28 13	06 02	05 54	04 04	04 17	05 28	28 15	05 23	03 57	12 31	01 03	16 55	02 03
S 9	9:16:30	20 16 42	09 ♓ 46	29 13	29 39	07 17	05 52	04 18	04 23	05 31	28 17	05 24	04 21	12 53	01 33	17 26	02 04
M 10	9:20:27	21 17 27	24 46	29 D 11	01 ≈ 05	08 32	05 49	04 32	04 29	05 35	28 20	05 25	04 44	13 16	02 02	17 57	02 04
T 11	9:24:23	22 18 10	09 ♈ 25	29 11	02 33	09 47	05 46	04 45	04 35	05 38	28 22	05 26	05 08	13 38	02 32	18 28	02 05
W 12	9:28:20	23 18 52	23 39	29 12	04 01	11 02	05 42	04 59	04 41	05 42	28 24	05 27	05 31	14 00	03 02	18 59	02 05
T 13	9:32:16	24 19 33	07 ♉ 27	29 14	05 31	12 17	05 37	05 13	04 48	05 45	28 26	05 27	05 54	14 22	03 32	19 30	02 05
F 14	9:36:13	25 20 12	20 49	29 15 ℞	07 01	13 32	05 31	05 27	04 54	05 48	28 28	05 28	06 18	14 44	04 02	20 00	02 05
S 15	9:40:09	26 20 50	03 ♊ 48	29 15	08 32	14 47	05 25	05 41	05 00	05 52	28 30	05 29	06 41	15 05	04 33	20 31	02 ℞ 05
S 16	9:44:06	27 21 25	16 28	29 14	10 05	16 02	05 17	05 54	05 07	05 55	28 32	05 30	07 04	15 27	05 03	21 02	02 05
M 17	9:48:02	28 22 00	28 52	29 11	11 38	17 17	05 09	06 08	05 13	05 58	28 34	05 30	07 27	15 49	05 34	21 33	02 05
T 18	9:51:59	29 22 32	11 ♋ 03	29 07	13 12	18 32	05 00	06 21	05 20	06 02	28 36	05 31	07 51	16 10	06 05	22 03	02 05
W 19	9:55:56	00 ♓ 23 02	23 05	29 02	14 47	19 48	04 51	06 35	05 26	06 05	28 38	05 32	08 14	16 32	06 35	22 34	02 04
T 20	9:59:52	01 23 31	05 ♌ 01	28 57	16 22	21 03	04 40	06 49	05 33	06 08	28 40	05 32	08 37	16 53	07 06	23 05	02 04
F 21	10:03:49	02 23 57	16 53	28 52	17 59	22 18	04 29	07 02	05 40	06 12	28 42	05 33	09 00	17 15	07 37	23 35	02 03
S 22	10:07:45	03 24 22	28 42	28 48	19 37	23 33	04 17	07 15	05 47	06 15	28 44	05 33	09 23	17 35	08 09	24 06	02 02
S 23	10:11:42	04 24 46	10 ♍ 31	28 45	21 15	24 48	04 04	07 29	05 53	06 18	28 46	05 34	09 46	17 56	08 40	24 36	02 01
M 24	10:15:38	05 25 08	22 22	28 D 44	22 55	26 03	03 51	07 42	06 00	06 21	28 48	05 34	10 09	18 17	09 11	25 07	02 00
T 25	10:19:35	06 25 28	04 ♎ 17	28 44	24 35	27 18	03 37	07 55	06 07	06 24	28 50	05 35	10 32	18 38	09 43	25 37	02 00
W 26	10:23:31	07 25 47	16 19	28 46	26 17	28 33	03 22	08 09	06 14	06 28	28 52	05 35	10 55	18 58	10 14	26 08	01 58
T 27	10:27:28	08 26 04	28 30	28 47	28 00	29 47	03 06	08 22	06 21	06 31	28 54	05 36	11 18	19 19	10 46	26 38	01 57
F 28	10:31:25	09 26 20	10 ♏ 53	28 49	29 43	01 ♓ 02	02 50	08 35	06 28	06 34	28 56	05 36	11 41	19 39	11 17	27 09	01 54

EPHEMERIS IS CALCULATED FOR MIDNIGHT GREENWICH MEAN TIME.

MARCH 1997

DAY	SID.TIME	SUN	MOON	NODE	MERCURY	VENUS	MARS	JUPITER	SATURN	URANUS	NEPTUNE	PLUTO	CERES	PALLAS	JUNO	VESTA	CHIRON
1	10:35:21	10 H 26 34	23 M, 33	28 mp R, 50	01 H 28	02 H 17	02 ≏ R, 33	08 ≈ 48	06 Y 35	06 ≈ 37	28 VS 57	05 ✗ 36	12 ≈ 03	19 VS 59	11 ర 49	27 ≈ 39	01 M, R, 53
2	10:39:18	11 26 47	06 ✗ 32	28 51	03 13	03 32	02 16	09 01	06 42	06 40	28 59	05 36	12 26	20 19	12 21	28 10	01 51
3	10:43:14	12 26 58	19 54	28 50	05 00	04 47	01 57	09 14	06 49	06 43	29 01	05 37	12 49	20 39	12 53	28 40	01 49
4	10:47:11	13 27 07	03 VS 41	28 49	06 48	06 02	01 38	09 27	06 56	06 46	29 03	05 37	13 11	20 59	13 25	29 10	01 47
5	10:51:07	14 27 15	17 54	28 47	08 36	07 17	01 19	09 40	07 03	06 49	29 04	05 37	13 34	21 19	13 57	29 40	01 45
6	10:55:04	15 27 22	02 ≈ 31	28 45	10 26	08 32	00 59	09 53	07 10	06 52	29 06	05 37	13 56	21 39	14 29	00 H 11	01 43
7	10:59:00	16 27 27	17 26	28 43	12 17	09 47	00 39	10 06	07 17	06 55	29 08	05 37	14 19	21 58	15 02	00 41	01 41
8	11:02:57	17 27 30	02 H 33	28 42	14 09	11 02	00 18	10 18	07 25	06 58	29 10	05 R, 37	14 41	22 17	15 34	01 11	01 38
9	11:06:54	18 27 31	17 43	28 D 41	16 02	12 17	29 mp 56	10 31	07 32	07 00	29 11	05 37	15 03	22 37	16 06	01 41	01 36
10	11:10:50	19 27 31	02 Y 46	28 41	17 56	13 31	29 34	10 44	07 39	07 03	29 13	05 37	15 25	22 56	16 39	02 11	01 33
11	11:14:47	20 27 28	17 34	28 42	19 51	14 46	29 12	10 56	07 46	07 06	29 14	05 37	15 48	23 15	17 12	02 41	01 31
12	11:18:43	21 27 23	02 ర 00	28 43	21 47	16 01	28 50	11 08	07 54	07 09	29 16	05 37	16 10	23 33	17 44	03 11	01 28
13	11:22:40	22 27 17	16 00	28 44	23 44	17 16	28 27	11 21	08 01	07 12	29 18	05 37	16 32	23 52	18 17	03 41	01 25
14	11:26:36	23 27 07	29 33	28 45	25 42	18 31	28 04	11 33	08 08	07 14	29 19	05 37	16 54	24 10	18 50	04 11	01 22
15	11:30:33	24 26 56	12 II 40	28 45	27 40	19 45	27 41	11 45	08 16	07 17	29 21	05 37	17 16	24 29	19 22	04 41	01 19
16	11:34:29	25 26 43	25 24	28 R, 46	29 39	21 00	27 17	11 58	08 23	07 20	29 22	05 36	17 37	24 47	19 55	05 11	01 16
17	11:38:26	26 26 27	07 ඉ 48	28 46	01 Y 38	22 15	26 54	12 10	08 31	07 22	29 24	05 36	17 59	25 05	20 28	05 40	01 13
18	11:42:22	27 26 09	19 57	28 46	03 38	23 30	26 30	12 22	08 38	07 25	29 25	05 36	18 21	25 23	21 01	06 10	01 09
19	11:46:19	28 25 49	01 ಖ 55	28 45	05 38	24 44	26 07	12 34	08 45	07 27	29 26	05 35	18 43	25 40	21 34	06 40	01 06
20	11:50:16	29 25 27	13 46	28 D 45	07 37	25 59	25 43	12 45	08 53	07 30	29 28	05 35	19 04	25 58	22 07	07 09	01 03
21	11:54:12	00 Y 25 02	25 35	28 46	09 36	27 14	25 20	12 57	09 00	07 32	29 29	05 35	19 26	26 15	22 40	07 39	00 59
22	11:58:09	01 24 35	07 mp 23	28 46	11 35	28 28	24 57	13 08	09 08	07 35	29 30	05 34	19 47	26 32	23 13	08 08	00 56
23	12:02:05	02 24 06	19 15	28 R, 46	13 32	29 43	24 33	13 20	09 15	07 37	29 32	05 34	20 08	26 49	23 47	08 38	00 52
24	12:06:02	03 23 35	01 ≏ 12	28 46	15 27	00 Y 58	24 10	13 32	09 23	07 40	29 33	05 33	20 30	27 06	24 20	09 07	00 48
25	12:09:58	04 23 02	13 17	28 46	17 21	02 12	23 48	13 43	09 30	07 42	29 34	05 33	20 51	27 23	24 53	09 37	00 44
26	12:13:55	05 22 27	25 31	28 46	19 13	03 27	23 25	13 55	09 38	07 44	29 35	05 32	21 12	27 39	25 26	10 06	00 40
27	12:17:51	06 21 50	07 M, 56	28 45	21 02	04 42	23 03	14 06	09 45	07 46	29 37	05 31	21 33	27 56	26 00	10 35	00 37
28	12:21:48	07 21 11	20 34	28 44	22 47	05 56	22 41	14 17	09 53	07 49	29 38	05 31	21 54	28 12	26 33	11 05	00 33
29	12:25:45	08 20 30	03 ✗ 25	28 43	24 30	07 11	22 20	14 28	10 00	07 51	29 39	05 30	22 15	28 28	27 07	11 34	00 28
30	12:29:41	09 19 48	16 32	28 41	26 08	08 25	21 59	14 39	10 08	07 53	29 40	05 29	22 35	28 43	27 40	12 03	00 24
31	12:33:38	10 19 04	29 56	28 40	27 42	09 40	21 39	14 50	10 15	07 55	29 41	05 29	22 56	28 59	28 13	12 32	00 20

EPHEMERIS IS CALCULATED FOR MIDNIGHT GREENWICH MEAN TIME.

APRIL 1997

DAY	SID.TIME	SUN	MOON	NODE	MERCURY	VENUS	MARS	JUPITER	SATURN	URANUS	NEPTUNE	PLUTO	CERES	PALLAS	JUNO	VESTA	CHIRON
T 1	12:37:34	11♈18'18"	13♑38	28♍40	29♈11	10♈54	21♍R.19	15≈01	10♈23	07≈57	29♑42	05♐R.28	23≈17	29♑14	28♉47	13✶01	00♏R.16
W 2	12:41:31	12♈17'31"	27♑38	28♍40	00♉35	12♈09	20♍59	15≈12	10♈30	07≈59	29♑43	05♐27	23≈37	29♑29	29♉20	13✶30	00♏12
T 3	12:45:27	13♈16'41"	11≈57	28♍41	01♉54	13♈23	20♍41	15≈22	10♈38	08≈01	29♑44	05♐26	23≈58	29♑44	29♉54	13✶59	00♏07
F 4	12:49:24	14♈15'49"	26≈30	28♍41	03♉08	14♈38	20♍22	15≈32	10♈46	08≈03	29♑45	05♐26	24≈18	29♑59	00♊28	14✶28	00♏03
S 5	12:53:20	15♈14'56"	11✶15	28♍42	04♉15	15♈52	20♍05	15≈43	10♈53	08≈05	29♑46	05♐25	24≈38	00≈14	01♊01	14✶56	29♎59
S 6	12:57:17	16♈14'00"	26✶05	28♍R.42	05♉16	17♈07	19♍48	15≈53	11♈01	08≈06	29♑47	05♐24	24≈58	00≈28	01♊35	15✶25	29♎54
M 7	13:01:13	17♈13'03"	10♈54	28♍41	06♉10	18♈21	19♍31	16≈03	11♈08	08≈08	29♑47	05♐23	25≈18	00≈42	02♊09	15✶54	29♎50
T 8	13:05:10	18♈12'04"	25♈34	28♍39	06♉57	19♈36	19♍16	16≈13	11♈16	08≈10	29♑48	05♐22	25≈38	00≈56	02♊42	16✶23	29♎45
W 9	13:09:07	19♈11'03"	09♉58	28♍36	07♉39	20♈50	19♍01	16≈23	11♈23	08≈12	29♑49	05♐21	25≈58	01≈10	03♊16	16✶51	29♎41
T 10	13:13:03	20♈10'00"	24♉00	28♍33	08♉19	22♈04	18♍47	16≈33	11♈31	08≈13	29♑50	05♐20	26≈18	01≈23	03♊50	17✶21	29♎36
F 11	13:17:00	21♈08'55"	07♊38	28♍31	08♉48	23♈19	18♍33	16≈43	11♈38	08≈15	29♑50	05♐19	26≈37	01≈36	04♊23	17✶48	29♎32
S 12	13:20:56	22♈07'47"	20♊51	28♍29	09♉11	24♈33	18♍21	16≈52	11♈45	08≈16	29♑51	05♐18	26≈57	01≈49	04♊57	18✶16	29♎27
S 13	13:24:53	23♈06'37"	03♋40	28♍27	09♉27	25♈47	18♍09	17≈02	11♈53	08≈18	29♑52	05♐17	27≈16	02≈02	05♊31	18✶45	29♎22
M 14	13:28:49	24♈05'26"	16♋08	28♍27	09♉36	27♈01	17♍58	17≈11	12♈00	08≈19	29♑52	05♐16	27≈36	02≈14	06♊05	19✶13	29♎18
T 15	13:32:46	25♈04'11"	28♋19	28♍27	09♉R.39	28♈16	17♍47	17≈21	12♈08	08≈21	29♑53	05♐15	27≈55	02≈26	06♊38	19✶41	29♎13
W 16	13:36:42	26♈02'55"	10♌17	28♍D	09♉36	29♈30	17♍38	17≈30	12♈15	08≈22	29♑53	05♐13	28≈14	02≈38	07♊12	20✶09	29♎08
T 17	13:40:39	27♈01'36"	22♌08	28♍30	09♉27	00♉44	17♍29	17≈38	12♈23	08≈23	29♑54	05♐12	28≈33	02≈50	07♊46	20✶37	29♎04
F 18	13:44:36	28♈00'15"	03♍56	28♍32	09♉09	01♉58	17♍21	17≈47	12♈30	08≈25	29♑54	05♐11	28≈52	03≈02	08♊20	21✶05	28♎59
S 19	13:48:32	28♈58'52"	15♍46	28♍34	08♉53	03♉13	17♍14	17≈56	12♈37	08≈26	29♑55	05♐10	29≈10	03≈13	08♊54	21✶33	28♎54
S 20	13:52:29	29♈57'26"	27♍41	28♍R.34	08♉28	04♉27	17♍07	18≈04	12♈45	08≈27	29♑55	05♐09	29≈29	03≈24	09♊27	22✶01	28♎50
M 21	13:56:25	00♉55'59"	09♎46	28♍31	07♉59	05♉41	17♍02	18≈13	12♈52	08≈28	29♑56	05♐07	29≈47	03≈34	10♊01	22✶29	28♎45
T 22	14:00:22	01♉54'30"	22♎03	28♍27	07♉26	06♉55	16♍57	18≈21	12♈59	08≈29	29♑56	05♐06	00✶06	03≈45	10♊35	22✶56	28♎40
W 23	14:04:18	02♉52'59"	04♏33	28♍21	06♉51	08♉09	16♍53	18≈29	13♈06	08≈30	29♑56	05♐05	00✶24	03≈55	11♊09	23✶24	28♎36
T 24	14:08:15	03♉51'26"	17♏17	28♍15	06♉13	09♉23	16♍50	18≈38	13♈14	08≈31	29♑57	05♐03	00✶42	04≈04	11♊43	23✶51	28♎31
F 25	14:12:11	04♉49'51"	00♐15	28♍09	05♉33	10♉37	16♍47	18≈45	13♈21	08≈32	29♑57	05♐02	01✶00	04≈14	12♊16	24✶19	28♎26
S 26	14:16:08	05♉48'14"	13♐27	28♍03	04♉53	11♉51	16♍45	18≈53	13♈28	08≈33	29♑57	05♐01	01✶18	04≈24	12♊50	24✶46	28♎22
S 27	14:20:05	06♉46'36"	26♐52	27♍59	04♉12	13♉05	16♍45	19≈01	13♈35	08≈34	29♑57	04♐59	01✶36	04≈33	13♊24	25✶14	28♎17
M 28	14:24:01	07♉44'56"	10♑29	27♍58	03♉32	14♉19	16♍D44	19≈08	13♈42	08≈35	29♑57	04♐58	01✶53	04≈41	13♊58	25✶41	28♎13
T 29	14:27:58	08♉43'14"	24♑17	27♍57	02♉54	15♉33	16♍45	19≈16	13♈49	08≈35	29♑58	04♐56	02✶11	04≈50	14♊32	26✶08	28♎08
W 30	14:31:54	09♉41'31"	08≈16	27♍D56	02♉17	16♉47	16♍46	19≈23	13♈56	08≈36	29♑58	04♐55	02✶28	04≈58	15♊05	26✶35	28♎04

EPHEMERIS IS CALCULATED FOR MIDNIGHT GREENWICH MEAN TIME.

MAY 1997

DAY	SID.TIME	SUN	MOON	NODE	MERCURY	VENUS	MARS	JUPITER	SATURN	URANUS	NEPTUNE	PLUTO	CERES	PALLAS	JUNO	VESTA	CHIRON
T 1	14:35:51	10♉39 47	22≈23	27♍56	01♉R43	18♉01	16♍48	19≈30	14♈03	08≈37	29♑R58	04♐R54	02♓45	05♈06	15♊39	27♓02	27♎R59
F 2	14:39:47	11 38 01	06♓39	27 57	01 12	19 15	16 51	19 37	14 10	08 37	29 58	04 52	03 02	05 13	16 13	29 29	27 55
S 3	14:43:44	12 36 14	21 00	27R58	00 44	20 29	16 54	19 44	14 17	08 38	29 58	04 51	03 19	05 20	16 47	27 56	27 50
S 4	14:47:40	13 34 25	05♈25	27 57	00 00	21 43	16 58	19 50	14 24	08 38	29 58	04 49	03 36	05 27	17 21	28 22	27 46
M 5	14:51:37	14 32 34	19 49	27 55	00 01	22 57	17 03	19 57	14 31	08 39	29 58	04 48	03 52	05 34	17 54	28 49	27 42
T 6	14:55:34	15 30 42	04♉07	27 51	29♈46	24 11	17 09	20 03	14 38	08 39	29 57	04 46	04 08	05 40	18 28	29 16	27 37
W 7	14:59:30	16 28 49	18 14	27 45	29D36	25 25	17 15	20 09	14 45	08 39	29 57	04 45	04 25	05 46	19 02	00♈42	27 33
T 8	15:03:27	17 26 53	02♊06	27 38	29 29	26 39	17 22	20 15	14 52	08 40	29 57	04 43	04 41	05 52	19 36	00 09	27 29
F 9	15:07:23	18 24 56	15 38	27 29	29 29	27 53	17 29	20 21	14 58	08 40	29 57	04 41	04 57	05 57	20 09	00 35	27 25
S 10	15:11:20	19 22 57	28 48	27 21	29 32	29 07	17 37	20 27	15 05	08 40	29 57	04 40	05 12	06 02	20 43	01 01	27 21
S 11	15:15:16	20 20 57	11♋37	27 14	29 40	00♊20	17 46	20 32	15 12	08 40	29 56	04 38	05 28	06 06	21 17	01 27	27 17
M 12	15:19:13	21 18 55	24 06	27 08	29 53	01 34	17 55	20 38	15 18	08 40	29 56	04 37	05 43	06 10	21 50	01 53	27 13
T 13	15:23:09	22 16 51	06♌18	27 05	00♊10	02 48	18 05	20 43	15 25	08R40	29 56	04 35	05 59	06 14	22 24	02 19	27 09
W 14	15:27:06	23 14 45	18 17	27D04	00 32	04 02	18 16	20 48	15 31	08 40	29 55	04 34	06 14	06 18	22 58	02 45	27 05
T 15	15:31:03	24 12 38	00♍08	27 04	00 58	05 16	18 27	20 53	15 38	08 40	29 55	04 32	06 28	06 21	23 31	03 11	27 01
F 16	15:34:59	25 10 29	11 56	27 06	01 28	06 29	18 39	20 58	15 44	08 40	29 55	04 30	06 43		24 05	03 38	26 57
S 17	15:38:56	26 08 17	23 48	27R07	02 02	07 43	18 51	21 06	15 51	08 40	29 54	04 29	06 58	06 26	24 38	04 04	26 54
S 18	15:42:52	27 06 04	05♎47	27 06	02 41	08 57	19 04	21 06	15 57	08 40	29 54	04 27	07 12	06 28	25 25	04 27	26 50
M 19	15:46:49	28 03 50	17 58	27 04	03 23	10 10	19 18	21 11	16 03	08 40	29 53	04 25	07 26	06 30	25 46	04 53	26 46
T 20	15:50:45	29 01 34	00♏25	26 58	04 08	11 24	19 31	21 15	16 09	08 39	29 52	04 24	07 40	06 31	25 19	05 18	26 43
W 21	15:54:42	29 59 17	13 10	26 51	04 57	12 38	19 46	21 18	16 15	08 39	29 52	04 22	07 54	06 32	25 53	05 43	26 40
T 22	15:58:38	00♊58 58	26 13	26 41	05 50	13 51	20 01	21 22	16 22	08 39	29 51	04 21	08 07	06 32	26 59	06 08	26 37
F 23	16:02:35	01 54 38	09♐34	26 30	06 46	15 05	20 16	21 26	16 28	08 38	29 51	04 19	08 20	06 32	27 59	06 33	26 33
S 24	16:06:32	02 52 17	23 12	26 19	07 45	16 18	20 32	21 29	16 34	08 37	29 50	04 17	08 34	06 32	28 33	06 58	26 30
S 25	16:10:28	03 49 55	07♑02	26 09	08 48	17 32	20 49	21 32	16 40	08 37	29 49	04 16	08 47	06 31	29 06	07 22	26 27
M 26	16:14:25	04 47 32	21 01	26 02	09 53	18 46	21 06	21 35	16 45	08 36	29 49	04 14	08 59	06 30	29 40	07 47	26 24
T 27	16:18:21	05 45 07	05≈05	25 58	11 02	19 59	21 23	21 38	16 51	08 36	29 48	04 12	09 12	06 29	00♋ ⊗	08 11	26 21
W 28	16:22:18	06 42 42	19 13	25 56	12 13	21 13	21 41	21 40	16 57	08 35	29 47	04 11	09 24	06 27	01 46	08 36	26 18
T 29	16:26:14	07 40 15	03♓22	25D55	13 27	22 26	21 59	21 43	17 03	08 34	29 46	04 09	09 36	06 25	01 20	09 00	26 16
F 30	16:30:11	08 37 48	17 29	25 52	14 44	23 40	22 18	21 45	17 08	08 33	29 45	04 07	09 48	06 22	01 53	09 24	26 13
S 31	16:34:07	09 35 20	01♈35	25R52	16 04	24 53	22 37	21 47	17 14	08 33	29 44	04 06	09 59	06 19	02 26	09 48	26 11

EPHEMERIS IS CALCULATED FOR MIDNIGHT GREENWICH MEAN TIME.

JUNE 1997

DAY	SID.TIME	SUN	MOON	NODE	MERCURY	VENUS	MARS	JUPITER	SATURN	URANUS	NEPTUNE	PLUTO	CERES	PALLAS	JUNO	VESTA	CHIRON
S 1	16:38:04	10 II 32 51	15 ♈ 38	25 ♏R 51	17 ♉ 27	26 II 07	22 ♍ 56	21 ≈ 49	17 ♈ 19	08 ≈R 32	29 ♑R 44	04 ♐R 04	10 ♓ 11	06 ≈R 16	02 ⊚ 59	10 ♈ 12	26 ≏R 08
M 2	16:42:01	11 30 21	29 37	25 47	18 52	27 20	23 16	21 50	17 25	08 31	29 43	04 02	10 22	06 12	03 32	10 36	26 06
T 3	16:45:57	12 27 51	13 ♉ 30	25 41	20 20	28 33	23 36	21 52	17 30	08 30	29 42	04 01	10 33	06 08	04 06	10 59	26 04
W 4	16:49:54	13 25 20	27 13	25 33	21 50	29 47	23 57	21 53	17 36	08 29	29 41	03 59	10 44	06 03	04 39	11 23	26 02
T 5	16:53:50	14 22 48	10 II 44	25 22	23 24	01 ⊚ 00	24 18	21 54	17 41	08 28	29 40	03 58	10 54	05 58	05 12	11 46	25 59
F 6	16:57:47	15 20 15	23 59	25 09	25 00	02 14	24 40	21 55	17 46	08 27	29 39	03 56	11 04	05 53	05 45	12 09	25 58
S 7	17:01:43	16 17 41	06 ⊚ 58	24 57	26 38	03 27	25 02	21 56	17 51	08 26	29 38	03 54	11 14	05 47	06 18	12 33	25 56
S 8	17:05:40	17 15 06	19 39	24 46	28 19	04 40	25 24	21 56	17 56	08 24	29 37	03 53	11 24	05 41	06 51	12 56	25 54
M 9	17:09:36	18 12 30	02 ♌ 04	24 36	00 II 03	05 54	25 47	21 56 R	18 01	08 23	29 36	03 51	11 33	05 34	07 24	13 18	25 52
T 10	17:13:33	19 09 53	14 13	24 30	01 49	07 07	26 09	21 56	18 06	08 22	29 34	03 50	11 42	05 27	07 57	13 41	25 51
W 11	17:17:30	20 07 15	27 01	24 26	03 37	08 20	26 33	21 56	18 11	08 21	29 33	03 48	11 51	05 19	08 30	14 04	25 49
T 12	17:21:26	21 04 36	08 ♍ 01	24 25	05 28	09 34	26 56	21 56	18 16	08 19	29 32	03 47	12 00	05 12	09 03	14 26	25 48
F 13	17:25:23	22 01 56	19 50	24 25	07 22	10 47	27 20	21 56	18 20	08 18	29 31	03 45	12 08	05 03	09 36	14 48	25 47
S 14	17:29:19	22 59 16	01 ≏ 41	24 25	09 18	12 00	27 45	21 55	18 25	08 16	29 30	03 43	12 16	04 55	10 08	15 10	25 46
S 15	17:33:16	23 56 34	13 42	24 25	11 16	13 13	28 09	21 54	18 29	08 15	29 28	03 42	12 24	04 46	10 41	15 32	25 45
M 16	17:37:12	24 53 51	25 56	24 22	13 17	14 27	28 34	21 53	18 34	08 14	29 27	03 40	12 31	04 36	11 14	15 54	25 44
T 17	17:41:09	25 51 08	08 ♏ 29	24 17	15 19	15 40	28 59	21 52	18 38	08 12	29 26	03 39	12 38	04 27	11 46	16 15	25 43
W 18	17:45:05	26 48 24	21 23	24 09	17 24	16 53	29 25	21 51	18 43	08 10	29 25	03 37	12 45	04 17	12 19	16 37	25 42
T 19	17:49:02	27 45 39	04 ✗ 40	23 58	19 30	18 06	29 51	21 49	18 47	08 09	29 23	03 36	12 52	04 06	12 52	16 58	25 42
F 20	17:52:59	28 42 54	18 20	23 46	21 37	19 19	00 ≏ 17	21 47	18 51	08 07	29 22	03 34	12 58	03 55	13 24	17 19	25 41
S 21	17:56:55	29 40 08	02 ♑ 20	23 34	23 46	20 32	00 43	21 45	18 55	08 05	29 21	03 33	13 04	03 44	13 57	17 40	25 41
S 22	18:00:52	00 ⊚ 37 21	16 35	23 23	25 56	21 45	01 10	21 43	18 59	08 04	29 19	03 32	13 10	03 33	14 29	18 01	25 41
M 23	18:04:48	01 34 35	01 ≈ 00	23 14	28 07	22 58	01 37	21 40	19 03	08 02	29 18	03 30	13 16	03 21	15 02	18 22	25 41
T 24	18:08:45	02 31 48	15 28	23 08	00 ⊚ 18	24 11	02 04	21 38	19 07	08 00	29 17	03 29	13 21	03 09	15 34	18 42	25 D 25
W 25	18:12:41	03 29 01	29 55	23 04	02 30	25 24	02 32	21 35	19 10	07 58	29 15	03 27	13 25	02 56	16 07	19 03	25 41
T 26	18:16:38	04 26 14	14 ✹ 15	23 03 D	04 41	26 37	02 59	21 32	19 14	07 57	29 14	03 26	13 30	02 43	16 39	19 23	25 41
F 27	18:20:34	05 23 27	28 27	23 R 02	06 52	27 50	03 27	21 29	19 18	07 55	29 12	03 25	13 34	02 30	17 11	19 43	25 41
S 28	18:24:31	06 20 40	12 ♈ 28	23 02	09 02	29 03	03 55	21 26	19 21	07 53	29 11	03 23	13 38	02 17	17 43	20 02	25 42
S 29	18:28:28	07 17 53	26 20	23 02	11 12	00 ♌ 16	04 24	21 22	19 24	07 51	29 09	03 22	13 41	02 03	18 16	20 22	25 42
M 30	18:32:24	08 15 06	10 ♉ 01	22 59	13 20	01 29	04 53	21 19	19 28	07 49	29 08	03 21	13 45	01 ≈R 50	18 48	20 41	25 43

EPHEMERIS IS CALCULATED FOR MIDNIGHT GREENWICH MEAN TIME.

JULY 1997

DAY	SID.TIME	SUN	MOON	NODE	MERCURY	VENUS	MARS	JUPITER	SATURN	URANUS	NEPTUNE	PLUTO	CERES	PALLAS	JUNO	VESTA	CHIRON
T 1	18:36:21	09♋12 19	23♉32	22♍R53	15♋28	02♌42	05♎22	21♒R15	19♈31	07♒R47	29♑R06	03♐R20	13♓48	01♒R35	19♋20	21♈00	25♎44
W 2	18:40:17	10 09 32	06♊52	22 45	17 34	03 55	05 51	21 11	19 34	07 45	29 05	03 18	13 50	01 21	19 52	21 19	25 45
T 3	18:44:14	11 06 45	20 00	22 35	19 38	05 08	06 20	21 07	19 37	07 43	29 03	03 17	13 52	01 06	20 24	21 38	25 45
F 4	18:48:10	12 03 59	02♋55	22 23	21 41	06 21	06 50	21 02	19 40	07 41	29 02	03 16	13 54	00 51	20 56	21 57	25 47
S 5	18:52:07	13 01 12	15 36	22 11	23 42	07 34	07 20	20 58	19 43	07 39	29 00	03 15	13 56	00 36	21 28	22 15	25 48
S 6	18:56:03	13 58 25	28 04	22 00	25 41	08 46	07 50	20 53	19 45	07 37	28 59	03 14	13 57	00 21	22 00	22 33	25 49
M 7	19:00:00	14 55 39	10♌19	21♍51	27 38	09 59	08 20	20 48	19 48	07 34	28 57	03 12	13 57	00 06	22 32	22 51	25 50
T 8	19:03:57	15 52 52	22 22	21 44	29 34	11 12	08 51	20 44	19 50	07 32	28 56	03 11	13 58	29♑50	23 04	23 09	25 52
W 9	19:07:53	16 50 05	04♍16	21 41	01♌28	12 25	09 22	20 38	19 53	07 30	28 54	03 10	13♓R58	29 34	23 35	23 26	25 54
T 10	19:11:50	17 47 19	16 05	21 D 39	03 19	13 37	09 52	20 33	19 55	07 28	28 53	03 09	13 58	29 18	24 07	23 44	25 55
F 11	19:15:46	18 44 32	27 52	21 40	05 05	14 50	10 24	20 28	19 58	07 26	28 51	03 08	13 57	29 02	24 39	24 01	25 57
S 12	19:19:43	19 41 45	09♎43	21 41	06 47	16 03	10 55	20 22	20 00	07 24	28 49	03 07	13 56	28 46	25 11	24 17	25 59
S 13	19:23:39	20 38 58	21 42	21♍R42	08 43	17 15	11 26	20 16	20 02	07 21	28 48	03 06	13 55	28 30	25 42	24 34	26♎01
M 14	19:27:36	21 36 11	03♏56	21 41	10 26	18 28	11 58	20 11	20 04	07 19	28 46	03 05	13 53	28 14	26 14	24 50	26 03
T 15	19:31:32	22 33 24	16 29	21 38	12 08	19 41	12 30	20 05	20 06	07 17	28 45	03 04	13 51	27 58	26 45	25 06	26 06
W 16	19:35:29	23 30 37	29 26	21 33	13 48	20 53	13 02	19 58	20 07	07 14	28 43	03 04	13 49	27 41	27 17	25 22	26 08
T 17	19:39:26	24 27 51	12♐48	21 26	15 25	22 06	13 35	19 52	20 09	07 12	28 41	03 03	13 47	27 25	27 48	25 38	26 11
F 18	19:43:22	25 25 04	26 37	21 17	17 02	23 18	14 07	19 46	20 10	07 10	28 40	03 02	13 43	27 09	28 19	25 53	26 13
S 19	19:47:19	26 22 19	10♑51	21 09	18 37	24 31	14 40	19 39	20 12	07 07	28 38	03 01	13 39	26 52	28 51	26 08	26 16
S 20	19:51:15	27 19 33	25 24	21 00	20 09	25 43	15 13	19 33	20 13	07 05	28 36	03 00	13 36	26 36	29 22	26 23	26 19
M 21	19:55:12	28 16 48	10♒11	20 54	21 39	26 55	15 46	19 26	20 15	07 03	28 35	03 00	13 32	26 20	29 53	26 37	26 22
T 22	19:59:08	29 14 04	25 03	20 49	23 07	28 08	16 19	19 19	20 16	07 00	28 33	02 59	13 27	26 03	00♌24	26 52	26 25
W 23	20:03:05	00♌11 19	09♓52	20 D 46	24 33	29 20	16 52	19 12	20 17	06 58	28 32	02 58	13 22	25 47	00 55	27 06	26 28
T 24	20:07:01	01 08 36	24 31	20 46	25 58	00♍32	17 25	19 05	20 18	06 56	28 30	02 57	13 17	25 31	01 26	27 19	26 31
F 25	20:10:58	02 05 54	08♈57	20 46	27 20	01 45	17 59	18 58	20 19	06 53	28 28	02 57	13 11	25 15	01 57	27 33	26 34
S 26	20:14:55	03 03 12	23 06	20 47	28 40	02 57	18 33	18 51	20 19	06 51	28 27	02 56	13 05	24 59	02 28	27 46	26 38
S 27	20:18:51	04 00 31	06♉57	20♍R48	29 58	04 09	19 07	18 44	20 20	06 48	28 25	02 56	12 59	24 44	02 59	27 59	26 41
M 28	20:22:48	04 57 52	20 31	20 47	01♍14	05 21	19 42	18 37	20 20	06 46	28 23	02 55	12 53	24 28	03 30	28 11	26 45
T 29	20:26:44	05 55 13	03♊49	20 45	02 27	06 33	20 16	18 29	20 21	06 44	28 22	02 55	12 46	24 13	04 01	28 24	26 48
W 30	20:30:41	06 52 36	16 51	20 40	03 38	07 45	20 51	18 22	20 21	06 41	28 20	02 54	12 38	23 57	04 32	28 35	26 52
T 31	20:34:37	07 50 00	29 40	20 34	04 47	08 58	21 25	18 14	20 21	06 39	28 19	02 54	12 31	23 42	05 02	28 47	26 56

EPHEMERIS IS CALCULATED FOR MIDNIGHT GREENWICH MEAN TIME.

AUGUST 1997

DAY	SID.TIME	SUN	MOON	NODE	MERCURY	VENUS	MARS	JUPITER	SATURN	URANUS	NEPTUNE	PLUTO	CERES	PALLAS	JUNO	VESTA	CHIRON
F 1	20:38:34	08♌47 24	12♋16	20♍R27	05♍53	10♍10	22♎00	18≈R06	20♈R22	06≈R36	28♑R17	02♐R53	12♓23	23♒27	05♌33	28♈58	27♎00
S 2	20:42:30	09 44 50	24 40	20 19	06 57	11 22	22 22	17 59	20 22	06 34	28 15	02 53	12♓R15	23♒R13	06 03	29 09	27 04
S 3	20:46:27	10 42 16	06♌53	20 13	07 58	12 34	23 10	17 51	20 22	06 32	28 14	02 52	12 06	22 58	06 34	29 20	27 08
M 4	20:50:24	11 39 44	18 56	20 07	08 57	13 45	23 46	17 43	20 21	06 29	28 12	02 52	11 57	22 44	07 04	29 30	27 13
T 5	20:54:20	12 37 12	00♍52	20 03	09 52	14 57	24 21	17 36	20 21	06 27	28 11	02 52	11 48	22 30	07 35	29 40	27 17
W 6	20:58:17	13 34 41	12 42	20 D 01	10 45	16 09	24 57	17 28	20 20	06 25	28 09	02 52	11 38	22 16	08 05	29 50	27 21
T 7	21:02:13	14 32 11	24 28	20 01	11 34	17 21	25 32	17 20	20 20	06 22	28 08	02 52	11 29	22 03	08 36	29 59	27 26
F 8	21:06:10	15 29 42	06♎15	20 03	12 20	18 33	26 08	17 12	20 20	06 20	28 06	02 51	11 18	21 50	09 06	00♉08	27 31
S 9	21:10:06	16 27 13	18 06	20 05	13 02	19 45	26 44	17 04	20 19	06 17	28 05	02 51	11 08	21 37	09 36	00 17	27 35
S 10	21:14:03	17 24 46	00♏05	20 07	13 41	20 56	27 21	16 57	20 18	06 15	28 03	02 51	10 58	21 24	10 06	00 25	27 40
M 11	21:17:59	18 22 20	12 18	20♍R08	14 16	22 08	27 57	16 49	20 17	06 13	28 02	02 51	10 47	21 12	10 36	00 33	27 45
T 12	21:21:56	19 19 54	24 48	20 08	14 47	23 20	28 33	16 41	20 16	06 11	28 00	02 51	10 36	21 00	11 06	00 40	27 50
W 13	21:25:53	20 17 30	07♐42	20 06	15 13	24 31	29 10	16 33	20 15	06 08	27 59	02 D 51	10 25	20 49	11 36	00 47	27 55
T 14	21:29:49	21 15 06	21 01	20 04	15 35	25 43	29 47	16 25	20 14	06 06	27 57	02 51	10 13	20 37	12 06	00 54	28 00
F 15	21:33:46	22 12 42	04♑49	20 00	15 53	26 54	00♏23	16 18	20 13	06 04	27 56	02 51	10 02	20 26	12 36	01 00	28 05
S 16	21:37:42	23 10 21	19 04	19 56	16 06	28 06	01 00	16 10	20 11	06 01	27 54	02 51	09 50	20 16	13 06	01 06	28 11
S 17	21:41:39	24 08 00	03≈42	19 53	16 12	29 17	01 38	16 02	20 10	05 59	27 53	02 51	09 38	20 06	13 35	01 11	28 16
M 18	21:45:35	25 05 41	18 39	19 50	16♍R14	00♎29	02 15	15 55	20 08	05 57	27 51	02 51	09 25	19 56	14 05	01 17	28 22
T 19	21:49:32	26 03 23	03♓46	19 48	16 10	01 41	02 52	15 47	20 06	05 55	27 50	02 51	09 13	19 46	14 34	01 22	28 27
W 20	21:53:28	27 01 06	18 54	19 D 47	16 01	02 51	03 30	15 39	20 04	05 52	27 49	02 51	09 00	19 37	15 04	01 26	28 33
T 21	21:57:25	27 58 51	03♈53	19 48	15 45	04 02	04 07	15 32	20 03	05 50	27 47	02 52	08 48	19 28	15 33	01 31	28 38
F 22	22:01:22	28 56 37	18 36	19 48	15 25	05 13	04 45	15 24	20 01	05 48	27 46	02 52	08 35	19 20	16 03	01 33	28 44
S 23	22:05:18	29 54 25	02♉59	19 50	14 58	06 24	05 23	15 17	19 59	05 46	27 45	02 52	08 22	19 12	16 32	01 36	28 50
S 24	22:09:15	00♍52 15	16 59	19♍R51	14 26	07 35	06 01	15 10	19 56	05 44	27 43	02 53	08 09	19 04	17 01	01 39	28 56
M 25	22:13:11	01 50 06	00♊36	19 51	13 48	08 46	06 39	15 03	19 54	05 42	27 42	02 53	07 56	18 57	17 31	01 41	29 02
T 26	22:17:08	02 47 59	13 50	19 51	13 06	09 57	07 17	14 55	19 52	05 40	27 41	02 53	07 43	18 50	18 00	01 43	29 08
W 27	22:21:04	03 45 54	26 44	19 50	12 19	11 08	07 56	14 48	19 49	05 38	27 40	02 54	07 30	18 43	18 29	01 44	29 14
T 28	22:25:01	04 43 50	09♋20	19 48	11 28	12 19	08 34	14 42	19 47	05 36	27 38	02 54	07 16	18 37	18 58	01 45	29 20
F 29	22:28:57	05 41 49	21 43	19 47	10 35	13 29	09 13	14 35	19 44	05 34	27 37	02 55	07 03	18 31	19 27	01 45	29 27
S 30	22:32:54	06 39 49	03♌53	19 45	09 39	14 40	09 51	14 28	19 41	05 32	27 36	02 55	06 49	18 26	19 56	01♉R45	29 33
S 31	22:36:51	07 37 51	15 54	19 43	08 43	15 51	10 30	14 21	19 39	05 30	27 35	02 56	06 36	18 21	20 25	01 45	29 39

EPHEMERIS IS CALCULATED FOR MIDNIGHT GREENWICH MEAN TIME.

SEPTEMBER 1997

DAY	SID.TIME	SUN	MOON	NODE	MERCURY	VENUS	MARS	JUPITER	SATURN	URANUS	NEPTUNE	PLUTO	CERES	PALLAS	JUNO	VESTA	CHIRON
M 1	22:40:47	08 ℗ 3555	27 ♌ 48	19 ℗℞ 42	07 ℗ 07	17 ♎ 01	11 ℠ 09	14 ♒℞ 15	19 ♈℞ 36	05 ♒℞ 28	27 ♑℞ 34	02 ♐ 56	06 ♍℞ 23	18 ♑℞ 16	20 ♌ 53	01 ♉ 44	29 ♎ 46
T 2	22:44:44	09 34 00	09 ℗ 38	19 D 42	06 53	18 12	11 48	14 08	19 33	05 26	27 33	02 57	06 09	18 12	21 22	01 ℞ 42	29 53
W 3	22:48:40	10 32 07	21 25	19 42	06 01	19 22	12 27	14 02	19 31	05 24	27 31	02 58	05 56	18 08	21 51	01 41	29 59
T 4	22:52:37	11 30 16	03 ♎ 12	19 42	05 13	20 33	13 07	13 56	19 30	05 23	27 30	02 58	05 43	18 04	22 19	01 38	00 ℠ 06
F 5	22:56:33	12 28 26	15 01	19 43	04 30	21 43	13 46	13 50	19 28	05 21	27 29	02 59	05 30	18 01	22 48	01 36	00 13
S 6	23:00:30	13 26 37	26 55	19 43	03 53	22 53	14 26	13 44	19 26	05 19	27 28	03 00	05 17	17 58	23 16	01 32	00 19
S 7	23:04:26	14 24 51	08 ♍ 58	19 44	03 23	24 03	15 05	13 38	19 23	05 17	27 27	03 01	05 04	17 55	23 44	01 29	00 26
M 8	23:08:23	15 23 05	21 13	19 44	03 01	25 14	15 45	13 33	19 20	05 16	27 26	03 02	04 51	17 52	24 12	01 25	00 33
T 9	23:12:19	16 21 22	03 ♐ 43	19 ℞ 44	02 47	26 24	16 24	13 27	19 17	05 14	27 25	03 02	04 38	17 49	24 41	01 20	00 40
W 10	23:16:16	17 19 40	16 34	19 44	02 ℗ 42	27 34	17 04	13 22	19 13	05 12	27 25	03 03	04 26	17 46	25 09	01 15	00 47
T 11	23:20:13	18 18 00	29 47	19 44	02 46	28 44	17 44	13 17	19 10	05 11	27 24	03 04	04 13	17 43	25 37	01 09	00 54
F 12	23:24:09	19 16 21	13 ♑ 25	19 D 44	02 59	29 53	18 23	13 12	19 06	05 09	27 23	03 05	04 00	17 40	26 05	01 03	01 01
S 13	23:28:06	20 14 44	27 30	19 44	03 21	01 ℠ 03	19 03	13 07	19 02	05 08	27 22	03 06	03 49	17 37	26 33	00 57	01 09
S 14	23:32:02	21 13 08	12 ♒ 01	19 44	03 52	02 13	19 46	13 03	18 58	05 07	27 21	03 07	03 37	17 D 34	27 00	00 50	01 16
M 15	23:35:59	22 11 34	26 52	19 44	04 32	03 22	20 26	12 58	18 54	05 06	27 20	03 08	03 25	17 32	27 27	00 43	01 23
T 16	23:39:55	23 10 01	11 ♓ 59	19 44	05 16	04 32	21 07	12 54	18 50	05 05	27 19	03 09	03 14	17 30	27 56	00 35	01 30
W 17	23:43:52	24 08 31	27 12	19 ℞ 45	06 41	05 42	21 47	12 50	18 46	05 04	27 19	03 11	03 02	17 28	28 23	00 27	01 38
T 18	23:47:48	25 07 02	12 ♈ 22	19 44	07 20	06 51	22 28	12 46	18 42	05 03	27 18	03 12	02 52	17 26	28 51	00 19	01 45
F 19	23:51:45	26 05 35	27 19	19 44	08 30	08 01	23 09	12 42	18 38	05 02	27 18	03 13	02 41	17 24	29 19	00 10	01 53
S 20	23:55:42	27 04 10	11 ♉ 57	19 43	09 46	09 10	23 50	12 38	18 35	04 59	27 17	03 14	02 30	17 22	29 48	00 02	02 00
S 21	23:59:38	28 02 48	26 09	19 42	11 11	10 18	24 31	12 35	18 32	04 58	27 16	03 15	02 20	18 20	00 ♍ 13	29 ♈ 51	02 08
M 22	00:03:35	29 01 28	09 ♊ 54	19 41	08 35	11 27	25 12	12 32	18 28	04 57	27 16	03 17	02 10	18 03	00 40	29 29	02 16
T 23	00:07:31	00 ♎ 0010	23 12	19 40	14 06	12 36	25 53	12 28	18 14	04 56	27 15	03 18	02 00	18 06	00 07	29 30	02 23
W 24	00:11:28	00 58 55	06 ♋ 06	19 D 40	15 41	13 45	26 35	12 25	18 09	04 54	27 15	03 19	01 51	18 10	01 34	29 18	02 31
T 25	00:15:24	01 57 41	18 39	19 40	15 41	14 53	27 16	12 23	18 05	04 53	27 14	03 21	01 42	18 14	01 01	29 08	02 39
F 26	00:19:21	02 56 30	00 ♌ 54	19 42	17 00	16 02	27 58	12 20	18 00	04 53	27 14	03 22	01 33	18 18	02 27	28 56	02 46
S 27	00:23:17	03 55 21	12 57	19 44	18 42	17 11	28 39	12 18	17 56	04 52	27 13	03 23	01 24	18 22	02 54	28 44	02 54
S 28	00:27:14	04 54 14	24 50	19 45	22 27	18 19	29 21	12 16	17 51	04 51	27 13	03 25	01 16	18 27	03 21	28 31	03 02
M 29	00:31:11	05 53 09	06 ℗ 39	19 47	24 13	19 27	00 ♐ 03	12 14	17 47	04 50	27 13	03 26	01 08	18 32	03 47	28 19	03 10
T 30	00:35:07	06 52 06	18 26	19 ℞ 48	25 59	20 35	00 45	12 12	17 42	04 49	27 12	03 28	01 01	18 38	04 14	28 06	03 18

EPHEMERIS IS CALCULATED FOR MIDNIGHT GREENWICH MEAN TIME.

OCTOBER 1997

DAY		SID.TIME	SUN	MOON	NODE	MERCURY	VENUS	MARS	JUPITER	SATURN	URANUS	NEPTUNE	PLUTO	CERES	PALLAS	JUNO	VESTA	CHIRON
W	1	0:39:04	07≏51 06	00≏13	19♍℞48	27♍47	21♏43	01✗27	12≈℞11	17♈℞38	04≈℞49	27♑℞12	03✗29	00♑℞54	18✗43	04♍40	27♈℞52	03♏26
T	2	0:43:00	08 50 07	12♏04	19 47	29 35	22 51	02 09	12 09	17 33	04 48	27 12	03 31	00 47	18 49	05 06	27 39	03 34
F	3	0:46:57	09 49 11	24 00	19 44	01≏23	23 59	02 51	12 08	17 28	04 47	27 12	03 32	00 40	18 56	05 33	27 25	03 42
S	4	0:50:53	10 48 17	06♏04	19 41	03 11	25 07	03 33	12 07	17 24	04 47	27 11	03 34	00 34	19 02	05 59	27 11	03 50
S	5	0:54:50	11 47 24	18 16	19 37	04 58	26 14	04 16	12 07	17 19	04 46	27 11	03 36	00 28	19 09	06 25	26 57	03 58
M	6	0:58:46	12 46 34	00✗40	19 33	06 46	27 22	04 58	12 06	17 14	04 46	27 11	03 37	00 23	19 16	06 50	26 42	04 06
T	7	1:02:43	13 45 45	13 17	19 29	08 31	28 29	05 41	12 06	17 10	04 46	27 11 D	03 39	00 18	19 24	07 16	26 27	04 14
W	8	1:06:39	14 44 58	26 09	19 27	10 19	29 36	06 23	12 06 D	17 05	04 45	27 11	03 41	00 13	19 31	07 42	26 13	04 23
T	9	1:10:36	15 44 12	09♑20	19 26	12 06	00✗44	07 06	12 06	17 00	04 45	27 11	03 42	00 09	19 39	08 07	25 57	04 31
F	10	1:14:33	16 43 29	22 50	19 D 26	13 51	01 50	07 49	12 06	16 55	04 44	27 11	03 44	00 05	19 47	08 33	25 42	04 39
S	11	1:18:29	17 42 47	06≈42	19 27	15 36	02 57	08 32	12 06	16 51	04 44	27 11	03 46	00 01	19 56	08 58	25 27	04 47
S	12	1:22:26	18 42 07	20 56	19 28	17 20	04 04	09 15	12 07	16 46	04 44	27 11	03 48	29♐58	20 04	09 24	25 12	04 56
M	13	1:26:22	19 41 29	05✶30	19 30	19 03	05 10	09 58	12 07	16 41	04 44	27 11	03 50	29 55	20 13	09 49	24 56	05 04
T	14	1:30:19	20 40 53	20 32	19℞29	20 46	06 17	10 41	12 08	16 36	04 44	27 11	03 51	29 53	20 22	10 14	24 41	05 12
W	15	1:34:15	21 40 19	05♈23	19 29	22 28	07 22	11 24	12 09	16 32	04 44 D	27 12	03 53	29 50	20 32	10 39	24 25	05 20
T	16	1:38:12	22 39 47	20 28	19 27	24 10	08 28	12 08	12 10	16 28	04 44	27 12	03 55	29 49	20 41	11 04	24 09	05 29
F	17	1:42:08	23 39 16	05♉25	19 23	25 50	09 34	12 51	12 13	16 23	04 44	27 12	03 57	29 47	20 51	11 29	23 54	05 37
S	18	1:46:05	24 38 48	20 08	19 18	27 31	10 39	13 34	12 15	16 18	04 44	27 12	03 59	29 46	21 01	11 54	23 38	05 46
S	19	1:50:02	25 38 22	04♊28	19 13	29 10	11 45	14 18	12 17	16 13	04 45	27 13	04 01	29 46	21 12	12 17	23 23	05 54
M	20	1:53:58	26 37 58	18 22	19 07	00♏49	12 50	15 02	12 19	16 08	04 45	27 13	04 03	29 45	21 22	12 42	23 07	06 02
T	21	1:57:55	27 37 36	01♋47	19 03	02 27	13 54	15 45	12 21	16 04	04 45	27 13	04 05	29 D 45	21 33	13 06	22 52	06 11
W	22	2:01:51	28 37 16	14 45	19 00	04 04	14 59	16 29	12 24	15 59	04 46	27 14	04 07	29 46	21 44	13 30	22 37	06 19
T	23	2:05:48	29 36 58	27 20	18 D 58	05 41	16 04	17 13	12 27	15 55	04 46	27 14	04 09	29 47	21 55	13 54	22 21	06 28
F	24	2:09:44	00♏36 43	09♌35	18 59	07 18	17 08	17 57	12 30	15 50	04 46	27 15	04 11	29 48	22 06	14 18	22 06	06 36
S	25	2:13:41	01 36 31	21 36	19 00	08 53	18 12	18 41	12 33	15 46	04 47	27 15	04 13	29 49	22 18	14 42	21 51	06 44
S	26	2:17:37	02 36 20	03♍27	19 02	10 29	19 16	19 25	12 37	15 41	04 48	27 16	04 15	29 51	22 30	15 06	21 37	06 53
M	27	2:21:34	03 36 12	15 13	19 03	12 03	20 19	20 09	12 40	15 37	04 48	27 16	04 17	29 53	22 42	15 29	21 22	07 01
T	28	2:25:31	04 36 05	27 00	19℞04	13 38	21 22	20 53	12 44	15 32	04 49	27 17	04 19	29 56	22 54	15 52	21 08	07 10
W	29	2:29:27	05 36 01	08≏51	19 01	15 11	22 25	21 38	12 48	15 28	04 50	27 18	04 21	29 59	23 06	16 16	20 54	07 18
T	30	2:33:24	06 35 59	20 48	18 57	16 45	23 28	22 22	12 52	15 24	04 50	27 18	04 24	00♓02	23 19	16 39	20 40	07 27
F	31	2:37:20	07 35 58	02♏55	18 50	18 17	24 30	23 06	12 57	15 20	04 51	27 19	04 26	00 00	23 31	17 02	20 26	07 35

EPHEMERIS IS CALCULATED FOR MIDNIGHT GREENWICH MEAN TIME.

NOVEMBER 1997

DAY		SID.TIME	SUN	MOON	NODE	MERCURY	VENUS	MARS	JUPITER	SATURN	URANUS	NEPTUNE	PLUTO	CERES	PALLAS	JUNO	VESTA	CHIRON
1	S	2:41:17	08 ᴍ,36:00	15 ᴍ, 12	18 ♍R, 41	19 ᴍ, 50	25 ✗ 32	23 ✗ 51	13 ≈ 01	15 ♈R, 15	04 ≈ 52	27 ♑ 20	04 ✗ 28	00 ♓ 10	23 ♑ 44	17 ♍ 25	20 ♏R, 13	07 ᴍ, 44
2	S	2:45:13	09 36 04	27 40	18 31	21 22	26 34	24 36	13 06	15 11	04 53	27 21	04 30	00 14	23 57	17 47	20 00	07 52
3	M	2:49:10	10 36 09	10 ✗ 20	18 22	22 53	27 36	25 20	13 11	15 07	04 54	27 21	04 32	00 19	24 11	18 10	19 47	08 01
4	T	2:53:06	11 36 16	23 13	18 13	24 24	28 37	26 05	13 16	15 03	04 55	27 22	04 34	00 24	24 24	18 33	19 35	08 09
5	W	2:57:03	12 36 25	06 ♑ 17	18 06	25 54	29 38	26 50	13 21	14 59	04 56	27 23	04 37	00 29	24 38	18 55	19 23	08 18
6	T	3:01:00	13 36 35	19 34	18 01	27 25	00 ♑ 38	27 35	13 26	14 56	04 57	27 24	04 39	00 35	24 51	19 17	19 11	08 26
7	F	3:04:56	14 36 47	03 ≈ 05	17 D 58	28 54	01 38	28 20	13 32	14 52	04 58	27 25	04 41	00 41	25 05	19 39	19 00	08 34
8	S	3:08:53	15 37 01	16 50	17 58	00 ✗ 23	02 38	29 05	13 38	14 48	04 59	27 26	04 43	00 47	25 19	20 01	18 49	08 43
9	S	3:12:49	16 37 15	00 ♓ 50	17 58	01 52	03 37	29 50	13 43	14 44	05 00	27 27	04 46	00 54	25 34	20 23	18 38	08 51
10	M	3:16:46	17 37 31	15 05	17 R, 56	03 20	04 36	00 ♑ 35	13 50	14 41	05 02	27 28	04 48	01 01	25 48	20 44	18 28	09 00
11	T	3:20:42	18 37 49	29 33	17 57	04 48	05 34	01 20	13 56	14 37	05 03	27 29	04 50	01 08	26 03	21 05	18 18	09 08
12	W	3:24:39	19 38 08	14 ♈ 12	17 55	06 15	06 32	02 05	14 02	14 34	05 04	27 30	04 52	01 15	26 17	21 27	18 08	09 16
13	T	3:28:35	20 38 29	28 55	17 49	07 42	07 30	02 50	14 09	14 30	05 06	27 31	04 55	01 23	26 32	21 48	17 59	09 25
14	F	3:32:32	21 38 51	13 ♉ 37	17 42	09 08	08 28	03 36	14 15	14 27	05 08	27 32	04 57	01 31	26 47	22 09	17 51	09 33
15	S	3:36:29	22 39 15	28 09	17 32	10 34	09 26	04 21	14 22	14 24	05 09	27 34	04 59	01 40	27 02	22 29	17 43	09 41
16	S	3:40:25	23 39 40	12 ♊ 24	17 21	11 58	10 19	05 07	14 29	14 21	05 11	27 35	05 02	01 48	27 17	22 50	17 35	09 50
17	M	3:44:22	24 40 07	26 17	17 11	13 22	11 14	05 52	14 37	14 18	05 13	27 36	05 04	01 57	27 33	23 10	17 28	09 58
18	T	3:48:18	25 40 37	09 ♋ 45	17 01	14 45	12 09	06 38	14 44	14 15	05 14	27 37	05 06	02 07	27 48	23 31	17 21	10 06
19	W	3:52:15	26 41 08	22 47	16 54	16 07	13 03	07 23	14 52	14 12	05 16	27 39	05 09	02 16	28 04	23 51	17 14	10 15
20	T	3:56:11	27 41 40	05 ♌ 24	16 48	17 29	13 57	08 09	14 59	14 09	05 18	27 40	05 11	02 26	28 20	24 11	17 08	10 23
21	F	4:00:08	28 42 14	17 42	16 46	18 48	14 50	08 55	15 07	14 07	05 20	27 41	05 13	02 36	28 36	24 30	17 03	10 31
22	S	4:04:04	29 42 50	29 44	16 D 45	20 07	15 42	09 40	15 15	14 04	05 22	27 43	05 16	02 46	28 52	24 50	16 58	10 39
23	S	4:08:01	00 ✗ 43 28	11 ♍ 35	16 R, 45	21 24	16 33	10 26	15 23	14 01	05 23	27 44	05 18	02 57	29 08	25 09	16 53	10 47
24	M	4:11:58	01 44 07	23 23	16 45	22 39	17 24	11 12	15 31	13 59	05 25	27 46	05 21	03 08	29 24	25 28	16 49	10 55
25	T	4:15:54	02 44 48	05 ♎ 11	16 43	23 52	18 14	11 58	15 40	13 57	05 27	27 47	05 23	03 19	29 40	25 47	16 45	11 04
26	W	4:19:51	03 45 30	17 04	16 40	25 02	19 04	12 44	15 48	13 55	05 29	27 49	05 25	03 31	29 57	26 06	16 42	11 12
27	T	4:23:47	04 46 14	29 08	16 33	26 12	19 52	13 30	15 57	13 52	05 32	27 50	05 28	03 42	00 ≈ 13	26 25	16 39	11 20
28	F	4:27:44	05 47 00	11 ᴍ, 24	16 23	27 17	20 40	14 16	16 06	13 50	05 34	27 52	05 30	03 54	00 30	26 43	16 37	11 28
29	S	4:31:40	06 47 47	23 55	16 11	28 19	21 26	15 02	16 15	13 48	05 36	27 53	05 32	04 06	00 47	27 01	16 35	11 36
30	S	4:35:37	07 48 35	06 ✗ 42	15 58	29 17	22 12	15 49	16 24	13 47	05 38	27 55	05 35	04 19	01 04	27 19	16 33	11 44

EPHEMERIS IS CALCULATED FOR MIDNIGHT GREENWICH MEAN TIME.

DECEMBER 1997

DAY	SID.TIME	SUN	MOON	NODE	MERCURY	VENUS	MARS	JUPITER	SATURN	URANUS	NEPTUNE	PLUTO	CERES	PALLAS	JUNO	VESTA	CHIRON
M 1	4:39:33	08 ✗ 49 24	19 ✗ 44	15 ♍ 45	00 ✅ 10	22 ✗ 57	16 ✅ 35	16 ≈ 33	13 ♈ 45	05 ≈ 40	27 ✅ 56	05 ✗ 37	04 ✗ 31	01 ≈ 21	27 ♍ 37	16 ♈ 32	11 ♏ 51
T 2	4:43:30	09 50 15	02 ✅ 59	15 32	00 59	23 41	17 21	16 42	13 43	05 43	27 58	05 39	04 44	01 38	27 55	16 31	11 59
W 3	4:47:27	10 51 06	16 25	15 22	01 42	24 24	18 08	16 52	13 42	05 45	28 00	05 42	04 57	01 55	28 12	16 D 31	12 07
T 4	4:51:23	11 51 59	00 ≈ 45	15 14	02 18	25 06	18 54	17 02	13 40	05 47	28 01	05 44	05 10	02 13	28 29	16 32	12 15
F 5	4:55:20	12 52 52	13 45	15 10	02 47	25 46	19 40	17 11	13 39	05 50	28 03	05 47	05 24	02 30	28 46	16 33	12 23
S 6	4:59:16	13 53 46	27 36	15 07	03 08	26 26	20 27	17 21	13 38	05 52	28 05	05 49	05 38	02 48	29 03	16 34	12 30
S 7	5:03:13	14 54 41	11 ✗ 34	15 06	03 20	27 04	21 13	17 31	13 37	05 55	28 07	05 51	05 52	03 05	29 19	16 35	12 38
M 8	5:07:09	15 55 37	25 38	15 06	03 22	27 41	22 00	17 41	13 36	05 57	28 08	05 54	06 06	03 23	29 35	16 38	12 45
T 9	5:11:06	16 56 34	09 ♈ 48	15 04	03 ✗ 13	28 16	22 46	17 51	13 35	06 00	28 10	05 56	06 20	03 41	29 51	16 40	12 53
W 10	5:15:02	17 57 31	24 03	15 01	03 03	28 50	23 33	18 02	13 34	06 02	28 12	05 58	06 35	03 58	00 ♎ 07 ◁	16 43	13 01
T 11	5:18:59	18 58 29	08 ♉ 19	14 54	02 54	29 23	24 20	18 12	13 34	06 05	28 14	06 01	06 49	04 16	00 22	16 46	13 08
F 12	5:22:56	19 59 27	22 34	14 46	02 23	29 54	25 06	18 23	13 33	06 08	28 16	06 03	07 04	04 34	00 38	16 49	13 15
S 13	5:26:52	21 00 26	06 ♊ 42	14 35	01 40	00 ✅ 24	25 53	18 33	13 33	06 10	28 18	06 05	07 20	04 52	00 53	16 54	13 23
S 14	5:30:49	22 01 26	20 38	14 22	00 47	00 51	26 40	18 44	13 32	06 13	28 20	06 07	07 35	05 11	01 07	16 59	13 30
M 15	5:34:45	23 02 26	04 ♋ 17	14 10	29 ✗ 44	01 18	27 27	18 55	13 32	06 16	28 22	06 10	07 50	05 29	01 22	17 04	13 37
T 16	5:38:42	24 03 28	17 36	13 58	28 32	01 42	28 13	19 06	13 D 32	06 19	28 24	06 12	08 06	05 47	01 36	17 09	13 44
W 17	5:42:38	25 04 30	00 ♌ 33	13 49	27 14	02 02	29 00	19 17	13 32	06 21	28 25	06 14	08 22	06 06	01 50	17 15	13 52
T 18	5:46:35	26 05 33	13 10	13 42	25 52	02 25	29 47	19 28	13 32	06 24	28 27	06 17	08 38	06 24	02 04	17 21	13 59
F 19	5:50:31	27 06 37	25 28	13 38	24 29	02 44	00 ≈ 34	19 40	13 32	06 27	28 29	06 19	08 54	06 42	02 17	17 28	14 06
S 20	5:54:28	28 07 41	07 ♍ 31	13 36 D	23 08	03 01	01 21	19 51	13 33	06 30	28 31	06 21	09 11	07 01	02 30	17 35	14 13
S 21	5:58:25	29 08 47	19 23	13 ♍ 36	21 51	03 15	02 08	20 03	13 33	06 33	28 34	06 23	09 27	07 20	02 43	17 42	14 19
M 22	6:02:21	00 ✅ 09 53	01 ♎ 11	13 36	20 41	03 28	02 55	20 14	13 34	06 36	28 36	06 26	09 44	07 38	02 56	17 49	14 26
T 23	6:06:18	01 11 00	13 00	13 35	19 39	03 38	03 42	20 26	13 34	06 39	28 38	06 28	10 01	07 57	03 08	17 57	14 33
W 24	6:10:14	02 12 07	24 55	13 32	18 47	03 46	04 29	20 38	13 35	06 42	28 40	06 30	10 18	08 16	03 20	18 06	14 40
T 25	6:14:11	03 13 15	07 ♏ 02	13 27	18 05	03 52	05 16	20 49	13 36	06 45	28 42	06 32	10 35	08 35	03 32	18 15	14 46
F 26	6:18:07	04 14 23	19 24	13 20	17 34	03 ♈ 55	06 03	21 01	13 37	06 48	28 44	06 34	10 53	08 54	03 43	18 24	14 53
S 27	6:22:04	05 15 33	02 ✗ 04	13 10	17 14	03 56	06 50	21 13	13 38	06 51	28 46	06 36	11 10	09 13	03 54	18 33	15 00
S 28	6:26:00	06 16 43	15 04	12 58	17 ✗ 05	03 55	07 37	21 26	13 39	06 54	28 48	06 39	11 28	09 32	04 05	18 43	15 06
M 29	6:29:57	07 17 53	28 25	12 47	17 05	03 51	08 24	21 38	13 41	06 58	28 50	06 41	11 46	09 51	04 16	18 53	15 12
T 30	6:33:54	08 19 03	12 ✅ 03	12 36	17 14	03 44	09 12	21 50	13 42	07 01	28 52	06 43	12 04	10 10	04 26	19 04	15 19
W 31	6:37:50	09 20 14	25 56	12 27	17 31	03 35	09 59	22 02	13 44	07 04	28 55	06 45	12 22	10 30	04 36	19 14	15 25

EPHEMERIS IS CALCULATED FOR MIDNIGHT GREENWICH MEAN TIME.

THE PLANETARY HOURS

The selection of an auspicious time for starting any affair is an important matter. When a thing is once commenced, its existence tends to be of a nature corresponding to the conditions under which it was begun. Not only should you select the appropriate date, but when possible you should also start the affair under an appropriate PLANETARY HOUR.

Each hour of the day is ruled by a planet, and so the nature of any time during the day corresponds to the nature of the planet ruling it. The nature of the planetary hours is the same as the description of each of the planets, except that you will not need to refer to the descriptions for Uranus, Neptune, and Pluto, as they are considered here as higher octaves of Mercury, Venus, and Mars, respectively. If something is ruled by Uranus, you can use the hour of Mercury.

The only other factor you need to know to use the Planetary Hours is the time of your local sunrise and sunset for any given day. This is given in the following chart.

EXAMPLE
Determine the planetary hours for January 2, 1997, 10° latitude

1) Find sunrise (table, page 182) and sunset (table, page 183) for January 2, 1997 at 10° latitude by following the 10° latitude column down to the January 2 row. In the case of our example, this is the first entry in the upper left hand corner of both the sunrise and sunset tables. You will see that sunrise for January 2, 1997 at 10° latitude is at 6 hours and 16 minutes (or 6:16 AM) and sunset is at 17 hours and 49 minutes (or 5:49 PM).

2) Subtract sunrise time (6 hours 16 minutes) from sunset time (17 hours 49 minutes) to get the number of astrological daylight hours. It is easier to do this if you convert the hours into minutes. For example, 6 hours and 16 minutes = 376 minutes (6 hours x 60 minutes each = 360 minutes + 16 minutes = 376 minutes). 17 hours and 49 minutes = 1069 minutes (17 hours x 60 minutes = 1020 minutes + 49 minutes = 1069 minutes). Now subtract: 1069 minutes - 376 minutes = 693 minutes. If we then convert this back to hours by dividing by 60, we have 11 hours and 33 minutes of Daylight Planetary Hours. However, it is easier to calculate the next step if you leave the number in minutes.

3) Next you should determine how many minutes are in a daylight planetary hour for that particular day (January 2, 1997, 10° latitude). To do this divide 693 minutes by 12 (the number of hours of daylight at the equinoxes). The answer is 58, rounded off. Therefore, a daylight planetary hour for January 2, 1997 at 10° latitude has 58 minutes. Remember that except on equinoxes, there is not an even amount of daylight and night time, so you will rarely have 60 minutes in a daylight hour.

4) Now you know that each daylight planetary hour is roughly 58 minutes. You also know, from step one, that sunrise is at 6:16 AM. To

determine the starting times of each planetary hour, simply add 58 minutes to the sunrise time for the first planetary hour, 58 minutes to that number for the second planetary hour, etc. So the daylight planetary hours for our example are as follows:1st hour 6:16 AM–7:14 AM; 2nd hour 7:15 AM–8:11 AM; 3rd hour 8:12 AM–9:08 AM; 4th hour 9:09 AM–10:05 AM; 5th hour 10:06 AM–11:02 AM; 6th hour 11:03 AM–11:59 AM; 7th hour 12:00 AM–12:56 PM; 8th hour 12:57 PM–1:53 PM; 9th hour 1:55 PM–2:50 PM; 10th hour 2:51 PM–3:47 PM; 11th hour 3:48 PM–4:44 PM; and 12th hour 4:45 PM–5:51 PM. Note that because you rounded up the number of minutes in a sunrise hour, that the last hour doesn't end where the Sunset Table says sunset begins. This is a good reason to give yourself a little "fudge space" when using planetary hours. (You could also skip the rounding up step.) For more accurate sunrise or sunset times, consult your local paper.

5) Now, to determine which sign rules which daylight planetary hour, consult your *Daily Planetary Guide* date pages to determine which day of the week January 2 falls on. You'll find it's a Thursday. Next, turn to page 184 to find the sunrise planetary hour chart. (It's the one on the top.) If you follow down the column for Thursday, you will see that the first planetary hour of the day is ruled by Jupiter, the second by Mars, the third by the Sun, and so on.

6) Now you've determined the daytime (sunrise) planetary hours. You can use the same formula to determine the night time (sunset) planetary hours. You know you have 11 hours and 33 minutes of sunrise planetary hours. Therefore subtract 11 hours and 33 minutes of sunrise hours from the 24 hours in a day to equal the number of sunset hours. 24 hours - 11 hours 13 minutes = 12 hours 47 minutes of sunset time. Now convert this to minutes $(12 \times 60) + 47 = (720) + 47 = 767$ minutes. (This equals 12.783 hours, but remember to leave it in minutes for now.)

7) Now go to step three and repeat the rest of the process for the sunset hours. When you get to step 5, remember to consult the **sunset** table on page 184 rather than the sunrise one. When you complete these steps you should get the following answers. There are (roughly) 63 minutes in a sunset planetary hour for this example. This means that the times for the sunset planetary hours are (starting from the 17:49 sunset time rather than the 6:16 sunrise time) first hour 5:49 PM; second 6:52 PM; third 7:55 PM; fourth 8:58 PM; fifth 10:01 PM; sixth 11:04 PM; seventh 12:07 AM; eighth 1:10 AM; ninth 2:13 AM; tenth 3:16 AM; eleventh 4:19 AM; twelfth 5:21 AM. You see which signs rule the hours by consulting the sunset chart on page 184. The first sunset hour is ruled by the Moon, the second by Saturn, the third by Jupiter, and so on.

Sunrise

Universal Time for Meridian of Greenwich

Latitude		+10°	+20°	+30°	+40°	+42°	+46°	+50°
		h:m	h:m	h:m	h:m	h:m	h:m	h:m
JAN	2	6:16	6:34	6:57	7:21	7:28	7:42	7:59
	14	6:21	6:34	6:55	7:20	7:26	7:39	7:53
	26	6:23	6:37	6:53	7:14	7:19	7:29	7:42
FEB	7	6:22	6:33	6:46	7:03	7:06	7:15	7:24
	19	6:18	6:27	6:36	6:48	6:50	6:56	7:03
	27	6:15	6:21	6:28	6:37	6:38	6:43	6:48
MAR	7	6:11	6:15	6:19	6:24	6:26	6:28	6:31
	19	6:05	6:05	6:05	6:05	6:05	6:05	6:05
	27	6:00	5:58	5:56	5:52	5:52	5:50	5:49
APR	12	5:51	5:44	5:37	5:27	5:25	5:19	5:14
	20	5:47	5:38	5:28	5:15	5:12	5:05	4:57
	28	5:44	5:33	5:20	5:04	5:00	4:52	4:42
MAY	6	5:41	5:28	5:13	4:54	4:50	4:40	4:28
	18	5:38	5:23	5:05	4:42	4:37	4:25	4:10
	26	5:38	5:21	5:01	4:36	4:30	4:17	4:01
JUN	3	5:38	5:20	4:59	4:32	4:26	4:12	3:54
	15	5:39	5:20	4:58	4:30	4:24	4:09	3:50
	23	5:41	5:22	5:00	4:32	4:25	4:10	3:51
JUL	1	5:43	5:24	5:02	4:35	4:28	4:13	3:55
	9	5:45	5:27	5:06	4:39	4:33	4:19	4:01
	17	5:47	5:30	5:10	4:45	4:39	4:26	4:10
	25	5:48	5:33	5:15	4:52	4:46	4:34	4:20
AUG	2	5:50	5:36	5:19	4:59	4:54	4:43	4:31
	10	5:51	5:38	5:24	5:07	5:02	4:53	4:42
	18	5:51	5:41	5:29	5:14	5:11	5:03	4:54
	26	5:51	5:43	5:34	5:22	5:19	5:13	5:06
SEP	3	5:51	5:45	5:38	5:29	5:27	5:23	5:18
	11	5:50	5:46	5:42	5:37	5:36	5:33	5:30
	19	5:49	5:48	5:47	5:45	5:44	5:43	5:42
	27	5:49	5:50	5:51	5:52	5:53	5:53	5:54
OCT	13	5:48	5:54	6:01	6:08	6:10	6:14	6:19
	21	5:49	5:57	6:06	6:17	6:19	6:25	6:31
	29	5:50	6:00	6:12	6:26	6:29	6:36	6:45
NOV	6	5:52	6:04	6:18	6:35	6:39	6:48	6:58
	14	5:54	6:08	6:24	6:44	6:49	6:59	7:11
	22	5:57	6:13	6:31	6:53	6:58	7:10	7:24
	30	6:01	6:18	6:37	7:02	7:07	7:20	7:35
DEC	8	6:05	6:23	6:44	7:09	7:15	7:29	7:45
	16	6:09	6:28	6:49	7:15	7:22	7:36	7:53
	24	6:13	6:32	6:53	7:20	7:26	7:40	7:57
	30	6:17	6:35	6:56	7:22	7:28	7:42	7:59

Sunset

Universal Time for Meridian of Greenwich

Latitude		+10°	+20°	+30°	+40°	+42°	+46°	+50°
		h:m	h:m	h:m	h:m	h:m	h:m	h:m
JAN	2	17:49	17:30	17:09	16:43	16:37	16:23	16:06
	14	17:57	17:41	17:22	16:58	16:52	16:40	16:25
	26	18:03	17:48	17:32	17:12	17:07	16:57	16:44
FEB	7	18:07	17:55	17:42	17:26	17:23	17:14	17:05
	19	18:09	18:01	17:52	17:40	17:38	17:32	17:25
	27	18:10	18:04	17:58	17:50	17:48	17:44	17:39
MAR	7	18:11	18:07	18:03	17:58	17:57	17:55	17:52
	19	18:11	18:11	18:11	18:11	18:11	18:11	18:11
	27	18:11	18:13	18:16	18:19	18:20	18:22	18:24
APR	12	18:10	18:17	18:25	18:35	18:38	18:43	18:49
	20	18:11	18:20	18:30	18:43	18:47	18:53	19:02
	28	18:11	18:22	18:35	18:52	18:55	19:04	19:14
MAY	6	18:12	18:25	18:41	19:00	19:04	19:14	19:26
	18	18:14	18:30	18:48	19:11	19:17	19:29	19:43
	26	18:16	18:33	18:53	19:18	19:24	19:38	19:54
JUN	3	18:18	18:37	18:57	19:24	19:30	19:45	20:02
	15	18:22	18:43	19:03	19:30	19:37	19:53	20:11
	23	18:23	18:42	19:05	19:33	19:39	19:55	20:13
JUL	1	18:25	18:43	19:05	19:33	19:39	19:54	20:12
	9	18:25	18:43	19:04	19:31	19:37	19:51	20:09
	17	18:25	18:42	19:02	19:27	19:33	19:46	20:02
	25	18:24	18:42	18:58	19:21	19:26	19:38	19:53
AUG	2	18:23	18:36	18:53	19:13	19:18	19:28	19:41
	10	18:20	18:32	18:46	19:03	19:07	19:17	19:28
	18	18:16	18:27	18:38	18:53	18:56	19:04	19:13
	26	18:12	18:20	18:30	18:41	18:44	18:50	18:57
SEP	3	18:08	18:14	18:20	18:28	18:30	18:35	18:40
	11	18:03	18:06	18:10	18:16	18:17	18:19	18:23
	19	17:58	17:59	18:00	18:02	18:03	18:04	18:05
	27	17:53	17:52	17:50	17:49	17:49	17:48	17:47
OCT	13	17:44	17:38	17:32	17:24	17:22	17:18	17:13
	21	17:40	17:32	17:23	17:12	17:09	17:04	16:57
	29	17:37	17:27	17:16	17:01	16:58	16:51	16:42
NOV	6	17:36	17:23	17:09	16:52	16:48	16:39	16:29
	14	17:35	17:21	17:04	16:45	16:40	16:30	16:17
	22	17:35	17:19	17:01	16:39	16:34	16:22	16:08
	30	17:36	17:19	17:00	16:36	16:30	16:17	16:02
DEC	8	17:39	17:21	17:00	16:35	16:28	16:15	15:58
	16	17:42	17:24	17:02	16:36	16:30	16:15	15:59
	24	17:46	17:27	17:06	16:40	16:33	16:19	16:02
	30	17:50	17:32	17:11	16:45	16:39	16:25	16:09

Sunrise and Sunset Hours Charts

Sunrise

Hour	Sun	Mon	Tue	Wed	Thu	Fri	Sat
1	☉	☽	♂	☿	♃	♀	♄
2	♀	♄	☉	☽	♂	☿	♃
3	☿	♃	♀	♄	☉	☽	♂
4	☽	♂	☿	♃	♀	♄	☉
5	♄	☉	☽	♂	☿	♃	♀
6	♃	♀	♄	☉	☽	♂	☿
7	♂	☿	♃	♀	♄	☉	☽
8	☉	☽	♂	☿	♃	♀	♄
9	♀	♄	☉	☽	♂	☿	♃
10	☿	♃	♀	♄	☉	☽	♂
11	☽	♂	☿	♃	♀	♄	☉
12	♄	☉	☽	♂	☿	♃	♀

Sunset

Hour	Sun	Mon	Tue	Wed	Thu	Fri	Sat
1	♃	♀	♄	☉	☽	♂	☿
2	♂	☿	♃	♀	♄	☉	☽
3	☉	☽	♂	☿	♃	♀	♄
4	♀	♄	☉	☽	♂	☿	♃
5	☿	♃	♀	♄	☉	☽	♂
6	☽	♂	☿	♃	♀	♄	☉
7	♄	☉	☽	♂	☿	♃	♀
8	♃	♀	♄	☉	☽	♂	☿
9	♂	☿	♃	♀	♄	☉	☽
10	☉	☽	♂	☿	♃	♀	♄
11	♀	♄	☉	☽	♂	☿	♃
12	☿	♃	♀	♄	☉	☽	♂

☉ Sun; ☿ Mercury; ♄ Saturn; ♂ Mars; ♀ Venus; ☽ Moon; ♃ Jupiter

Quick Table of Rising Signs

Your ascendant is the following if your time of birth was:

Sun sign:	6-8 am	8-10 am	10 am-12 pm	12-2 pm	2-4 pm	4-6 pm
Aries	Taurus	Gemini	Cancer	Leo	Virgo	Libra
Taurus	Gemini	Cancer	Leo	Virgo	Libra	Scorpio
Gemini	Cancer	Leo	Virgo	Libra	Scorpio	Sagittarius
Cancer	Leo	Virgo	Libra	Scorpio	Sagittarius	Capricorn
Leo	Virgo	Libra	Scorpio	Sagittarius	Capricorn	Aquarius
Virgo	Libra	Scorpio	Sagittarius	Capricorn	Aquarius	Pisces
Libra	Scorpio	Sagittarius	Capricorn	Aquarius	Pisces	Aries
Scorpio	Sagittarius	Capricorn	Aquarius	Pisces	Aries	Taurus
Sagittarius	Capricorn	Aquarius	Pisces	Aries	Taurus	Gemini
Capricorn	Aquarius	Pisces	Aries	Taurus	Gemini	Cancer
Aquarius	Pisces	Aries	Taurus	Gemini	Cancer	Leo
Pisces	Aries	Taurus	Gemini	Cancer	Leo	Virgo

Sun sign:	6-8 pm	8-10 pm	10 pm-12 am	12-2 am	2-4 am	4-6 am
Aries	Scorpio	Sagittarius	Capricorn	Aquarius	Pisces	Aries
Taurus	Sagittarius	Capricorn	Aquarius	Pisces	Aries	Taurus
Gemini	Capricorn	Aquarius	Pisces	Aries	Taurus	Gemini
Cancer	Aquarius	Pisces	Aries	Taurus	Gemini	Cancer
Leo	Pisces	Aries	Taurus	Gemini	Cancer	Leo
Virgo	Aries	Taurus	Gemini	Cancer	Leo	Virgo
Libra	Taurus	Gemini	Cancer	Leo	Virgo	Libra
Scorpio	Gemini	Cancer	Leo	Virgo	Libra	Scorpio
Sagittarius	Cancer	Leo	Virgo	Libra	Scorpio	Sagittarius
Capricorn	Leo	Virgo	Libra	Scorpio	Sagittarius	Capricorn
Aquarius	Virgo	Libra	Scorpio	Sagittarius	Capricorn	Aquarius
Pisces	Libra	Scorpio	Sagittarius	Capricorn	Aquarius	Pisces

1) Find your Sun sign in the left column.
2) Determine correct approximate time of birth.
3) Line up your Sun sign with birth time to find ascendant.
Note: This table will give you your *approximate* ascendant. To obtain your *exact* ascendant you must consult your natal chart.

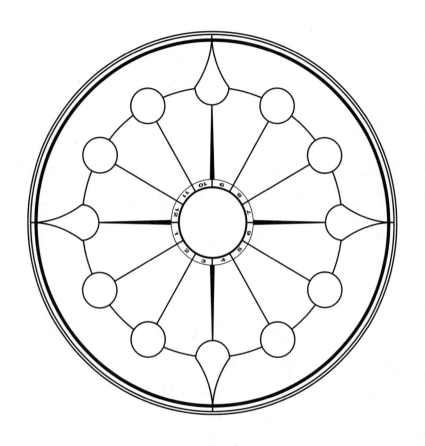

NAME

ADDRESS

CITY, STATE, ZIP

HOME PHONE   OFFICE PHONE

BIRTHDAY

NAME

ADDRESS

CITY, STATE, ZIP

HOME PHONE   OFFICE PHONE

BIRTHDAY

NAME

ADDRESS

CITY, STATE, ZIP

HOME PHONE   OFFICE PHONE

BIRTHDAY

NAME

ADDRESS

CITY, STATE, ZIP

HOME PHONE   OFFICE PHONE

BIRTHDAY

NAME

ADDRESS

CITY, STATE, ZIP

HOME PHONE   OFFICE PHONE

BIRTHDAY

NAME

ADDRESS

CITY, STATE, ZIP

HOME PHONE   OFFICE PHONE

BIRTHDAY

NAME

ADDRESS

CITY, STATE, ZIP

HOME PHONE   OFFICE PHONE

BIRTHDAY

NAME

ADDRESS

CITY, STATE, ZIP

HOME PHONE   OFFICE PHONE

BIRTHDAY

NAME

ADDRESS

CITY, STATE, ZIP

HOME PHONE   OFFICE PHONE

BIRTHDAY

NAME

ADDRESS

CITY, STATE, ZIP

HOME PHONE   OFFICE PHONE

BIRTHDAY

NAME

ADDRESS

CITY, STATE, ZIP

HOME PHONE   OFFICE PHONE

BIRTHDAY

NAME

ADDRESS

CITY, STATE, ZIP

HOME PHONE   OFFICE PHONE

BIRTHDAY

NAME

ADDRESS

CITY, STATE, ZIP

HOME PHONE   OFFICE PHONE

BIRTHDAY

NAME

ADDRESS

CITY, STATE, ZIP

HOME PHONE   OFFICE PHONE

BIRTHDAY

NAME

ADDRESS

CITY, STATE, ZIP

HOME PHONE   OFFICE PHONE

BIRTHDAY

NAME

ADDRESS

CITY, STATE, ZIP

HOME PHONE   OFFICE PHONE

BIRTHDAY

NAME

ADDRESS

CITY, STATE, ZIP

HOME PHONE   OFFICE PHONE

BIRTHDAY

NAME

ADDRESS

CITY, STATE, ZIP

HOME PHONE   OFFICE PHONE

BIRTHDAY

NAME

ADDRESS

CITY, STATE, ZIP

HOME PHONE   OFFICE PHONE

BIRTHDAY

NAME

ADDRESS

CITY, STATE, ZIP

HOME PHONE   OFFICE PHONE

BIRTHDAY

NAME

ADDRESS

CITY, STATE, ZIP

HOME PHONE   OFFICE PHONE

BIRTHDAY

NAME

ADDRESS

CITY, STATE, ZIP

HOME PHONE   OFFICE PHONE

BIRTHDAY

NAME

ADDRESS

CITY, STATE, ZIP

HOME PHONE   OFFICE PHONE

BIRTHDAY

NAME

ADDRESS

CITY, STATE, ZIP

HOME PHONE   OFFICE PHONE

BIRTHDAY

NAME

ADDRESS

CITY, STATE, ZIP

HOME PHONE   OFFICE PHONE

BIRTHDAY

NAME

ADDRESS

CITY, STATE, ZIP

HOME PHONE   OFFICE PHONE

BIRTHDAY

NAME

ADDRESS

CITY, STATE, ZIP

HOME PHONE   OFFICE PHONE

BIRTHDAY

NAME

ADDRESS

CITY, STATE, ZIP

HOME PHONE   OFFICE PHONE

BIRTHDAY

NAME

ADDRESS

CITY, STATE, ZIP

HOME PHONE   OFFICE PHONE

BIRTHDAY

NAME

ADDRESS

CITY, STATE, ZIP

HOME PHONE   OFFICE PHONE

BIRTHDAY

NAME

ADDRESS

CITY, STATE, ZIP

HOME PHONE   OFFICE PHONE

BIRTHDAY

NAME

ADDRESS

CITY, STATE, ZIP

HOME PHONE   OFFICE PHONE

BIRTHDAY

DIRECTORY OF PRODUCTS AND SERVICES

BUSINESS CARD DIRECTORY

BUSINESS CARD DIRECTORY

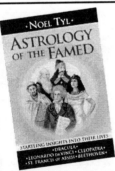

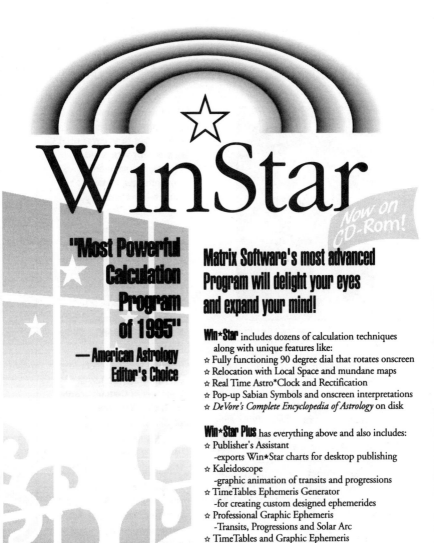

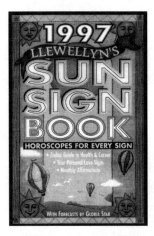

Be a Natural Success

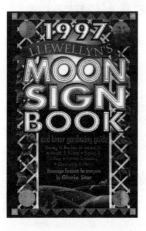

No other almanac supplies as much sound advice for daily success as *Llewellyn's Moon Sign Book*. Lively lunar horoscopes for every sign ... weather and earthquake forecasts ... practical business and gardening advice ... economic and political predictions ... timing events for successful outcomes—all based on the well-known influence the Moon has on our lives!

This is the only almanac that deals with every aspect of living better—the lunar way. See for yourself why *Llewellyn's Moon Sign Book* has been a best-selling guide to successful living for nearly a century!

- Find the best dates to accomplish almost any activity: plant crops, ask for a raise, get a haircut, or marry for happiness

- Learn all about the Moon through ancient Moon lore and current scientific knowledge

- Find the best fishing, hunting, and gardening dates

- Read accurate and personal lunar forecasts each month by renowned astrologer Gloria Star

- Prepare for inclement conditions with the weather and earthquake forecasts for your area

- New information on using the energies of Moon voids and Mercury retrograde

- Explore your natural intuitive abilities ... learn which Moon-ruled vegetables fight cancer ... find out what's in store in politics and economics ... surface-mine for moonstones ... work with the moon void-of-course to your advantage ... visit a lunar sacred site

LLEWELLYN'S 1997 MOON SIGN BOOK

384 pp. • 5 ¼" x 8" • Order # K-912 • $6.95
Please use order form on last page.

All the Monthly Astrological Data You Want—At A Glance!

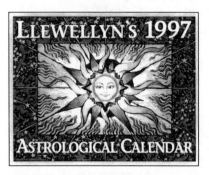

• Get a jump on your future with accurate, concise monthly forecasts by Rose Murray!

• Enjoy radiant new artwork by Anne Marie Garrison

• Quickly check best fishing and planting dates

• Reference Moon void-of-course times

• Plan ahead with daily aspects and monthly ephemerides

• Know your upcoming rewarding and challenging days

• Browse the thorough introduction to basic astrology

• Glimpse the international outlook for 1997 by the "Master of Astrological Prediction," Noel Tyl

• Jot down appointments and birthdays

Snatch up your copy of the most-trusted, best-selling astrological calendar on earth! Colorful, contemporary art by Anne Marie Garrison and monthly horoscopes by Rose Murray kick off each month, which highlights the most rewarding and challenging dates for each sign; major daily aspects; planetary sign changes; the Moon's sign, phase and void-of-course dates; monthly ephemerides; a retrograde table; planet visibility dates; and best dates for undertaking dozens of activities. Plus, previews by professional astrologers on travel, business and international events focus on using planetary vibrations to maximize their advantage! Includes an introduction to astrology for beginners and an easy-to-understand guide on how to use the calendar. Eastern Standard Times are listed along with a fold-out international time conversion chart.

LLEWELLYN'S 1997 ASTROLOGICAL CALENDAR

48 pp. • full-color • 13" x 10" • Order # K-923 • $12.00
Please use order form on last page.

The Gods and Goddesses Are Alive Within You!

Nourish your soul with this monthly mythological feast for 1997, rendered by visionary artists Kris Waldherr and Moon Deer. Evocative images blend seamlessly with mythic stories to speak to you on a level as deep and mysterious as the Underworld itself.

If these evocative images resonate strongly with you, then the gods and goddesses are surely alive within. When you see Ra in the blazing Sun, Thor in the thunder and lightning, Can Nü in the green leaves of a mulberry tree, or elves under your hearthstone, you'll know they do live in the world around you!

- **Can Nü (Chinese "Lady Silkworm")**
- **Thor (Norse god of sky and thunder)**
- **Aengus and Caer (Celtic god of love and swan-maiden)**
- **Cimidyue (Heroine of the Tucuna Indians of Brazil)**
- **Maui (Polynesian god of fire)**
- **Domovoi (Slavic elves)**
- **Venus and Vulcan (Roman goddess of love and the forger of thunderbolts)**
- **Durga (Indian war goddess)**
- **Ra (Egyptian sun god)**
- **Wakinyan Tanka (Brule Sioux thunderbirds)**
- **Manman Brigitte (Haitian voodoo spirit of the dead)**
- **Pale Fox (African trickster)**

LLEWELLYN'S 1997 MYTHS OF THE GODS & GODDESSES CALENDAR

24 pp. • full-color • 12" x 12" • Order # K-924 • $12.00
Please use order form on last page.

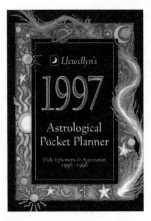

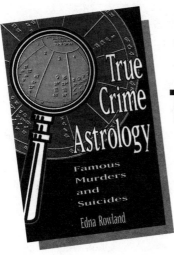

Llewellyn's Computerized Astrological Services

Llewellyn has been a leading authority in astrological chart readings for more than 30 years. We feature a wide variety of readings with the intent to satisfy the needs of any astrological enthusiast. Our goal is to give you the best possible service so that you can achieve your goals and live your life successfully. **Be sure to give accurate and complete birth data on the order form. This includes exact time (A.M. or P.M.), date, year, city, county and country of birth. Note: Noon will be used as your birthtime if you don't provide an exact time. Check your birth certificate for this information! Llewellyn will not be responsible for mistakes from inaccurate information.** An order form follows these listings.

SIMPLE NATAL CHART
Learn the locations of your midpoints and aspects, elements, and more. Discover your planets and house cusps, retrogrades, and other valuable data necessary to make a complete interpretation. Matrix Software programs and designs The Simple Natal Chart printout.
APS03-119 . . . . $5.00

PERSONALITY PROFILE
Our most popular reading also makes the perfect gift! This 10-part profile depicts your "natal imprint" and how the planets mark your destiny. Examine emotional needs and inner feelings. Explore your imagination and read about your general characteristics and life patterns.
APS03-503 . . . . $20.00

LIFE PROGRESSION
Progressions are a special system astrologers use to map how the "natal you" develops through specified periods of your present and future life. With this report you can discover the "now you!" This incredible reading covers a year's time and is designed to complement the Personality Profile Reading. **Specify present residence.**
APS03-507 . . . .$20.00

COMPATIBILITY PROFILE
Are you compatible with your lover, spouse, friend, or business partner? Find out with this in-depth look at each person's approach to the relationship. Evaluate goals, values, potential conflicts. This service includes planetary placements for both individuals, so send birth data for both. **Indicate each person's gender and the type of relationship involved** (romance, business, etc.).
APS03-504 . . . .$30.00

PERSONAL RELATIONSHIP INTERPRETATION

If you've just called it quits on one relationship and know you need to understand more about yourself before testing the waters again, then this is the report for you! This reading will tell you how you approach relationships in general, what kind of people you look for and what kind of people might rub you the wrong way. Important for anyone!

APS03-506 ....$20.00

TRANSIT REPORT

Keep abreast of positive trends and challenging periods in your life. Transits are the relationships between the planets today and their positions at your birth. They are an invaluable timing and decision-making aid. This report starts on the first day of the month, devotes a paragraph to each of your transit aspects and their effective dates. *Be sure to specify your present residence.*

APS03-500 – 3-month report $12.00
APS03-501 – 6-month report $20.00
APS03-502 – 1-year report $30.00

BIORHYTHM REPORT

Some days you have unlimited energy, then the next day you feel sluggish and awkward. These cycles are called biorhythms. This individual report accurately maps your daily biorhythms and thoroughly discusses each day. Now you can plan your days to the fullest!

APS03-515 – 3-month report $12.00
APS03-516 – 6-month report $18.00
APS03-517 – 1-year report $25.00

TAROT READING

Find out what the cards have in store for you with this 12-page report that features a 10-card "Celtic Cross" spread shuffled and selected especially for you. For every card that turns up there is a detailed corresponding explanation of what each means for you. Order this tarot reading today! *Indicate the number of shuffles you want.*

APS03-120 ....$10.00

LUCKY LOTTO REPORT (State Lottery Report)

Do you play the state lotteries? This report will determine your luckiest sequence of numbers for each day based on specific planets, degrees, and other indicators in your own chart. Give your full birth data and middle name. *Tell us how many numbers your state lottery requires in sequence, and the highest possible numeral. Indicate the month you want to start.*

APS03-512 – 3-month report $10.00
APS03-513 – 6-month report $15.00
APS03-514 – 1-year report $25.00

NUMEROLOGY REPORT

Find out which numbers are right for you with this insightful report. This report uses an ancient form of numerology invented by Pythagoras to determine the significant numbers in your life. Using both your name and date of birth, this report will calculate those numbers that stand out as yours. With these numbers, you can tell when the important periods of your life will occur. *Please indicate your full birth name.*

APS03-508 – 3-month report $12.00
APS03-509 – 6-month report $18.00
APS03-510 – 1-year report $25.00

ULTIMATE ASTRO-PROFILE

More than 40 pages of insightful descriptions of your qualities and talents. Read about your burn rate (thirst for change). Explore your personal patterns (inside and outside). The Astro-Profile doesn't repeat what you've already learned from other personality profiles, but considers the natal influence of the lunar nodes, plus much more.

APS03-505 ....$40.00

Special Combo Offer!

Personality Profile & Life Progression

This powerful combination of readings will help you understand what challenges lie ahead for you and what resources you have to achieve the success you want.

Special Combo Price!

APS03-216 $30.00

ASTROLOGICAL SERVICES ORDER FORM

SERVICE NAME & NUMBER_____

_____

Provide the following data on all persons receiving a service:

1ST PERSON'S FULL NAME, including current middle & last name(s)

_____

Birthplace (city, county, state, country) _____

_____

Birthtime _____ ☐ A.M. ☐ P.M. **Month** _____ **Day** _____ **Year** _____

2ND PERSON'S FULL NAME (if ordering for more than one person)

_____

Birthplace (city, county, state, country) _____

_____

Birthtime _____ ☐ A.M. ☐ P.M. **Month** _____ **Day** _____ **Year** _____

BILLING INFORMATION

Name _____

Address _____

_____

City _____ **State** _____ **Zip** _____

Country _____ **Day phone:** _____

Make check or money order payable to Llewellyn Publications, or charge it!
Check one: ☐ Visa ☐ MasterCard ☐ American Express

Acct. No. _____ Exp. Date _____

Cardholder Signature _____

Mail this form and payment to:

LLEWELLYN'S PERSONAL SERVICES
P.O. BOX 64383-K926 • ST. PAUL, MN 55164-0383

Allow 4-6 weeks for delivery.